Early Praise for *Adopting Elixir*

Adopting Elixir is brilliant: a practical, no-frills guide for all teams who want to use Elixir and get it right the first time. All ideas completely overlap with my consulting experience and I'll be sure to recommend it to all customers I work with.

➤ **Claudio Ortolina**
  Consultant and Head of Elixir, Erlang Solutions Ltd.

Adopting Elixir is the comprehensive guide I only wish we, one of the earliest adopters of Elixir, had available years ago. Whether you are still considering Elixir or actively coding and scaling your team, this book distills the lessons we learned into a detailed and thorough adoption plan.

➤ **David Marks**
  Senior Director of Engineering, Bleacher Report

Required reading for anyone considering or planning to use Elixir in production. It picks up where other books left off, with great higher-level discussions of development, deployment, and production.

➤ **Saša Jurić**
  Author of *Elixir in Action* and Developer at Aircloak, Aircloak

If you're looking to bring Elixir into your organization, you will find no better source of information than the team who wrote this book. They've walked the walk of using Elixir in production from the earliest days of the language. They introduce a wide range of topics—from staffing to tricky technical bits like distributed Erlang. Then they give you the knowledge you need, at just the right level of detail, to make great decisions for your team.

➤ **Lance Halvorsen**
  Senior Software Architect, Le Tote

Adopting Elixir

From Concept to Production

Ben Marx
José Valim
Bruce Tate

The Pragmatic Bookshelf

Raleigh, North Carolina

Many of the designations used by manufacturers and sellers to distinguish their products are claimed as trademarks. Where those designations appear in this book, and The Pragmatic Programmers, LLC was aware of a trademark claim, the designations have been printed in initial capital letters or in all capitals. The Pragmatic Starter Kit, The Pragmatic Programmer, Pragmatic Programming, Pragmatic Bookshelf, PragProg and the linking *g* device are trademarks of The Pragmatic Programmers, LLC.

Every precaution was taken in the preparation of this book. However, the publisher assumes no responsibility for errors or omissions, or for damages that may result from the use of information (including program listings) contained herein.

Our Pragmatic books, screencasts, and audio books can help you and your team create better software and have more fun. Visit us at *https://pragprog.com*.

The team that produced this book includes:

Publisher: Andy Hunt
VP of Operations: Janet Furlow
Managing Editor: Brian MacDonald
Supervising Editor: Jacquelyn Carter
Copy Editor: Jasmine Kwityn
Indexing: Potomac Indexing, LLC
Layout: Gilson Graphics

For sales, volume licensing, and support, please contact *support@pragprog.com*.

For international rights, please contact *rights@pragprog.com*.

ISBN-13: 978-1-68050-252-7

Book version: P1.0—March 2018

Contents

Part II — Development

Part III — Production

      Instrumenting Your System   172
      Instrumenting Ecto   178
      Instrumenting Phoenix   180
      Performance Assessment Workflow   182
      Load Testing   183
      Profiling   186
      Benchmarking   189
      Wrapping Up   191

10.   **Making Your App Production Ready** **193**
      Logs and Errors   193
      SASL Reports   199
      Tracing   201
      Using Other Advanced Tools   205
      Wrapping Up   207

      Bibliography **209**
      Index **211**

Acknowledgments

More than any other Elixir book that's ever been written, this book is a community book. The early adopters we profile shared their experiences directly in time-consuming interviews; inventors and committers for hundreds of projects made the very libraries we describe in these pages; beta testers tried new releases; and beta readers helped refine each word you find here. We owe our deepest gratitude to each of you and this book is dedicated to you. We can't possibly enumerate all of those that made this book possible, but we have to try.

We would like to thank the prags for believing in this concept. Our dear friend Jackie helped shape the words, Andy has been a constant source of support, Susannah made the start smooth, and Janet has guided the process from end to end. Many others shaped this book, from indexers to artists and copy editors. Thanks to each of you.

Thanks to all of our technical reviewers: Alexandre Hamez, Claudio Ortolina, Dave Marks, Kim Shrier, Maurice Kelly, Nigel Lowry, Saša Jurić, Sean Callahan, Shaun Collette, and Xavier Noria. Whether the suggestions were technical or stylistic, or a sounding board to bounce ideas off of, the book is that much richer and we are grateful for the reviews.

Thanks to Daniel Perez, Dave Marks, Hidetaka Kojo, Lauren Tan, Myron Marston, Pejvan Beigui, Shaun Collett, Steve Cohen, Tetiana Dushenkivska, Tsunenori Oharam, and Yusuke Tanaka for perspective and insight in their interviews. One of the goals of the book was to not only tell our Elixir adoption stories but to hear from varied members of the Elixir community. Each person's interview helped illuminate a different area of Elixir adoption.

From Ben:

I'm eternally grateful to Dave Marks for not only hiring me at Bleacher Report but encouraging and supporting me—and our entire team—as we undertook the monumental task of moving from our legacy sytem to the new Elixir-based platform. He's been an insightful mentor and has become a dear friend over these last years.

Many thanks to everyone at Bleacher Report; this was a team effort and we revamped everything from back end to front end to design and we have great plans for a bright future. Thanks especially to Miguel DeAvila for all that you've done to support me over the last year and also to Dave Finocchio for permission to write about Bleacher Report and leading a company I'm proud to be a part of.

This book wouldn't have happened had Bruce not approached me after a talk in Mexico about Elixir adoption. Bruce has been an excellent and encouraging mentor and co-author as the book came together. From our first call talking about the book, José has been nothing but a supportive and collaborative co-author. It's been an unforgettable and treasured experience.

Thanks to the Elixir core team, the Phoenix and Nerves core teams, and to the Elixir community and ElixirBridge for all the hard work you do to make this community innovative and inclusive.

And of course, the person who has supported me throughout this entire process and really in everything that I do, Aoi Yamaguchi. When I spent nights and weekends writing, she was there to encourage me to keep going and see this through to the end. I look forward to the continued adventures and excitement that we'll share together.

From José:

I have been working on Elixir for the past six years and Elixir wouldn't exist without Plataformatec. They adopted Elixir when it was only an idea and they were the first ones to invest in it. As the language grew, Plataformatec reached different companies using Elixir around the world, providing the challenges and insights that made this book possible.

We also wouldn't have gotten this far without Elixir's early adopters. In the first years of the language, there was a great amount of uncertainty. Every person who sent a pull request, wrote about it, started an event, or deployed it to production gave us confidence to move forward. You helped move Elixir beyond a personal project and shaped it into one driven by a community.

I also want to thank the Elixir team, past and current members: Aleksei Magusev, Alexei Sholik, Andrea Leopardi, Eric Meadows-Jönsson, and James Fish. You bring different perspectives into the project and help me grow professionaly and personally.

Bruce and Ben, my co-authors, you have been great friends throughout this journey and made me a better writer.

Finally, all of this wouldn't have been possible without the unconditional support of my wife, Małgosia, on this long journey: you are a constant source of inspiration and encouragement. I also want to thank my parents and friends for teaching me the lessons that still guide me on this journey.

From Bruce:

Thanks so much to my employers at LRW. Shaun, Paul, and Matt, thanks for being patient with those professional activities you've supported like this one that help us be good citizens in the Elixir space.

Thanks to my good friends José and Ben for your great attitudes and insights. Our readers will tell us if the efforts are worthwhile. I think they will be.

Thank you to Jim Freeze and Dave Thomas. Without your efforts, we wouldn't have the same Elixir community we do today.

It's always the family that pays the biggest cost for books like these. Julia and Kayla, I love you very much. Maggie, you're my love and inspiration.

To my readers and the Elixir community, books exist to be read (and bought!). Thanks for making this writing thing possible and enjoyable.

Introduction

Elixir is a rapidly growing functional language and the first production applications are emerging. Still, early adopters may find some important details missing. As with any emerging language, common questions arise:

- At what point do the promising rewards of the Elixir platform outweigh the risks?

- How do you recruit and train teammates who might never have used a functional language before to build consistent code?

- How do you wrestle with the trade-offs with distributed systems?

- What tools do the pros use to test, deploy, and measure your applications?

- What critical but less popular tools are available to solve issues like integrating external code or measuring performance trade-offs in production?

We wrote *Adopting Elixir* to change that. Rather than write another Elixir book about some narrow aspect of the language, we decided to write an experiential book containing the kinds of details that are typically difficult to find for an emerging language. It's a daunting task.

Said another way, you can find plenty of books out there to cover known topics. This book is more of an exploration of the expansive field of resources for new Elixir developers. Most often, we won't give you all of the answers. Instead, we'll help you know what you don't know, help you build a limited foundation with the basic trade-offs between possible solutions to a problem, and point you to the community for more answers.

Who This Book Is For

Each adoption story has many actors, and many of them have broadly different roles and responsibilities. Our book cuts across all adoption stories.

Such a book will have many different types of readers, and no single reader will find everything covered here relevant to them. Team leads and technical managers will want to know how to recruit and train, but pure programmers will probably find such details distracting. Beginners from traditional languages like Java or Ruby will crave more information on making the transition to a more functional, concurrent language.

We decided to write this book anyway, because the information is important right now for the greater community. We hope you'll agree.

Still, this book is not for everyone. If you're the type of reader who is likely to be frustrated when you find content that is not specifically for you, we don't think you'll be happy. The Pragmatic Bookshelf has the biggest selection of Elixir books in the industry and we'll gladly help you find one that's right for you, but you may want to pass on this one.

If you are a CTO looking for a book to help you build a business case for using Elixir, we don't believe such a book exists. The first couple of chapters will introduce you to a few stories that you may find instructive, with some hints toward financial justifications beyond "It scales well." But in the end, we decided we did not want to build a full business case in this book. This book may help some technical managers who code, but is probably not for the C-level executive.

We're writing this book for those in the technical Elixir community who find themselves adopting Elixir (or who plan to in the near future). Look, Elixir adoption can be hard because the collective problems we're solving are demanding. It's a functional, concurrent, distributed language. Any one of those concepts is difficult to understand. Many of our readers will be learning all of them at once. Have courage, though. We also know that many teams are making the successful transition.

Our combined experience suggests there is a growing segment of Elixir programmers who need to walk with successful Elixir practitioners. That list includes day-to-day developers looking for help making the transition from other languages. Experienced programmers may be deploying their solution from the experimental staging servers into production for the first time, or learning to scale their solution, or beginning to dabble in distribution for better fault tolerance. We can't promise you'll like everything in this book, but we can guarantee that you'll find something you'll like, something you've not seen before.

About the Authors

Ben Marx is one of the first developers to use Elixir at scale. As a lead developer at Bleacher Report, he was intimately involved in their transition from Ruby on Rails. His involvement spans the whole development cycle, from the initial plans for the Elixir migration through recruiting, development, production, and debugging that live system.

José Valim is the creator of the Elixir programming language and was once a member of the Rails Core Team. He graduated with an engineering degree from São Paulo University, Brazil, and has a Master of Science from Politecnico di Torino, Italy. He is also co-founder and Director of R&D at Plataformatec, a consultancy firm based in Brazil. He is the author of *Programming Phoenix [TV16]* and *Crafting Rails 4 Applications [Val13]*. He now lives in Kraków, Poland, with his wife and children.

Based out of Chattanooga, Tennessee, Bruce Tate is a father of two, as well as a climber and mountain biker. As CTO, he helped grow icanmakeitbetter.com, the insight community platform, from a cocktail napkin drawing in 2010 to its acquisition in 2016. As of this writing, he is leading the company through an Elixir migration. He's an international speaker and the author of several other books, including *Programming Phoenix [TV16]* and *Seven Languages in Seven Weeks [Tat10]*.

Now you know us. Let's get to the book.

How To Read This Book

We'll cover the whole adoption lifecycle in three parts, from concept to development and finally into production. As you progress through the book, the chapters will go deeper into technical details. This is intentional, as we're working to fill the many holes we've seen our teams and customers encounter. We'll try to provide enough detail to lay the right theoretical foundations and point you toward the right solution, and then move on.

Feel free to read the individual parts in any order, or not at all based on your needs. We've designed the code and prose so that you can do so. We'll tell you if there's something from an earlier chapter we think you should know. For example, if you have already built and trained your Elixir team, you may find more value in the development and production lessons explored in Parts II and III. On the other hand, if you are early in your adoption journey and you are still deciding if Elixir is the right tool for you, you will likely get more mileage from the first chapters and you can revisit the production discussion once development starts.

We understand that's not the typical experience, but we made that trade-off because each adopting developer has a different set of needs. No simplistic grouping of technologies can cover everything that needs to be said. We're willing to take our lumps in the review process because we believe in the need for this book in the greater community.

With those bits of housekeeping done, let's dive into the parts of the book. We'll also highlight which parts will be of particular interest based on your individual use case.

Part I: Concept

Adoption is in part a social problem. Adopting an emerging technology means becoming a salesperson. Helping stakeholders, teammates, and potential new hires understand that our technical decisions are wise and in the best interests of the companies we serve is a critical part of the process. New languages often mean new hiring and team-building strategies. Adoption *is* changing habits and practices to take best advantage of our new platform. This book will give you tools to help automate those things you can and lay out experiences to help you handle the things you can't. We'll walk you through the discussion in three chapters:

Team Building
Building a team for an emerging language is a little different than ramping up for a well-known, established technology. We'll tell you what we did to train and recruit talent, set expectations, and keep folks motivated. If you have an established effective team and a good handle on recruiting and training, you will probably want to skip this chapter. If you find yourself ramping up or training for a new adoption or if you're concerned about finding talent, this chapter will help you in your efforts.

Ensuring Code Consistency
It's easy to fall into old habits when you're learning a new language, but that would limit the benefits you'd reap. This chapter will show you how to use automated tools to gently nudge your team toward a more beautiful idiomatic coding style. If you have a comfortable cadence and are already well versed with lexers like Credo, Elixir's testing ecosystem, and Elixir's documentation tools, you may not give this chapter more than a quick

skim, but most developers will appreciate the concepts outlined in this chapter. You *can* automate many different aspects of code quality.

Legacy Systems and Dependencies

Many of the companies adopting Elixir are choosing it to replace a legacy system, and we'll cover that topic. Dealing with legacy systems also means carefully considering each new line of code you write and each new dependency you add. Sometimes code becomes legacy because of business needs, other times because the code becomes less healthy. In this chapter we will talk about how to replace legacy systems, building tomorrow's friendlier legacy systems as you write code today, and working with internal and external dependencies.

If you're a manager, an executive, or a team lead tasked with building a team and establishing culture, Part I is for you. The chapters in this part will also be of interest if you are starting your own project and need to understand what tools can help you build consistent code.

When you're through with Part I, you'll understand how to build a unified tool that writes uniform code. You'll then think about the best ways to think about taking that old system apart to adopt the new, should that be your chosen path.

Part II: Development

This part will show you how others have successfully built Elixir applications using new development teams or retooled teams who wrote in some other language. We'll focus on how to write code to do things beyond what you'd find in most typical technology books. We'll focus specifically on ideas and tools we've found difficult to find elsewhere. In particular, we've divided this part into the following chapters:

Making the Functional Transition

Object-oriented developers sometimes have trouble learning functional languages. This chapter gives advice to help make that transition. It is tailored specifically for beginning and intermediate Elixir developers, especially those who have come from other ecosystems.

Distributed Elixir

Adopting a new language is hard enough when you're only concerned about one system. It takes experience to learn to split concepts across the wire. This chapter provides exactly that. We'll talk about how to name things, the role of OTP, and how to think about distribution. If you're a technical lead or looking to break Elixir out of a single box, this chapter will help you reason about the next level of challenges you're likely to face.

Integrating with External Code

Sometimes, Elixir is not enough. When your code needs to step out of its universe, Erlang and Elixir provide several tools to do exactly that. This chapter covers those tools, whether you decide to stay in the same memory space, or use different processes or different machines altogether. If you plan to stay within the Elixir ecosystem for all of your application needs, you'll likely want to skip this chapter. Just give it a quick skim so you'll know the techniques available to you should the need arise.

If you're a new Elixir developer making the transition from OOP to FP, the early chapters in this part will help. If you're an experienced developer but struggling with what it means to write a distributed project or the approaches to integrating external code, the later chapters in this part will have something you find useful.

When you've completed Part II, you'll have more tools to think about the things that trip up early adopters from functional programming to concurrency, even distributed systems. Then, in the final part, we'll worry about deployment.

Part III: Production

Every new language community has to work out what to do with deployment. Elixir is no different. It's not surprising that one of the most common questions Plataformatec received was how to deploy, and how to monitor the system once deployed. This part of the book will point to some prevailing wisdom in these areas. In particular, you'll see chapters for:

Coordinating Deployments

Deploying a simple system on a single server is a pretty easy problem, but modern applications no longer fit that profile. This chapter will show how successful DevOps folks think about releases and the tools they use to deploy. In some teams, the folks that write the code are the same ones that deploy and support it in production. If you're involved in any way in deploying Elixir or packaging your code for deployment, this chapter is for you.

Metrics and Performance Expectations

Typically, new languages have some lesser-utilized areas with less documentation than others. Since performance measurements often happen after production applications are close to ready, this topic is one of the last to develop. When it's time to push Elixir to the limits and test performance, you'll need to know how to measure your performance and report those results. This chapter will tell you what you need to know. The techniques are advanced and the topics specialized, so you'll want your Elixir foundations to be pretty solid to attack this material.

Making Your App Production Ready

Once a system reaches deployment, the debugging and monitoring tools change. That throws many developers off, but Elixir has some unique capabilities that greatly simplify this process. This chapter will focus on instrumenting, measuring, and monitoring production systems. Just about all developers need to know about the debugging, logging, and reporting techniques in this chapter.

If you're in operations or responsible for seeing that your application is easy to deploy and manage, this part will be invaluable to you. Leads and architects will also want to understand how the deployment story fits together.

When you've finished this part, you'll know how others deploy with confidence. You'll learn what to measure, how to instrument your code, and how to monitor for the best possible reliability and information.

About the Code

The sample code and examples included in this book are written using the Elixir programming language, and will walk you through many broadly different Elixir concepts. Some of those are just fragments and some are full working examples. We'll show you how to use each example in the context of the book.

This book is about showing you a wider picture of the evolving greater Elixir ecosystem. Keep in mind that the nature of this book is that some of these code examples are just snippets, or segments of a fully working system. We can't possibly show you whole working systems for all of the examples in this book. Such a book would be many times the size of this one and take much longer to write.

Instead, we will let the prose and the code work together. Let the prose guide you through the proper use of the code examples. If you find any concepts that are not clear, just let us know in the forums. We will help you the best we can.

Online Resources

You can find all the example code for this book on its Pragmatic Bookshelf website,[1] alongside a handy community forum if you'd like to reach out for help along the way.

While we've worked hard to make our code examples and explanations bug-free and clear in every way for our readers, we've written enough software to know that we're fallible. Thanks in advance for reporting any issues that you find in the book code or text via the errata form, also conveniently found on the book website.

Thank you for joining us in your Elixir adoption story! We are excited to have you with us.

Ben Marx, José Valim, & Bruce Tate
March 2018

---

1. https://pragprog.com/book/tvmelixir/adopting-elixir

## CHAPTER 1

Three Adoption Stories

As we were putting the finishing touches on this book, a solar eclipse crossed the United States, moving as fast as 2,400 miles per hour. Many were near the path of totality, but not quite in that magic zone. Ben, in San Francisco, didn't have to move an inch to see 80% of the sun covered by the moon. Bruce could have stepped outside and witnessed 99.8% coverage, avoiding the worst predicted traffic in ten years. He decided to make the two-hour trip to the full eclipse zone rather than staying at home because *a partial eclipse and a total eclipse are not the same.*

In the same way, instead of writing about adoption of Elixir as a whole, we might have chosen to write exclusively about some single tool, problem, or technology. Such a book would have been easier to conceive and most likely far easier to write. In a world where publishers focus on an increasingly narrow set of topics, language adoption books are becoming rarer. Some will doubtlessly believe that if you understand the sum of the technologies surrounding a language, you'll know what it takes to adopt them.

We are writing a book about adoption because we believe *books about the individual pieces and books about adoption of the whole are not the same.* As a team of early adopters, we each have special insight into details that could smooth adoption for others. Where most other books in this space focus on *answers*, we'll focus on *questions.* We'll examine several problem spaces, talking to others who have experience and laying enough of a foundation to help you understand what the trade-offs between solutions might be as we understand them. Then we'll point you to solutions or resources in the industry for further study. If a chapter isn't useful to you, feel free to skip it. We've designed the book to make sense either way.

In this chapter, we'll tell our adoption stories and let you know what questions these experiences prompted. We'll start with Bruce's company and the icanmakeitbetter.com acquisition.

The Acquisition of icanmakeitbetter

Our first story is one of acquisition. We tell this tale because acquisitions highlight the tensions between risk versus reward at the heart of every other adoption story. It starts with an entrepreneur, a few slices of pizza, and a dirty napkin. You see, icanmakeitbetter was a tech startup.

In 2011, Paul Janowitz was a young entrepreneur with a growing market research company and an idea. He came to understand that asking folks the best questions, even with excellent effort and world-class analysis, wouldn't mean anything if you asked the wrong people. He met with Bruce Tate over pizza to talk about ways to automate the process of building research communities to find and engage the best customers. They brainstormed and sketched, and days later icanmakeitbetter was formed. Alas, that first napkin went into the trash because of irredeemable sauce stains.

The freshly merged company had just two programmers, and one worked his first full year from New Zealand. They stood up a product quickly and landed a few whales to feed the company as it grew. They knew the business model would be fluid so they chose a software stack that optimized the developer rapid-prototyping experience. Scalability could come later.

Growing the Business

Over the next few years, the young startup tweaked their platform to hone in on a business model that could better scale. They encountered several technical problems along the way. Their initial idea platform scaled easily because it was built primarily of pages that were easy to cache, and because the traffic moved to the platform organically, with a steady, equally distributed traffic load throughout the day.

As the company moved into new areas (including surveys), performance problems emerged. Complex survey platforms are tricky to scale with caching because the content and structure of each page depends on the answers to questions on previous pages.

Survey platforms also depend heavily on email and push notifications. When a researcher invites tens of thousands of people through an automated invitation, they tend to show up at the same time. Since it's tough to determine which surveys will have high completion rates, the traffic can be unpredictable. The platform started to show signs of strain under the weight. The caching strategy wouldn't work anymore, and Bruce started looking for potential solutions.

After attending dozens of conferences internationally over a two-year period, icanmakeitbetter landed on Elixir to solve these scalability problems and to offer more interactive experiences to their users. Elixir was a functional language with strong concurrency and fault tolerance, so it would scale. The fledgling language supported an advanced and readable syntax with excellent metaprogramming, so it would support their highly productive programming environment. The Erlang foundation underneath Elixir gave the team confidence in long-term stability and reliability.

Bruce began to get involved with José, the creator of the language, and other members of the community to help jump-start the libraries, conferences, and publishing that Elixir would need to emerge as a serious language. They hired Elixir's second committer, Eric Meadows-Jönsson, to give the language some stability. Then, icanmakeitbetter first launched an Elixir chat application blending the concepts of quantitative and qualitative research. When that project proved successful, they then migrated their core survey platform to Elixir and the company started to see benefits trickling in.

The icanmakeitbetter team assumed their association with this new technology would make their company more attractive to potential suitors. Better technology meant better scalability and stability. You'll soon see this assumption was not necessarily accurate.

The Acquisition

While the technical team worked on the long process of migrating to their new language, the business side of the company was enjoying newfound success with their research communities. At a time when traditional research firms were having trouble growing, icanmakeitbetter grew because they found ways to better engage their customers by providing research communities, leading to a sense of connection and better research.

Others noticed too. LRW is a family of market research companies in an industry going through substantial change. As part of a new growth strategy, they wanted to acquire icanmakeitbetter to compete in a fast-growing space called insight communities. Shaun Collett, their CTO, and his team were responsible for evaluating icanmakeitbetter's technology stack for business risks.

Then the questions started coming, fast and furious. Initially, Shaun was quite concerned about adopting a new language, based on the difficulty of finding developers and tools to work with it. As a good businessman and experienced CTO, he understood what could happen when good developers adopted leading-edge technologies for the wrong reasons. Let's hear what he had to say, in his own words:

Bruce: *Can you tell me a bit more about why LRW and ISA were interested in acquiring icanmakeitbetter?*

Shaun: *The market research industry is undergoing rapid change. Today's businesses need to make decisions faster and more iteratively to fuel growth. Community platforms have emerged in the past five to eight years to address this, offering tools and technologies to help clients make more meaningful business decisions in ways previously not possible or which were otherwise cost prohibitive. We knew we were late to the game and to catch up quickly, sought to acquire icanmakeitbetter. The platform was one of the most advanced community platforms in the industry and had great potential to grow even more, especially after looking under the hood.*

Bruce: *Through the acquisition process, did you have any concerns with icanmakeitbetter's strategy to move toward Elixir?*

Shaun: *The short answer is "yes." As a business leader and technologist, I'm always mindful to separate technologies that are simply "cool" with those that create real business value, or present meaningful business risk. I had never heard of Elixir before meeting Bruce and his team. After learning more about it, I thought it had potential to create real business value, but I also had significant concern about how new it was. While promising, new languages come with inherent risks, specifically surrounding people and development speed. I was worried through the acquisition process that if anyone left, we'd have a very hard time backfilling that position in a timely manner. Additionally, I worried about the speed of development, as immature languages don't give you many packages or "plugs" to get started, which can slow development speed and increase cost. After seeing our Ruby engineers pick up Elixir and experiencing early success building an incredibly successful chat feature, we felt both were worthwhile risks to take on and decided to move forward with the acquisition.*

Bruce: *Did the business face any challenges as we proceeded with this migration strategy?*

Shaun: *After cutting our teeth with the chat feature, next we tackled a core business feature that was suffering from inherent performance and scalability limitations from our Ruby codebase: our data collection process, our surveys. Our scalability issues were more than just performance. The complexity of our codebase suffocated us. The reality of business is that it doesn't stop changing, which in fact is a good thing. We knew we had to continue supporting critical business changes while we moved surveys to Elixir. This took longer than we expected, created some angst among business leaders as not as many features could be worked on, and created long weeks for the team, but we got through it, launching a totally new platform roughly six months after start. The most important thing was trust—we leaned on it significantly as we asked business leaders to be patient while we re-laid the tracks under a fast-moving train.*

Bruce: *Since migrating the platform, what benefits have you seen?*

Shaun: *Sure, we were able to scale, but that value was secondary. More importantly, we could quickly develop and release complex features across our survey platform that the business had been asking for. We couldn't (or shouldn't) have built these features on our old Ruby platform, as it wouldn't have scaled well enough to serve the business, so we felt great that we could finally deliver this. Once the business saw the features and understood that it was the work of the previous six months that enabled this—as well as many other features on our roadmap—to be possible, it created a lot of positive momentum, trust, and support for our work. I'm delighted to say that we're truly rocking and rolling!*

Shaun's comments show that adoption is more than a technology problem. He had some well-founded concerns about acquiring a company in the midst of transition.

Over the next year, progress slowed. icanmakeitbetter didn't stop working on the Elixir migration, but the focus was divided across some features they needed to build to stay competitive and maintain growth. As their platform stabilized and gained critical mass, they started to deliver new features at an accelerated rate.

As this story unfolded, Bruce began to think of Elixir in a different light, through the eyes of other early adopters. He spent two years speaking about technology adoption, making it easier for developers who were struggling with older technologies to make a case for Elixir based on the needs of their businesses. In short, he was helping adopters to discover new questions to ask and where to go to find the answers.

Leadership Questions for Early Adopters

As the startup joined the acquirer, Bruce and Shaun began to work together more closely. Bruce invited Shaun to ElixirConf 2016 in Orlando and the two attended other events together. They began to work on the political side of technology adoption, asking themselves:

- How do you fully involve upper management stakeholders at the earliest stages of the decision process?

- Where can you find developers to work on new technologies?

- Where can programmers go to learn about how to write functional, concurrent code?

As you get deeper into this book, you'll see new questions form about each of these topics. We'll also interview others who dealt with some of those questions before you.

If this first story highlights the inherent risks of early adoption, the next highlights the rewards. It is the story of Elixir at Bleacher Report.

Bleacher Report Improves Performance and Reliability

Our second story concerns migration. We tell it because adoption is tense business, and early adopters need to dream together. The story begins with a good dream, an angry clock, and a cup of coffee. You see, Ben had pager duty and the site wasn't working. Let's go back to the beginning.

Bleacher Report is the second biggest sports platform in the world and quickly grew to that size by offering sports fans something that no one else did: personalization and rapid content production, while following local to international sports. Most early users accessed the site through a computer or from newsletters that would, in turn, lead them back to the site.

In general, it was a passive model—you had to go to the site to get the information. Since most pages were static, they could cache them for performance. Spikes were relatively gentle, even when news broke.

Mobile Changes the Rules of the Game

Almost overnight, that landscape changed. When the iPhone exploded, companies quickly developed apps that transformed the way customers interact with the web. Suddenly, when news broke, push notifications or emails would send everyone to their favorite sports site at once. Spikes were instant and violently sharp.

It's hard to express just how much impact this kind of change could have. Say a famous star like Kevin Durant, one of the most famous basketball players in the world, suddenly gets traded to the San Francisco area. The news site would push out ten million notifications. If only 5% clicked, they'd have an instant spike of a half million users, and the site couldn't handle it.

With a mobile phone in everyone's pocket, the definition of what was major news changed too. Now, the end of a good game or an upset became major news. While this shift certainly wasn't limited to Bleacher Report, it hit them particularly hard. They knew they had to do something, but deciding exactly what to do wasn't easy.

Early Responses to the Challenge

At first, the sports news publisher did what everyone does. They threw hardware at the problem. For a while, it worked. Then, an unexpected guest named "Success" crashed the party. As more sports junkies found the site, the cost for scaling through hardware went up too quickly to absorb. Soon the site was running on over a hundred servers. To save money, the team introduced *auto scaling* to add servers on demand. That too failed because ramping up a new environment takes time, and they were failing users at peak demands.

They had to make their next logical play. They cached. The early results were promising, serving content many times faster. At this point, another guest named "Personalization" slammed through the door without an invitation. As athletes published their own Twitter feeds and they started showing highly variable content like scores, caching made less sense because *each user saw something different.* Imagine the user subscribes to college basketball, international soccer, major league baseball, and a couple of the streams that are topic-focused. You simply can't cache that. Increasingly, the scrambling software engineers decided to only build pages based on what they could cache, drastically hurting personalization. They realized that caching was a deal with the devil, and he had collected his price: the very innovation that made Bleacher Report great.

So Bleacher Report developers were on call because *their existing technology stack was not up to the problems the next few years would throw at it.* The industry was changing, the servers were overloaded, and the developers were going as hard as they could go. Something had to give.

At some point, the development leadership and management teams both agreed that they had to take some bitter medicine to get better. For many of the same reasons as icanmakeitbetter, they settled on Elixir: they wanted scalability and reliability without compromising productivity. And with that decision made, they set out to find some problems to prove their hypothesis.

Establishing Early Wins

Matt Pruitt and Michael Schäfermeyer were the Elixir advocates at Bleacher Report who first championed the language. They were able to quickly develop a proof of concept. It was still a prototype when Ben came to Bleacher Report but they'd done the hard work of demonstrating its viability to the company.

Ben first worked on a tiny service that fetched titles, descriptions, and the like from external services. By fetching all of the metadata concurrently instead of doing each request sequentially, his tiny team reduced the response time dramatically. The simple service took a day to prototype, a few more to finish out and deploy, and solved a key business need.

Neither prototype was *aesthetically* pleasing, but both were *conceptually* beautiful. The code was explicit, concurrent, and well organized, running much faster with better stability than the code it replaced. They'd established a few quick political wins.

Based on the early success, the anxious but excited initial group made a firm commitment to Elixir and sought ways to expand on their initial successes and kept chipping away. It wasn't always easy. Those were the early days of the Elixir community. Elixir and Phoenix, the dominant web framework in the community, were changing rapidly, so early code had a great deal of churn. Elixir's flexibility for rapid prototyping mitigated the damage somewhat, and the team was eager to rewrite early attempts to more idiomatic Elixir.

Over time, Bleacher Report increased the scope of their prototypes and moved more substantial pieces of their application into production. Elixir was improving both scale and reliability, one bottleneck at a time. The developers gathered confidence. Management and customers also started to notice.

Eventually, over four years, they'd moved the bulk of their system. The benefits weren't just tangible. They were transforming.

Enjoying the Benefits on Draft Day

For the first time in years, the platform was stable and response times were largely traffic independent. The following graph shows the number of requests (y) over time (x) for the sports site's busiest week of the year, the NFL draft for 2017, *after* the migration. The massive peaks and valleys are the first three draft rounds. The specific details are proprietary, but it's the highest number of concurrent users in their history:

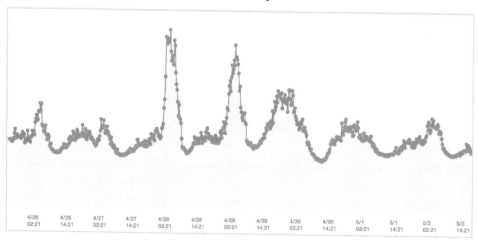

Traffic is higher than usual throughout the week because of the news coming out about the draft. They expected to see a relative increase in traffic on the first nights of the draft but they didn't expect to break their highest number of concurrent users by almost 30,000!

In the past, when traffic would ebb and flow, there would be corresponding, sustained fluctuations in the response times. This NFL draft also happened to be the first NFL draft where the majority of their stack was Elixir. The following figure shows how the Elixir app API gateway that serves their client apps—iOS, Android, and web—fared during this record-breaking time.

Now, for the kicker. Let's look at the response times in seconds (y) against time (x):

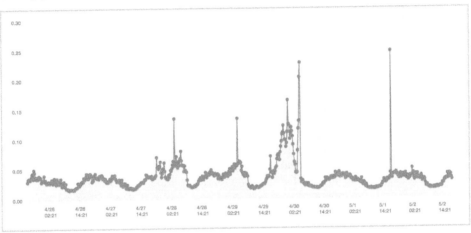

The average response time hovers around 50ms, and remains rock solid. On April 29th, around 10 p.m. EST, when the traffic shot up to the highest number of concurrent users, the response time only increases to around 170ms! The response times hovered around 170ms for a few minutes even as the number of requests were fairly constant for a much longer time.

In years past, the NFL draft meant everyone was on-call and quite often many needed to come in. In 2017, folks were relaxed, laughing and marveling at how the system fared. Soon after, people started to go home.

That's what a planned event looks like today. Unplanned events are very much the same. You may recall our mention of NBA MVP Kevin Durant's announcement to join his team's biggest rival. The news broke suddenly, flinging the sports universe into a maelstrom of conjecture and speculation. At the office, *nothing happened.* There were no alarms, no new servers spinning up, nothing buckled, and the response times hovered around 100ms. The biggest unplanned story of the year was a sports blockbuster, but a technical non-event.

The View from Management

You've heard some anecdotes from the Bleacher Report rank and file. Sometimes, a manager's words can be more convincing. Let's talk to Dave Marks, the Senior Engineering Director at Bleacher Report. He'll tell you about Elixir adoption from a senior manager's perspective:

> *Ben: As someone who doesn't have a background in Elixir, how did you assess the risk and reward of adopting it?*
>
> *Dave: It was clear we needed to change what we were doing to meet the demands of our growing user base and it was a big gamble to choose Elixir. I had confidence in our developers to make a reasonable choice and as the prototypes yielded better-than-expected results, I was more convinced. What really showed the power of Elixir was how resilient our apps are when traffic spikes. Now we can rest assured that our platform can handle breaking news spikes without any issue. In fact, duplexing and multiplying production traffic to a test environment showed that we can handle about ten times our current load before any response time increases.*
>
> *Ben: Did you have any doubts along the way?*
>
> *Dave: In the beginning we had only three or four developers who could write Elixir. If one or more of them left, it might have caused us some headaches as we trained other developers. That, of course, didn't come to pass. The fact that we use Elixir so extensively has attracted a lot of talent and retained our developers who enjoy working with the language so much. And now, we've trained all of our back-end developers to use Elixir so it's a moot point.*
>
> *Ben: What other benefits has Elixir provided?*
>
> *Dave: It's simplified our stack. Previously we used third-party integrations to help us handle our scaling needs. Now we can do what we do with just Elixir. It's saved us not insubstantial amounts of money and has also, as it turns out, made our system faster. Server savings is another big win. It's sometimes hard to explain to stakeholders why moving to a new language is a good idea because it cuts down on feature development. If, however, you can show tangible savings and a faster and more stable platform, it's much easier to convince them that you've made a worthwhile choice.*
>
> *We've been able to largely do away with caching at the application layer and only cache at the CDN level. Our system is simpler now and easier to reason about. It's, as always, a work in progress as we improve but Elixir has given us the tools to move forward and go from firefighting to feature development and platform expansion.*

That's powerful stuff. A development director's two biggest goals for cutting costs are often at odds. Choosing to emphasize development productivity often reduces the size and cost of the development staff. Sometimes this thrust comes at the cost of performance, as it once did at Bleacher Report. This project, though, shows a *simplification* of the development stack and better development buy-in. It reduced the costs of feature development and made it easier to bring in new staff when it's necessary.

Questions and Answers About Development

The Bleacher Report story is a struggle that took several years. They successfully waded through the politics we identified in the first story, setting expectations and building consensus. They identified a problem that was too big for their current technology stack and solved it by establishing some quick wins. Then, they methodically migrated the rest of their system, piece by piece. Though they're still not done, they're close enough to reap major rewards of a more effective development staff, better stability, and excellent performance.

Getting to that point was hard. Ben made it his mission to write articles and speak at conferences to tell others about questions Bleacher Report developed through their process:

- With a larger migration, how do you decide what to do first?
- How do you train a large team on Elixir?
- How do you address a legacy monolith?
- How do you maintain good code quality with measurable heuristics for quality given an inexperienced team?

Ben and Bruce met at a conference in Mexico City and decided to write a book about their growing number of questions surrounding adoption. Bleacher Report is the most pervasive adoption story in this book. We'll help you identify the questions *you* should be asking as you develop *your* application. We'll then help you build some intuition around potential solutions and point you toward tools and techniques that can help you find the answers you seek.

Now you've seen the two individual stories. The third is a collective one.

Plataformatec Supports Early Adopters

Our third story is comprised of the many tales that were spun as Plataformatec supported the first few Elixir adoptions. You might be tempted to think that each new adoption is a snowflake with its own intricate set of unique circumstances, but as this example illustrates, they have many lessons in common. The story begins with a keyboard, a rebellious wrist, and a restless mind. You see, José was one of the most helpless creatures in all of nature: a programmer with a wrist injury.

José had been typing too much with the wrong keyboard setup and his body was telling him to slow down. He couldn't *type*, so he had to stop to *think*. He started reading a paper on concurrency, then chased that one with an article on type systems, a book on languages, and a blog post on virtual machines. He was planting a seed deep within himself that would sprout when that wrist was healthy enough to brave his new ergonomic keyboard. He began to build a prototype that would become Elixir.

The Plataformatec cofounder and consultant took his new language to his founding partners and together they decided that with some time and investment Elixir could become something special. José began to work part time on the emerging language.

Over time, success stories began to emerge, many of which had no connection whatsoever to Plataformatec. Some early promising benchmarks showed staggering numbers, especially with many cores, that rivaled the top frameworks in the industry. Gaming companies used it to work efficiently with in-memory systems instead of putting everything in the database. Embedded systems vendors used Elixir to build faster systems with a much simpler and efficient tool chain. Plain old web programmers used the new language to make their systems more scalable and productive. Others simply applied it to odd jobs that needed a better solution than the ones they already had.

For example, Pinterest used Elixir for focused, high-volume, high-impact service around performance tooling and monitoring. Steve Cohen is a software engineer who's been working with their early adoption teams:

> *José:*   *Why did you choose Elixir?*
>
> *Steve:*   *We chose Elixir because we were looking for a system that was easy for programmers to understand and could take better advantage of our servers. I was intrigued at Elixir's combination of friendly syntax, powerful metaprogramming features, and incorporation of the Actor model.*
>
> *José:*   *In what capacity are you using Elixir?*
>
> *Steve:*   *We're using Elixir as a rate limiter in our developer ecosystem, an ads API, and heavily inside our spam detection and remediation systems. The spam-fighting systems process all the write requests sent to Pinterest and handle many tens of megabytes of data per second per server. It's also not one monolithic system, but several interconnected systems, many of which are Elixir based. The spam team consists of five engineers, though we have maybe 15 engineers that have contributed to our Elixir codebases.*
>
> *José:*   *What was your biggest concern when first approached to use Elixir?*
>
> *Steve:*   *Our first use of Elixir was fairly early in its evolution, so I was a little concerned with whether or not it'd be successful as a language. Thankfully, that concern appears to be unfounded. I was also concerned by the perception of others about introducing a new language. People's natural desire to work with technologies they're familiar with means that introducing something new is difficult. Add to the*

fact that Elixir runs on an unfamiliar VM and introduces an often-new programming paradigm, and you have the recipe for difficult adoption. We had our detractors, but over time won over most people with the advantages that Elixir offers: performance, efficiency, fault tolerance, and fewer bugs.

José: *How has your company benefited from Elixir?*

Steve: *That's pretty easy. When I started on the spam team, we had close to 1,400 servers running. When we converted several parts to Elixir, we reduced that by around 95%. One of the systems that ran on 200 Python servers now runs on four Elixir servers (it can actually run on two servers, but we felt that four provided more fault tolerance). The combined effect of better architecture and Elixir saved Pinterest over $2 million per year in server costs. In addition, the performance and reliability of the systems went up despite running on drastically less hardware. When our notifications system was running on Java, it was on 30 c32.xl instances. When we switched over to Elixir, we could run on 15. Despite running on less hardware, the response times dropped significantly, as did errors.*

This story is a microcosm of what's been happening in the Elixir space. icanmakeitbetter and Bleacher Report both experienced early success with stunning scalability numbers. In fact, most new Elixir deployments experience significant performance improvements. What you might not know is the impact of performance beyond the cost of servers.

Performance matters to development productivity every bit as much as it matters in production. icanmakeitbetter's test suites in Elixir all run in under 20 seconds. About two-thirds of the total codebase is written in Ruby, and runs tests in just under 10 minutes. Both suites measure 100% code coverage, and have about the same density per function. Productive developers demand fast cycles because they impact programming flow. Nothing disrupts flow more than waiting helplessly for a lethargic compilation cycle, glacially slow tests, or tedious wait times for deployments to staging. Concurrent tests and well-conceived tools to lend concurrency to deployments or tests mean happier and more productive developers.

Performance is also one of the most important criteria for customer acquisition and retention. As time goes on and user interfaces get more responsive, you need to respond in a short, predictable time frame. You'll need to respond even faster if you have a higher percentage of mobile users since mobile platforms have greater latencies.

From the growing list of users, customers in the midst of early adoption began to call Plataformatec. The early Elixir investment was beginning to pay dividends. At the same time, they understood they could not support all companies interested in Elixir directly. They had to scale and decentralize Elixir's adoption by bringing to light the common questions all early adopters face.

By answering those questions, Plataformatec and their clients could focus on the business, rather than on the adoption mechanics. The company began meeting with customers to answer the inevitable blocking questions all early adopters face.

Common Questions

Some of the earliest questions were difficult and at times impossible to answer. Folks would wonder about web frameworks before Phoenix or Ecto, only to be told to use Erlang libraries that had questionable support for Elixir. Over time, though, the platform matured and the questions started to get more interesting.

As the folks in the community began to fill the obvious gaps of web servers, database layers, and the like, a more sophisticated family of questions surfaced, especially in the context of the private conversations in the design reviews Plataformatec was doing. Some of those questions were specific to a business problem or implementation detail, but others were common across most customers:

- How do I architect my application and integrate with my existing infrastructure?

- How do I deploy, monitor, and measure my live system?

- When should I use hot code swapping?

- When should I use processes or genservers instead of just functions?

- What are the security implications of distributed Elixir?

Every one of these questions had reasonable answers, and Plataformatec could satisfy each customer inquiry with a report with reasonable responses based on well-studied foundations. That's what they did for a while. Once the questions settled down long enough, José realized that the story should be told to a broader audience, so he joined the team to write this book.

Embracing End-To-End Adoption

We strongly believe the Elixir community needs a holistic book with broad lessons, both technical and political, across the whole application development perspective. We think new teams need a place to go for how to introduce this new language into their own environments. In short, we'll try to give the wide variety of readers advice we and our customers could have used.

When you encounter topics that are not interesting to you, please understand that this book has been rigorously reviewed. We've cut away material that is not broadly interesting. If it's in the book, someone cares.

If you're adopting Elixir, we do think you'll find something you can use. Stories have power. We'll show you how Bleacher Report and others have successfully answered many of the same questions you're likely to face. You've also seen that stories have values, so we'll show you more of them in the form of interviews with the folks who did the work, or those whose job was on the line. We want to help weave them together in a way that helps you see what's worked for others in the past.

Wrapping Up

In this chapter, we've introduced three adoption stories. In the icanmakeitbetter story, an acquisition, you learned that adoption is a political problem. Though new language adopters speak in glowing terms about the finished product, you saw how upper management and talented developers perceive the real risks. The Bleacher Report migration showed what kind of rewards are possible if you're careful. The Plataformatec experience showed how adoption stories are important, with critical similarities we can mine.

Now you are ready to begin in earnest. Turn the page and we'll begin with Part I!

Part I

Concept

For any application, success begins when you write the first line of code. When you're adopting a new language, that's doubly true. In this part, you'll get ready to adopt Elixir. You'll start with a compelling business case and address the factors compelling you to make a move, from financial considerations to the health of your team and codebase. We'll then discuss how to convince business stakeholders and key technical staff. Throughout, we'll mix our own stories with circumstantial evidence, objective facts, and interviews so you're armed with convincing arguments that will help you think about the case you have to make.

From there, you'll begin to think about your own Elixir team. You'll see up close how we built our team—we'll talk you through the tools we use every day to objectively provide more consistent code with standards and tools to help ensure quality. Then, you'll explore tools and techniques to support a migration from existing technologies. While you won't generally find books on these techniques, each of them can help contribute to your success.

## CHAPTER 2

Team Building

Each time you adopt a new technology, you need to address talent acquisition. Whether you're dealing with a small team or a larger one, your training and recruiting processes will necessarily change. We understand this chapter isn't for everyone. If you're confident in your training and recruiting, you'll want to skip ahead to Chapter 3, *Ensuring Code Consistency*, on page 37, knowing you're already prepared to recruit, hire, and train an effective Elixir team. If you're nervous about this topic or know others in your organization who might be, you might want to give it a careful read, or at least a quick skim.

Imagine this: you've convinced your boss that your company can't stay on your current technology stack. You've put in your time to research all of the alternatives. You sell the stakeholders one by one. Some come grudgingly and some immediately, but eventually you win them over.

You can almost touch the tangible sense of excitement in the room as you get the green light to start building prototypes using technology you all believe in. The stakeholders are patiently waiting for the payoffs you've promised, and then it hits you. There's exactly one developer in the whole company who knows Elixir. It's a scary feeling.

Take heart. One of the reasons you should be adopting Elixir is to retain, attract, and motivate top talent. Let's talk about how to do so.

To thrive, you're going to need to build a team of Elixir developers, perhaps without breaking the bank. A recurring theme that all of us hear is that *working with good, new technologies helps companies attract and retain good developers.*

We'll talk about two ways to find Elixir developers. You can build them or buy them. In this chapter, we're going to show you techniques we've learned to build a team by training your existing staff, or augment it by getting new developers. Don't kid yourself. Both practices are a little different when you're adopting a new technology. Let's get started.

Training Developers

Training developers for a new language is more than simply sending a few of them at a time to classes and conferences. A holistic approach is better. Early adopters are learning and deploying a new technology at the same time and you want to minimize where things can go wrong.

Once you decide to make a commitment to Elixir, your first goal should be to solve a single, focused problem. That may be a small web service, a prototype, or the sketch of a system you plan to rewrite.

It is also worth shaping your first team of Elixir developers with the future in mind. Experienced developers will be more comfortable with leading the project and working as mentors. Some may have been exposed to functional programming, which will ease the migration to Elixir, and others may have deep domain knowledge.

Remember you don't have to immediately train everyone at once to write Elixir. At Bleacher Report, they had only two to four full-time Elixir developers in the first year. This strategy gave developers time to learn the language and get the prototype apps into production. Once you have established early success and momentum, you will be ready to engage the rest of the development staff bit by bit.

Let's take a closer look.

Establish Momentum with Early Prototypes

Your first prototype will have a tremendous impact on the adopting of Elixir at your company. Start by establishing what the language can do and what it can't. Since you're reading this book, you are already on the right track. An early prototype has to balance the following aspects:

Tangible business value
> You need to quickly reward the business side of the house with a quick win. That win might be fixing a problem they're seeing in their existing application or establishing a new capability that's cost-prohibitive using older technology.

Central enough to be seen and big enough to matter
> You need a visible political win and a technical win. A trivial problem may not give you either.

Small enough to permit failure

You don't want to bet the company on success because you didn't have enough experience to take on such a large risk.

In essence, you should aim for low risk and high reward, both on the technical side and the business side. At some companies, picking up a new technology is a straightforward process. In other companies, you may need to involve your stakeholders in the decision making and planning to get the maximum political value for the win.

Your adoption decision is the most fragile at the very beginning. With the first political win, you are actually doing three things at once: you're giving stakeholders a view of the business benefit, you're offering technical staff a taste of the success, and you're also establishing some new team members.

Developers Training Developers

Once your first Elixir projects hit production, you should expect more team members to get enthusiastic about learning Elixir. This early buy-in is critical. You need to manage technology adoption *by consensus instead of by decree* because you're going to have to build trust for when you need to dictate, and that will happen more often than you think. When you've invested in trust, the more difficult decisions that come later in your adoption curve will be easier.

You'll have early hurdles to overcome, and if the team isn't willing to work through them, it's a non-starter. It's also OK for a few to disagree. You'll want to build some excitement, and small gestures matter. Bleacher Report got the team a copy of *Programming Elixir 1.3* by Dave Thomas and gave them some office time to start working through it, alone or in groups. Slowly the team built an overall feel for the language. Developers can learn the theory in books and open up your codebase to see how things work in practice. Your earliest code won't be polished, but that's fine.

If you'd like to take the same approach, you have several good books to choose from, and the Elixir website is a good start when looking up Elixir resources.[1]

There are many other techniques we've seen successfully employed to engage teams:

- Spread out the Elixir maintenance work for the new prototypes to new members. Assign some relatively easy tickets to new developers and let them add some simple functionality to an existing feature.

---

1. elixir-lang.org/learning.html

- When working with legacy systems, assign porting of legacy functionality to new Elixir developers. In many ways, it's easier to port existing legacy functionality to a new Elixir app if you already understand how the code works. We will explore this exact scenario in Chapter 4, *Legacy Systems and Dependencies*, on page 61.

- Set aside time for refactoring and make sure new developers get feedback from experienced ones. If not, you could be reinforcing bad habits instead of breaking them in favor of good ones.

- Set aside time to talk about bad habits that show up in the codebase, and let the leaders talk about why the discussion matters. An old Japanese proverb applies here. *Fix the problem, not the blame.*

- Write tests. It's easy to write tests in Elixir, especially when you're assigned relatively simple, small amounts of functionality. Tests force decoupled code with small functions and will give confidence to developers that join the codebase later on.

Each of these approaches has a time and place for establishing coding skills in a real-world context. It's real-life experience with production problems that best accelerates adoption.

At each step, look for chances to pair, review, or mentor. When you're adopting any new technology, much of the risk is consolidated into two critically important times. The first is your initial ramp up of your novice developers. The second is keeping your developers from blocking when critical problems happen. Building a program to train and develop those programmers is critical to your success.

As you ramp up with Elixir, you will learn that a great deal of thought has gone into making the language work for new developers. The Elixir website is enough for developers to get started and the language documentation is extensive and accessible. The built-in tooling takes care of everything from creating a new project, to managing dependencies and running tests. Still, language adoption is never easy. It pays to be prepared for the inevitable problems you'll encounter.

When Things Go Wrong

You've built your first prototype and your new leaders are starting to, well, lead. It may seem like a feedback loop that's just too suspiciously positive. Don't worry. Things will eventually break. Expect periods of success followed by frustration. At some point, your team *will* stall on your learning curve, and how you address that challenge will make or break your adoption.

Keep in mind how much you're asking your developers to learn. *The old languages don't work as well anymore precisely because they are missing core concepts your new systems need.* Functional programming, concurrency, and distribution are all demanding disciplines. Learning them won't happen overnight. If you expect some pushback from your team and yourself, you'll be better equipped to handle it.

The trick to breaking through with a new concept is to minimize the time each developer is stuck. You do that by pairing inexperienced developers with experienced ones. Whether that happens in a classroom setting, a conference, pairing sessions, or code review is up to you. The key is to keep attitudes receptive and positive while you're opening learning channels through real coding experience.

Some concepts may be hard to break through. What clicks immediately for one developer may require time for other developers to digest. When that happens, it's OK to put it aside and revisit it later.

Programmers are a sum of their experience. When you're learning a new language, it's inevitable that your old programming habits carry over to your new language. Some will work in your favor, and you'll have to break others. When you're learning a new programming paradigm, that's doubly true. In this section, let's see how the Bleacher Report team was able to break through the concept of "functions transform data" and the importance of managing expectations along the way.

Functions Transform Data

When we say "functions transform data" what do we mean? It's a deceptively simple statement. It's easy to understand how a single function transforms data. Give some function an input, and it'll produce an output. The same input always yields the same output. As you might imagine, it gets more challenging when you move beyond simple functions to applications and more complex systems.

Bleacher Report is a news and content company first and foremost. The users come to the app and site because they want to read breaking news or gain insight into various sports happenings. The content programmers at Bleacher Report want to engage with the users in new and exciting ways, and they do that in part by using different content types.

One business requirement made the team realize that the current data model would be unsustainable. The business wanted the ability to switch content types. For instance, when news breaks, Twitter is usually the place where people first report it. After some time, articles or videos come to add more detail. Bleacher Report wanted to simulate that concept in code so that the user would have the whole experience through Bleacher Report instead of having to sift through different sources.

The initial modeling represented each content type as a distinct data structure, each with its own database table. As the system grew, common logic and requirements between content types were moved to shared modules. Later, that database structure bit them because changes to this shared functionality affected content types in unexpected ways. Eventually they found themselves scattering conditionals around the code to manage the different types and depending on heuristics that often failed.

The trouble here is that they were still too hung up on the names and nouns in their systems. They created artificial boundaries between content types and they were struggling with the dependencies between those boundaries. The solution that they came up with was a watershed moment for understanding functional programming. Since most content types have overlapping features, what if the team generalized the modeling and used functions to validate and transform that data before inserting it into the database?

Fortunately, they were using Ecto as their database abstraction and Ecto Changesets[2] was exactly what Bleacher Report needed. Changesets are quintessential functions that transform data. With changesets you validate and modify the data through a series of functions. Different content types should be in a different pipeline of functions, all working on the same data.

Whenever the content publisher added or modified an article, the content_type field would tell the application which functions and validations to use. Here is a simplified version of what the team did:

```
def changeset(post, content_type, params) do
  data
  |> cast(params, @required_fields)
  |> cast_content_type(content_type, params)
  # other general validations
end
```

2.　https://hexdocs.pm/ecto/Ecto.Changeset.html

```
defp cast_content_type(audio, "audio", params) do
  validate_extension(audio, :url, [:mp3])
end
defp cast_content_type(video, "video", params) do
  validate_extension(video, :url, [:mp4])
end
defp cast_content_type(tweet, "tweet", params) do
  ...
end
```

With this schema, the team broke out of the traditional database-backed model pattern and embraced a new confident, declarative pattern more in line with functional programming paradigms.

An unexpected pleasant side effect of moving to this new schema was that it lowered the barrier to entry for developers working on Elixir. The team now had a great pattern for adding new content types and an easily teachable one, too. Developers who were learning Elixir could quickly add a new content type; it inspired confidence, and it was discrete functionality that the developer could see in the app.

This is just one example but these are the ways in which you can build your team. Lower the barrier to entry by setting up defined patterns and then teach them to the enthusiastic developers. Their enthusiasm will spread to others and then suddenly you'll find yourself with a team full of Elixir developers. That's exactly what happened at Bleacher Report.

Managing Expectations

As you work to establish your initial wins, it's easy for your team or your management to get frustrated or concerned when things take too long. You've likely promised plenty of benefits for your new language, but initially, you'll likely take longer to do the most trivial tasks because it's new. To prevent all-out mutiny, you'll need to manage the expectations of the involved parties.

Once your team comes up to speed, you will find that you are able to move at a faster pace, but sometimes to realize those improvements, you need to rework some of your past infrastructure. When Bleacher Report developers realized that they could model their data in a much more efficient and extensible way using Elixir, they had to negotiate how to validate those ideas and move forward.

Re-modeling the data was no small undertaking, and it took more time than they had initially anticipated. They did their best to explain why this was worth the time it took, and the stakeholders agreed. After they finished the project, the benefits were immediate. It's now a trivial amount of work—an hour or two—to add a new content type. The initial delay in feature work paid for itself and more with the rate at which they can now develop new features.

Building a new team by training your existing developers is not easy, but it's possible. It's the primary technique used by this whole author team. If you're careful to slow down and manage expectations, you can do quite well with this approach.

Sometimes, this strategy isn't enough. Whether you need to grow or add a critical skill you don't have on staff, you'll need to find a way to bring in external developers. Elixir has not quite grown to the point where there are more developers than jobs, so you may need to adjust your typical staffing routine. That's the subject of the next section.

Hiring Elixir Developers

Training your existing staff is only one way to build a team of skilled Elixir developers. Another way is to recruit them. It's not easy; finding good developers in any language is tough, and the pool of Elixir talent is still small, though growing. All in all, it's a deviously complex process, so let's cover two topics. Since we're Elixir programmers, let's deal with that complexity the same way we deal with the complexity of our codebase, with function transformations. Here's a good starting point.

```
candidate_pool
|> interview
|> offer
```

This pipeline starts with a pool of candidates. The interview process is fundamentally a filter and ends with an offer. The offer process is highly dependent on business parameters such as how much you can spend, where your candidates can live, job stability, and the growth you can offer. Such topics are beyond the scope of this book. Beyond the flippant "Paying more will improve your closing percentage," we just can't offer much.

The other two are very much front and center in an adoption story. You can improve your hiring process by either increasing your candidate pool or refining your filter (or both). Let's start at the top of the pipeline.

Expanding Your Pool

If your process has the right kinds of filters, improving your candidate pool will improve the quality of your hires. We'll talk about two different ways to improve your candidate pool. The first is to get involved in the community. The second is to find good developers from other programming communities and train them.

Go Where They Go

As with all new languages, the total pool of programmers is relatively smaller, but don't lose heart. They are also often among the most motivated candidates to make a move. If you make yourself visible in the Elixir community, you'll often have opportunities that others don't.

When you want to find Elixir developers, get involved in the Elixir community. As you contribute, you'll meet folks and start to understand where to go to find talent. At icanmakeitbetter, Bruce had great luck going to conferences and listening. They initially met Eric Meadows-Jönnson in Stockholm at the Erlang User Community. They'd worked with José on establishing the Plug library and asked him how best to help the Elixir community. José mentioned Eric, a graduating college student who built the Hex package manger and the Ecto library. They hired Eric to help them build their initial Elixir implementation. The initial push was a great success. When the Swedish market matured allowing Eric to take a job closer to home, they were able to tap the conference circuit once again in Orlando, Florida, and Austin, Texas. They hired James Edward Gray II, who was a speaker at both events and is now writing a book on application design.

When companies invest in building the ecosystem, good things happen for everyone. In Tokyo, Japan, Elixir is growing in the gaming, media, and advertisement industries. In 2013, Japan overtook the United States to become the world's number one country in mobile systems revenue, thanks to the growth of smartphone and tablet games. It is a large market with increasing competition and demand. With pressure to improve the reliability and performance of those services, many companies looked to new technologies, including Elixir.

Though Japanese programmers and managers had watched Elixir because of its Ruby heritage and its established Erlang underpinnings, this familiarity wasn't enough. They still had to convince their bosses who had reservations about hiring and building their teams. Rather than just wait for the Elixir community to grow organically, they decided to take matters into their own hands.

To address this issue, CTOs and engineers of five different companies—XFLAG/mixi,[3] Akatsuki,[4] Drecom,[5] dwango,[6] and gumi[7]—decided to team up and organize meetups and others activities, leading to elixirconf.jp, a one-day Elixir conference in Tokyo with more than 300 attendees. This conference served as a platform to grow the Elixir presence in Japan, provided a platform for companies to recruit and train developers, and established the language as a less risky alternative. José was lucky enough to speak at the event and to have a round table discussion with their engineering leads:

José: *Why did you choose Elixir?*

Tsunenori Ohara (Drecom): *We were planning to use Erlang and when Elixir v1.0 came out we ended up evaluating four options: Scala, Erlang, Elixir, and Ruby. We were looking for reliability and performance and Elixir faired well in our trials. We also have many Ruby engineers and the similarities between languages played an important role.*

Yusuke Tanaka (Akatsuki): *We are mostly a Ruby company and we were looking at languages with better performance. In the end, we were conflicted between Elixir and Go. Elixir came out ahead thanks to its active development and community. We also had engineers familiar with Erlang and brought a couple more onboard, which helped with the migration to this new runtime.*

José: *In what capacity are you using Elixir?*

Yusuke Tanaka (Akatsuki): *We first built a contact management system in Phoenix as our proof of concept. Then we developed two new services, related to authentication and payments, which are also running with no hiccups. Now that we are comfortable with the language and runtime, we are planning to build our next game in Elixir.*

Hidetaka Kojo (XFLAG/mixi): *Since we are used to working with different technology stacks, establishing new technologies internally has always been relatively straightforward. Today we already have three services running in Elixir and a fourth in development, being worked on by about twenty engineers.*

José: *What was your biggest concern when you were first approached to use Elixir?*

Yusuke Tanaka (Akatsuki): *While our engineering teams were sold on Elixir, we still had to convince our bosses about the stability of the language and the community. Our solution was to invest in them ourselves and help the community grow in Japan.*

---

3. https://xflag.com/
4. https://aktsk.jp/
5. http://www.drecom.co.jp/
6. http://dwango.co.jp/
7. https://gu3.co.jp/

> *Tsunenori Ohara (Drecom):* *The same here. After we convinced our bosses with prototypes and benchmark results, they were still worried about finding engineers.*

You can see that these leads adopted Elixir for many of the same reasons as others around the world. All were worried about the future of the community and hiring prospects. Even so, to date the adoption stories have been successful. To mitigate their recruiting risk, they invested in the Elixir community to grow the new language locally. We'll watch this story closely to see how the community grows for them.

When you're hiring, you don't have to run a full conference yourself. Many meetups are looking for meeting spaces or sponsors to bring in speakers or food. Organize your own or find one and invest. Get the lay of the land before you announce a job posting. Then, when you know the local community and they know you, tell them what you're looking for.

Hiring Programmers from Other Language Communities

When you can't find an Elixir developer who's ready on day one, you need to evaluate your development needs. You have several options beyond simply increasing what you're willing to pay a full-time employee.

If you need immediate help but you're OK with a temporary solution, you might consider an Elixir consultancy. Plataformatec is the company behind Elixir and has an excellent team of developers led by José Valim. Chris McCord, creator of Phoenix, works at Dockyard, a consultancy with increasing investment in Elixir. Supporting them means also investing in the ecosystem.

Even within the realm of consultants and contractors, you have options. If you have a more limited budget and some knowledge in house, you can hire occasional consulting help to do design reviews at critical junctures in your development. Your bet is that an experienced consultancy can keep you from making big mistakes. It was during one of many of those reviews that José Valim realized the impact this book could have in Elixir's adoption.

Other times, you may want to focus on in-house, full-time employees. If you have some time to invest, the best approach is often to hire excellent programmers and teach them Elixir. The directors from Drecom and Akatsuki successfully tapped Ruby and Erlang engineers to supplement their teams. The process goes about like you'd expect. Look for the skills or attributes that are most important to you, and those that predict good success in learning functional languages. These are some areas that you might consider:

- Hiring people with past successes often leads to future success.

- Functional programming and concurrency are sometimes more important than syntax. Think Erlang or Scala, which both have a very close concurrency model to Elixir.

- If you'll need domain-specific languages, Lisp developers often work well. Building languages and tweaking syntax within Elixir often means working with macros, and Elixir's macros are based on similar features in Lisp.

- Focus on your problem domain such as machine learning or mapping. If you're working in a demanding discipline, learning Elixir will be easier than learning your domain.

These are a few strategies you can use for finding senior development talent when you can't find or afford an Elixir developer. Select a skill that's critical for your project and look for that instead. If your candidate knows Clojure and is applying for an Elixir job, they're willing to learn. If they are outstanding with Clojure, they'll learn Elixir just fine. At icanmakeitbetter, Bruce's finalists included an Erlang developer, a Ruby developer, and a Clojure developer. Bruce is confident that any of those three would have worked just fine.

A Case Study for Hiring Developers

EasyMile is a company from Toulouse, France, that has a similar experience. They develop software for autonomous vehicles and aim to provide turnkey solutions—such as geolocation, managing fleets, and so on—for any kind of autonomous vehicles. They support vehicles around the world, so they need robust systems to manage them. The system *must stay up* while people are inside the vehicles. Elixir, and OTP in particular, is a great addition to EasyMile's tech stack.

Autonomous vehicles are a relatively new industry. The odds EasyMile will find candidates that are familiar with their domain and OTP at the same time is virtually zero, so they need to build skills from within. They hire smart engineers and developers who are eager to learn. They must compete with big local companies such as Airbus, so they also need an edge, and Elixir may be it. Here's what Pejvan Beigui, EasyMile's CTO, had to say:

José: *Why did you choose Elixir?*

Pejvan: *My personal opinion had been for a while that a functional programming approach with a focus on concurrency would be a better fit for our particular use case. And having played around with Erlang and its VM, I thought we could benefit from its distinctive features such as fault tolerance and live upgrades. From there, it's easy to get attracted to Elixir, which builds on the strength of Erlang, while adding a modern and productive feel to the platform.*

But since I would not be involved in the actual coding, I didn't want to impose a language on the team who would be writing the code, so while the team was studying multiple stacks, such as Node.js, I just threw in a one-liner: "You might also want to have a look at this new language called Elixir."

As the CTO, it was a very proud moment because a week later, when I came back to the office, I discovered that they had not only settled on using Elixir for the platform but had also gone so far as to completely rewrite our initial C++ prototype using it. It was amazing to see them build this so quickly, with far less code and complexity, and for the prototype to be already much more stable than the C++ one.

José: *How has your company benefited from Elixir?*

Pejvan: *First of all, the fact we are doing Elixir has attracted developers. There are some developers who applied only because we are exploring new technologies such as Elixir. The whole approach that we have for recruitment is very opportunistic. If we find great developers, we hire them even if we don't have a place right now. We are also organizing meetups and sponsoring events such as ElixirConf Europe. And that's also a benefit. Elixir's young and growing community is such that a small company such as EasyMile can have an impact, whereas it would have been very hard for us to do the same in the PHP or Java community.*

When talking about our platform to clients and investors, we also mention that our system is built on the Erlang VM, with its background in telecommunication and building robust and fault-tolerant systems. We consider it a competitive edge and it has been well received.

José: *Have you had hiccups or roadblocks along the way? How did you overcome them?*

Pejvan: *We have been proactively removing the roadblocks that we expect in the future. Still, we're learning how to leverage OTP, and OTP itself is a big beast. There is a learning curve, but the codebase is more compact and organized than we would expect so we are looking forward to benefits in the long run.*

For doing things in the right way, we have also brought companies like Plataformatec to help with code reviews and architectural decisions.

The bottom line is that only you know what you need. If you need someone to be productive from day one in Elixir, you'll need to find a way to hire an Elixir developer. If you're willing to expand your search a bit, you can add some excellent candidates by looking for domain-specific knowledge across similar families of languages. You'll be able to quickly shape such folks into productive developers. In fact, a great Erlang developer would probably contribute sooner than a decent Ruby developer with six months of Elixir experience. If you've chosen well, the process will go smoothly. Let's talk about how to find good candidates and make the right choice for your situation.

Conducting Interviews

So far, we've been talking about recruiting as if it were an Elixir pipeline. Recall the flow:

```
candidate_pool
|> interview
|> offer
```

We've discussed some ways to increase the talent pool, possibly beyond Elixir developers. Let's look at the second way to improve the quality of your recruits. You can improve the *interview* filter. That's the topic of this section.

After exchanging experiences, we realized the processes we coordinate at our respective companies were fairly similar. In this section, we'll highlight what has been working for us. You are free to try those ideas and cherry-pick what best suits you. Let's break down that interview pipeline:

```
candidate_pool
|> phone_screen
|> code_test
|> onsite_interviews
```

In programming terms, the phone_screen, the code_test, and the onsite_interviews are all *filters*. The strength of the filters in your chain shapes your recruiting progress, but the source for your filter matters too. Your filters can be more selective if your candidate_pool is deeper.

Whenever there is an open position and résumés arrive, the process generally works the same. The recruiting team looks at a résumé and at any attached project links. If all are in agreement, it is time for a phone screen.

Phone Screens

The first filter is the phone screen. It is an opportunity to reduce your candidate pool without much energy. Since you'll invest many hours in recruiting and interviewing a single candidate, removing pretenders from the pool as early as possible is important.

Phone screens can be aggressive or conservative. An aggressive approach tends to want to let only the top fraction of applicants through. For example, at icanmakeitbetter, phone screens recently trimmed a list of ten résumés to the top two. At Bleacher Report, phone screens usually just weed out the obvious pretenders. Their phone screens usually take about fifteen to twenty minutes, and unless the candidate inflated their résumé or ducks the call, they are invited to do a code test and then an in-person interview.

In general, open-ended questions based on personal experience are the hardest ones to fake. Here are a few sample questions we've used in the past for Elixir candidates:

- What's been your most difficult problem?
- What's your open source history?
- What don't you like about Elixir?

These questions provide a good gauge to see how much the candidate is interested and if they've *done* anything with the language. Serious candidates can speak about their experience confidently; an ideal candidate can freely discuss language fundamentals, what they like and what they don't. If a candidate has Elixir projects to show off, take notes. An open source project can be worth ten coding tests.

Once they've passed the screen, it is time to ask them to write some code.

The Code Test

Sometimes, once you've identified what you think is an ideal candidate, you can enter a contract-to-hire relationship. Other times, you may have direct professional knowledge from another job or project. If you don't know first-hand whether a candidate can code, you'll need to measure their ability to do so. The best way to do so is with a code test.

The goal of the code test is the second filter, and perhaps the most important one. Use it to assess critical thought and real-world problem-solving. There are at least four different kinds of coding tests:

- Whiteboard tests ask a candidate to sketch solutions to difficult problems.

- In-office coding tests put a candidate in a room with a keyboard and a problem.

- Pairing interviews let the candidate work with senior members of a development team.

- Take-home tests allow a candidate to work on the problem outside of the interview setting and submit the solution by a certain deadline.

The test should be an accurate gauge of skills that apply directly to your problems. Like many others,[8] we recommend you forgo puzzle questions. Instead, you should ask the types of questions that your developers would have to solve in a typical workday. It's much harder to fake critical thought

---

8. https://github.com/poteto/hiring-without-whiteboards

than to memorize puzzle question answers. Almost all developers need documentation to look up functions, parameters, and other language characteristics. Often, you'll read different blog posts if you're developing a new feature to get insight on how other developers have done it. This is how most of us work, so we should evaluate developers in the same way.

Take-Home Tests

Bleacher Report and Plataformatec use take-home tests. If your company infrastructure is composed of multiple services and you need a back-end developer, you may want them to integrate with a mock version of an internal API. You'll need to provide a basic set of instructions: what their implementation should do, what it should return, and other details. The design and implementation details should be left up to the applicant.

The candidate should spend roughly three hours writing the API. It's enough time to write something more than a trivial API, but it's not so much time that it feels like a burden. Try to make it a worthwhile investment for both the applicant and you. Also give them plenty of time to complete the test, typically a week. If a candidate asks for more time, don't fret—it is a great opportunity to assess how the candidate communicates on such situations.

Even though we're all busy, carving three hours out of the week to finish a test for a job you want isn't excessive. It's also self-selecting in some ways. If a programmer disagrees, you can part ways knowing that hiring this person involves *more risk than you're willing to take.*

It's also easier on the candidate; on-site interviews can be up to a full day of work. It's troublesome to arrange time off to go to an on-site interview for a job they might not get. With the take-home test, they have more flexibility to manage their working hours.

After wrapping up the code test, you should talk to the programmer. It's important to talk about the candidate's decisions as a part of the code test. We'll talk about that step in *The Interview*, on page 35. For now, let's look at some other ways to evaluate a programmer's technical skills.

The Pairing Test

At icanmakeitbetter, the approach is very much the same, but often uses pairing instead. The test can be local or remote, depending on your interview process. It's best that the pairing mirrors the feel of your office development as closely as it can. With the right interviewers on staff you can learn a surprising amount about an applicant in a pairing session. Problems with many different requirements of escalating difficulty are excellent choices.

Like a take-home test, a pairing test measures skill, but it also eliminates cheating and measures the ability to interact while coding. It's much easier to get feedback throughout the process on the reasoning behind choices for data structures, algorithms, and style. You can do an extended pairing test by working with a paid contractor for a short time before hiring them as a full-time employee.

It's important to watch a candidate navigate their tool chain. Pay attention to whether they automate and how they interact with both command-line and graphical tools. Watch them switch context. See how they handle information flow across user interfaces. These can be good indicators of whether the candidate's experience level matches the résumé.

Both the pairing test and the take-home test can put the candidate at ease in ways a simple in-office test can't. Keep in mind *neither of these approaches require Elixir knowledge*. You can ask for a coding test in any language. If you were recruiting a Scala or Clojure developer, you'd just provide a JSON block or a straightforward HTTP response and ask for a simple passing test. You confirm the ability to think critically and check parameters against desired outcomes.

We pay attention to the API design, extensibility, code hygiene, documentation, and tests, but we don't ask those things in an interview. We let the code do the talking. "Do you write tests?" is an easy interview question to beat. The code, though, doesn't lie.

The Interview

We won't try to shape your full interview process, because that's beyond the scope of this book. Still, when you're adopting a new language, there are a few things you should know. Having competition is usually critically important because it's easier to negotiate a fair deal, leading to reasonable expectations and generally a better relationship. The interview's role is to reduce the pool of candidates, eventually to the one you decide to hire.

On-site interviews are expensive in terms of time, so it's important to do all you can to evaluate the candidate before they ever reach your doorstep. In most places, in-person interviews are the central part of the technical evaluation of a candidate, but if you've followed the advice in this chapter, they don't need to be your sole source of information. Having a good take-home test or open source evaluation takes some of the guesswork out of a technical evaluation, and removes unnecessary pressure from the process. Interviews with enough space between provide a much better experience with more natural interactions that lead to better decisions.

Regardless of whether the candidate passes or fails, give them feedback. Tell them what was lacking and where they can improve. This rewards them for their time investment and can cause a positive impression, even if they are not hired. Maybe the code test reveals the candidate doesn't quite fit a senior role today but they might in a year or two.

After you've chosen your candidate and they've accepted, you know what to do. The process is similar to the flow of ramping up your existing developers. It's a good place to pause and reflect on this material.

Wrapping Up

In this chapter, we talked about how to build a team. We looked at techniques to train existing staff or hire new developers. Many companies will need to know how to do both to have a successful adoption experience.

The chapter began by walking through how our companies initially ramped up with Elixir. When we trained our developers, we started by choosing a small part of the application and put together a small team of potential leaders to do that work. We used techniques like pairing and code reviews to quickly ramp them up. After our initial prototype, we had a finished application, a win for the business advocates, and a small and growing list of assets in new leaders and code.

When we had to hire new developers, we sometimes needed to look beyond our typical staffing techniques because the language is still relatively new. You saw that giving back to the community paid dividends later by expanding our exposure to new Elixir developers. You also learned how to find and hire developers who might not have Elixir experience. We talked about the critical data that a code test can provide, examining both take-home and pairing versions of that technique.

After a whole chapter troubleshooting problems you'll find when hiring for a new technology, it's important to emphasize the converse too. You can use the excitement around Elixir to attract and retain talent too. In the next chapter, you'll learn to take the next step with those new developers. You'll learn how to build consistent code with repeatable, measurable quality. Don't stop now! You're almost through Part I. Turn the page!

## CHAPTER 3

Ensuring Code Consistency

In the past ten years, programmers have made tremendous strides in crafts-manship. Collectively, we're paying more attention to code structure, testing, types, and more because *these concepts matter*. New adopters might not have enough experience to completely control every implementation detail, but they can embrace code consistency.

Whether you're working on a big team or a young team, you'll want to establish a baseline so that your code stays *fresh*, and the coding stays *fun*. It's natural that technical debt accrues more quickly as inexperienced programmers learn the best ways to write code that's easy to understand and maintain. That's why code standards are so crucial. Churn without boundaries is chaotic; churn within a framework is annoying but tolerable.

In this chapter, we're going to walk you through code quality. We'll provide some guidance in five primary areas:

Coding standards
    The Elixir community has settled on coding standards so code looks the same not just from one module to the next, but also one project to the next.

Types
    Type annotations provide documentation for the programmer and infor-mation for tools that help you find bugs.

Documentation
    For your public-facing modules, documentation will help you describe what's happening in your codebase so others will know how to best use your code.

Tests

Testing for functional languages is different. The focus on immutability will let you build shorter, simpler tests.

Reviews

Fungus grows in the dark. Each different set of eyes is like sunlight into a damp, dark corner, improving quality and adding accountability.

Many of the tools we'll show you are not just guidelines you have to police yourself. They're *automations*. That way, you can continuously get many of these benefits with a fraction of the cost of manual intervention. When you commit to guidelines throughout your organization and as part of your whole lifecycle, from setting expectations when you hire your first developer to maintaining code that's already in production, you'll profit.

Before we get started, let's do one bit of housekeeping. You may be asking yourself, "How much is too much?" We don't have an answer for you. Which tools you install will depend on the size and experience levels for your team, the size and complexity of your codebase, and your affinity for the approaches we suggest. We'll offer two pieces of advice:

- You almost certainly don't want to implement all of this at once.
- If it feels good, do it more. If it hurts, stop.

None of the authors on this team use all of the tools in this chapter. We all select the best tools for our teams and circumstances. We suggest you do the same. With that guidance in mind, let's get to work. We'll start with automated coding standards.

Coding Standards

Every programming language has built-in idioms and practices that collectively shape the look and feel of a codebase's structure and contents. That's coding *style*. Good style is especially important to adoption because it reduces friction between developers and makes a collective codebase easier to read.

As you can imagine, some tools can help you manage many of these elements automatically. Such tools are typically divided in two categories:

- *Code formatters* focus on code layout concerns, such as indentation, use of spaces and newlines, line length, and the like.

- *Linters* focus on code quality and code structure concerns that go beyond layout, such as function and variable names.

The Elixir community embraced linters years ago but formatters are a more recent addition. Let's start with them.

Code Formatters

You and your teams have probably already had one or more heated discussions about code style. Should you use tabs or spaces? Should you add spaces after commas or not? To mature, all new language communities must go through these discussions at some point.

Even when teams are in perfect agreement and choose a style guide that already exists in the community, enforcing such guidelines requires constant effort during development as well as code reviews. To make matters worse, as your company grows, each new developer needs to get acquainted with the house rules, and that may take some time getting used to.

The Elixir team has heard those complaints loud and clear. To address them, they have recently announced that Elixir will include a Code Formatter starting with release v1.6. This new feature can format your code using a consistent style. Assume a file like this one:

```elixir
defmodule HelloWorld do
  def greet( first, last ) do
    name = first<>" "<>last
    IO.puts "Hello #{ name }!"
  end
end
```

mix format will rewrite that code to:

```elixir
defmodule HelloWorld do
  def greet(first, last) do
    name = first <> " " <> last
    IO.puts("Hello #{name}!")
  end
end
```

We strongly advise all teams and companies to adopt Elixir's code formatter. With it, your team no longer needs to worry about small style decisions that sap productivity. They can now focus on the issues that matter.

The Elixir formatter is also a great teaching tool. If a new developer joins your team and they are not yet familiar with Elixir, they can learn how to write idiomatic code that is consistent with your company and the whole community by simply running the formatter as they program. They get immediate feedback and grow more confident their code will fit right in.

Elixir's code formatter provides as little configuration as possible. A formatter with too many options would lead to many different sets of rules, causing fragmentation inside companies and in the community. Instead, the community gets greater consistency and new hires or open source contributors know exactly what to expect.

Finally, note that the formatter will never change the code semantics. The formatter guarantees any code before and after formatting will behave exactly the same. This guarantee implies Elixir won't be able to handle all code style rules such as underscored_names versus camelCase because such a change would impact the meaning of the code.

Luckily, the Elixir community provides other tools, such as linters, to handle all other concerns that the formatter cannot.

Credo: Linter as Teacher

Linters are important because they automate tedious style and code quality checks. Linter rules don't exist in a vacuum; the coding rules come from the language community. As the language evolves, so does the linter. One of the most useful libraries for code consistency you'll find is René Föhring's Credo.[1] It's a linter like Ruby's Rubocop or JSLint for JavaScript, but as it proclaims in the tagline on GitHub, it's a linter "with a focus on code consistency and teaching." That aim is what makes Credo so interesting.

With a standard linter, you might get some warning or suggestion, and instead of understanding the issue you make the change and move on. The linter helps improve the quality of the code, but it doesn't give the developer much context as to why these changes are necessary.

Credo, too, tells you "what," but also answers "why."

Let's look at a contrived simple Mix application. Elixir has a package manager called Hex.[2] Every time you add a dependency to your project, Hex is responsible for downloading it. Many packages in Hex are named after the package domain followed by an _ex prefix, such as html_sanitize_ex, kafka_ex, and many others.

Our application will "hexify" library names by appending _ex to the given string unless one already exists. Let's create it:

```
$ mix new belief_structure
```

---

1.   https://github.com/rrrene/credo
2.   https://hex.pm/

The BeliefStructure module in lib/belief_structure.ex defines the main hexify function:

```
ensuring_code_consistency/belief_structure/lib/belief_structure.ex
defmodule BeliefStructure do
  def hexify(package) do
    case String.ends_with?(package, "ex") do
      true  -> package
      false -> BeliefStructure.Hexify.name(package)
    end
  end
end
```

And in lib/belief_structure/hexify.ex, you'll find this:

```
ensuring_code_consistency/belief_structure/lib/belief_structure/hexify.ex
defmodule BeliefStructure.Hexify do
  def name(package) do
    package(package)
  end

  defp package(package) do
    package <> "_ex"
  end
end
```

As you can guess, it works like this:

```
iex(1)> BeliefStructure.hexify("warden")
"warden_ex"

iex(2)> BeliefStructure.hexify("aws_ex")
"aws_ex"
```

It works fine, and the code looks OK, but let's run Credo to check our code. First, add Credo to your deps:

```
ensuring_code_consistency/belief_structure/mix.exs
defp deps do
  [
    {:credo, "~> 0.8.8", only: [:dev], runtime: false}
  ]
end
```

From the command line, run the command mix credo. Credo has multiple levels of warnings and suggestions. If you'd like to see all levels, run mix credo --strict, which should return the following output:

```
Software Design
?
? [D] ? Nested modules could be aliased at the top of the invoking module.
?        lib/belief_structure.ex:6:16 (BeliefStructure.hexify)
```

```
Code Readability
?
? [R] ? Modules should have a @moduledoc tag.
?       lib/hexify.ex:1:11 (BeliefStructure.Hexify)
? [R] ? Modules should have a @moduledoc tag.
?       lib/belief_structure.ex:1:11 (BeliefStructure)

Please report incorrect results: https://github.com/rrrene/credo/issues

Analysis took 0.1 seconds (0.00s to load, 0.1s running checks)
5 mods/funs, 2 code readability issues, 1 software design suggestion.
```

Credo reports improvements over a wide range of categories. While those suggested improvements may quickly resonate with experienced Elixir developers, new adopters may not understand what they mean or why they matter. That's why Credo goes a step further. Let's try it out (note that your output might vary based on the particular version of Credo you're running):

```
    mix credo lib/belief_structure.ex:1:11
?
?   [R] Category: readability
?    ?  Priority: normal
?
?       Modules should have a @moduledoc tag.
?       lib/hexify.ex:1:11 (BeliefStructure.Hexify)
?
?   __ CODE IN QUESTION
?
?    1 defmodule BeliefStructure.Hexify do
?              ^^^^^^^^^^^^^^^^^^^^^^^^
?    2   def name(package) do
?    3      package(package)
?
?   __ WHY IT MATTERS
?
?       Every module should contain comprehensive documentation.
?
?       Many times a sentence or two in plain english, explaining why
?       the module exists, will suffice. Documenting your train of
?       thought this way will help both your co-workers and your
?       future-self.
?
?       Other times you will want to elaborate even further and show some
?       examples of how the module's functions can and should be used.
?
?       In some cases however, you might not want to document things about
?       a module, e.g. it is part of a private API inside your project.
?       Since Elixir prefers explicitness over implicit behavior, you
?       should "tag" these modules with
?
```

```
?          @moduledoc false
?
?       to make it clear that there is no intention in documenting it.
?
?    __ CONFIGURATION OPTIONS
?
?       You can disable this check by using this tuple
?
?         {Credo.Check.Readability.ModuleDoc, false}
?
?       There are no other configuration options.
```

It's concise and clear. With such an explanation, anyone in the organization could act on it. If your organization doesn't use these tags, or at least uses them sparsely, you can add {Credo.Check.Readability.ModuleDoc, false} to your .credo.exs and supress such warnings as suggested by Credo here.

Credo has significantly helped Elixir adoption at Bleacher Report for all of the reasons just mentioned. They adopted Elixir around October 2014 when the language was quite young. Credo didn't yet exist and style guides were just developing. Each app had its own personality but since the team at Bleacher Report was all learning Elixir, there were varying degrees of technical debt and experimentation. This state of constant churn made it harder to switch between apps and no one was exactly sure how to style or unify the apps in development.

As the community grew, tools started to emerge and they nudged the Bleacher Report team in the right direction. Most of the tools came in the form of documents outlining advice or coding suggestions. Using such manuals, developers can often miss these stylistic and design inconsistencies, or worse will only focus on these types of issues during a code review and miss critical logical errors or regressions. With code formatters and linters such as Credo, most of those concerns are automated away.

Other elements of code consistency go much deeper. In the next section, we will work on consistency of types.

Typespecs and Dialyxir

Functional languages depend heavily on types to determine how functions interact with one another. You can dramatically improve a function's declaration of intent with *typespecs*. A typespec annotates the expected input and outputs of a function. Typespecs aren't required, but they may be worthwhile because they require the developer to explicitly state what a function accepts and what it returns.

Since many bugs creep in at system boundaries such as function interfaces, declaring and enforcing types when you make your function definitions lets you find bugs and improve documentation for your programs. Typespecs are a consistent and repeatable way to document your system and decrease bugs. They're especially useful for teams adopting functional languages for the first time:

- To use them effectively, programmers must reason through how their functions interact.

- They help tools find bugs that tests might not.

In this section, we'll show you how to write typespecs and use them to find bugs in your programs. We'll work through some code examples, use some Elixir type specs, and then use an automated tool called Dialyxir to look for type bugs.

Conscious Coding

By default, Elixir checks the arity, or the number of arguments each function requires. A type spec is an extra annotation for a function that does more. Creating one is declaring your intent that your function takes specific types as arguments and produces a return value of a specific type.

Think of a function that adds two integers and returns the sum. Here's the function:

```
def add(x, y), do: x + y
```

Both inputs and the output might be of type integer(), so your typespec would look like this:

```
@spec add(integer(), integer()) :: integer()
def add(x, y), do: x + y
```

Comments and documentation are subjective *opinions*; typespecs are objective *facts*. Many programmers think of types as a hurdle to satisfy compilers. But types can be a great communication tool when extended to your domain.

Imagine you are writing a function that computes the distance between two points:

```
@spec distance({number(), number()}, {number(), number()}) :: float()
def distance({x1, y1}, {x2, y2}) do
  :math.sqrt(:math.pow(x2 - x1, 2) + :math.pow(y2 - y1, 2))
end
```

The typespec tells us about the inputs and outputs but it is devoid of any domain knowledge. That makes it hard to read and even full of duplication, as seen in the {number(), number()} tuple.

Let's rewrite it to rely on user-defined types:

```
@type point() :: {number(), number()}
@type distance() :: float()

@spec distance(point(), point()) :: distance()
def distance({x1, y1}, {x2, y2}) do
  :math.sqrt(:math.pow(x2 - x1, 2) + :math.pow(y2 - y1, 2))
end
```

User-defined types have more semantic meaning than the default Elixir types for the developers reading and writing the code. As the module grows, you will re-use those types, leading to clearer and more understandable code. The full reference for typespecs in Elixir can be found in the Elixir documentation.[3] They are interesting on their own, but get more useful once you start automating error checking.

Dialyxir

Since Elixir is a dynamically typed language, the compiler doesn't bother to evaluate whether your typespecs are correct. The compiler only cares if the number of function arguments, or arity, and function name match.

Typespecs don't seem useful; you can remove them without upsetting the compiler. You might ask yourself why you'd ever go through the effort for extraneous typespecs. Worse, typespecs could easily fall out of alignment with the functions they support and lead to confusion. We need some kind of tool to automate type checking just as Credo automates style checks.

Jeremy Huffman[4] has written a library called Dialyxir,[5] which is a set of easy-to-use mix tasks for Dialyzer, an Erlang tool named from the characters in *DIscrepancy AnaLYZer for ERlang*. The tool actually analyzes your code for type consistency using your typespecs for extra information. Let's give Dialyxir a try. In the same hexify project from the previous section, add Dialyxir to your dependencies in mix.exs:

```
ensuring_code_consistency/belief_structure/mix_1.exs
defp deps do
  [
    {:credo, "~> 0.8.8", only: [:dev], runtime: false},
    {:dialyxir, "~> 0.5", only: [:dev], runtime: false}
  ]
end
```

---

3. https://hexdocs.pm/elixir/typespecs.html
4. https://github.com/jeremyjh
5. https://github.com/jeremyjh/dialyxir

and now let's configure it:

```
ensuring_code_consistency/belief_structure/mix_1.exs
def project do
  [
    app: :belief_structure,
    dialyzer: [plt_add_deps: :transitive],
```

You're likely wondering what plt does. The *Persistent Lookup Table* (PLT) is a compiled cache containing the analysis of your application. Otherwise, running Dialyxir would take ages. First run:

```
> mix dialyzer
```

Wait some time for it to run. And continue to wait a bit more. You'll eventually need to cancel it. And *now* you understand why building this cache is important.

Let's add some incorrect specs to see what Dialyxir says. Crack open hexify.ex again, and add these typespecs:

```
ensuring_code_consistency/belief_structure/lib/belief_structure/hexify_1.ex
defmodule BeliefStructure.Hexify do
  @spec name(integer) :: integer
  def name(package) do
    package(package)
  end

  @spec package(boolean) :: boolean
  def package(package) do
    package <> "_ex"
  end
end
```

After mix dialyzer, you'll clearly see what's broken:

```
    >> mix dialyzer

...

  hexify.ex:2: Invalid type specification
    for function 'Elixir.BeliefStructure.Hexify':name/1.
    The success typing is (binary()) -> <<_:24,_:_*8>>
  hexify.ex:7: Invalid type specification
    for function 'Elixir.BeliefStructure.Hexify':package/1.
    The success typing is (binary()) -> <<_:24,_:_*8>>

  done in 0m1.12s
  done (warnings were emitted)
```

Mercifully this only took 0m1.12s to analyze. The Invalid type specification warning shows that the both name/1 and package/1 expect a binary. You can infer both from the code, but Dialyxir makes it explicit. Fix the specs and rerun Dialyxir, like this:

```
ensuring_code_consistency/belief_structure/lib/belief_structure/hexify_2.ex
defmodule BeliefStructure.Hexify do
  @spec name(String.t) :: String.t
  def name(package) do
    package(package )
  end

  @spec package(String.t) :: String.t
  defp package( package ) do
    package <> "_ex"
  end
end
```

Now when you run mix dialyzer, you get a successful report. All our types are correct, and we're confident these functions expect a string and return a string. These typespecs, in turn, lead to better tests and better documentation.

One thing to be aware of is that Dialyzer warnings can be difficult to understand and troubleshoot. You can potentially lose a lot of time trying to sort out somewhat cryptic errors, and it could even spook some of your team while they are learning Elixir. Take a look at the following warnings emitted by Dialyzer:

1. Function handle_cast/2 has no local return

2. The return type tuple() in the specification of init/1 is not a subtype of 'ignore' | {'ok',_} | {'stop',_} | {'ok',_,'hibernate' | 'infinity' | non_neg_integer()}, which is the expected return type for the callback of 'Elixir.GenServer' behaviour

Both of them are relatively easily solved. For the no local return warning, you must explicitly declare the handle_cast/2 function will fail by adding no_return() as the return type of its @spec. The second warning happens when the return type of your @spec does not match the return type defined for the callback by Elixir's GenServer.

The point is, though, that these kinds of warnings can be overwhelming if you're retroactively adding in the typespecs or you've been adding typespecs along the way without testing them against Dialyzer.

Finally, even if you spec all your functions in your application correctly, warnings might still pop up from external libraries you include in your application, just as you'd get compiler warnings from included libraries.

Dialyzer does require an explicit step to run and it produces cryptic errors, so it is an acquired taste. But if you tend to like the safety types can offer, typespecs with Dialyzer may provide just enough support for you. We will explore one of those areas next. Let's talk about documentation.

Documentation

We've discussed strategies for how to enforce consistent coding standards and typespecs. These are arguably objective metrics. Documentation, on the other hand, is essential to maintaining a consistent codebase, but since it's for human readers, it's much more subjective.

For experienced developers, documentation of public and common interfaces allows rapid ramp up and removes friction. For new adopters, documentation is essential. Documentation will help them internalize how your new application works, and serves as a first point of communication between the code producer and consumer. In this section, we're going to look at ways to help automate aspects of your documentation. We'll look at tools to help you build tested examples into your code and check the health of your documentation with a single automated metric.

The Elixir team emphasizes first-class documentation support. The documentation for your application should be easy to write and easy to read. For writing, use the @doc and @moduledoc attributes. The former documents public functions and macros, and the latter describes the module. Write Elixir documentation in Markdown.[6]

Elixir makes a strong distinction between documentation and code comments. Documentation is written for developers that consume your APIs, and must be understandable without opening the source code. In contrast, code comments should be reserved for important observations that developers might otherwise miss, and should be used sparingly.

The Elixir guides provide an overview on how to write documentation[7] and a couple of ground rules. As with the other tools mentioned in this chapter, the most important rules will come from within your team and organization, especially when it comes to what to document.

For reading documentation, you may be able to access it in IEx via the h helper or directly from your editor. But most commonly, developers access documentation via the browser, in the form of HTML pages. To build those, you'll use ExDoc.

---

6. https://guides.github.com/features/mastering-markdown/
7. https://hexdocs.pm/elixir/writing-documentation.html

Using ExDoc

Using ExDoc is easy because it feels like any other tool in the Elixir ecosystem. Add ExDoc to your mix.exs as you would any other library, like this:

```
{:ex_doc, "~> 0.18", only: [:dev], runtime: false}
```

Run mix deps.get and then mix docs to output the documentation. There are many configuration options detailed on the GitHub page to configure ExDoc as you see fit.

To see examples of ExDoc check any of the packages on hex.pm. For example, if we browse over to hexdocs.pm/ecto we can see its output. If you point your browser at hexdocs.pm/ecto you'll see something like the following figure:

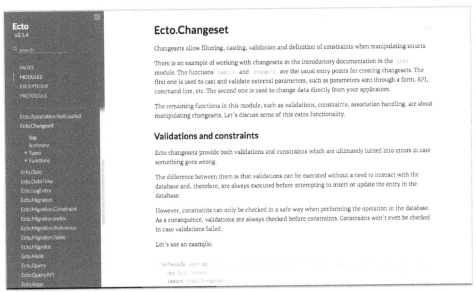

One of the benefits to how ExDoc outputs the documentation is that it feels like annotated code rather than a division between code and documentation. It's accessible and therefore useful. You can see the results of your module tags. With ExDoc, you can keep minimal focus on the contents of your documentation and leave the more mechanical elements to your tool chain.

While ExDoc automates how you document each piece of code, InchEx measures the level of your code's documentation coverage.

InchEx

InchEx is another tool written by Credo's René Föhring, and it takes a more laissez-faire approach to measuring documentation coverage. Instead of assigning an overall percentage of covered documentation, it evaluates and grades each module. You can decide how much is enough. A more experienced team might work for a grade of say 50%. A newer team might aim higher because such programmers need more support. OpenSource frameworks might aim especially high.

Let's start adding some documentation for InchEx to measure. Examples complement even the most basic of functions. Elixir promotes such practices by providing doctests, automatically running the examples in the documentation when running tests:

```
ensuring_code_consistency/belief_structure/lib/belief_structure_1.ex
defmodule BeliefStructure do
  @doc """
  Adds the "_ex" suffix to the package name if necessary.

  ## Examples

      iex> BeliefStructure.hexify("math_ex")
      "math_ex"

  """
  @spec hexify(String.t) :: String.t
  def hexify(package) do
    case String.ends_with?(package, "ex") do
      true -> package
      false -> BeliefStructure.Hexify.name(package)
    end
  end
end
```

Now that we've added some documentation, we can run InchEx on our codebase like any other hex package. Add it to your deps in mix.exs:

```
{:inch_ex, "~> 0.5", only: [:dev, :test], runtime: false}
```

Then run mix deps.get and then mix inch. It'll return something like this:

```
$ mix inch

# Properly documented, could be improved:
 |  B  ↑  Hexify.package/1

# Undocumented:
 |  U  ↑  BeliefStructure
 |  U  ↗  BeliefStructure.hexify/1

Grade distribution (undocumented, C, B, A):  █ _ ▄ ▄
```

mix inch can give reviewers a quick snapshot of the documentation health. Important open source projects, such as Plug and Ecto, rely on InchEx to guarantee their APIs are well documented and help to spot any undocumented code. Documentation is essential on any codebase that is meant to be used by a group of developers beyond the team who maintains it.

Tests and Code Coverage

In the past fifteen years, we've seen a tremendous growth in automated software testing. Elixir embraces this trend. Rather than give you a deep dive into any single tool, we're going to walk you through a few important ones that will help ease your adoption.

ExUnit

Elixir ships with a unit testing framework called ExUnit.[8] Based on longstanding principles, it serves as the basic building block for almost all other Elixir testing frameworks.

The Elixir community expects applications and libraries to be well tested. We'll not give you more than a brief overview here, but we will touch on some ExUnit basics:

- Tests are a series of scripts that mix discovers and runs based on their name.

- Each test runs a flow of setup, test, teardown.

- After setup, a test executes some piece of application code and then makes one or more assertions about what should be true.

- If an assertion is not true or there's an unplanned application exception, the test fails.

ExUnit has a strong focus on usability. Every time an assertion fails, you get detailed reporting on what went wrong. Recent Elixir versions even show colored diffs in those reports, making it trivial to spot errors.

Most of your interactions with the test suite happen through mix test.[9] Because it integrates with ExUnit tags, mix test provides plenty of control of what to test on every invocation. For example, if you have tests that need to talk to external services, you may want to hide those behind an external tag and run those only when necessary with mix test --only external. We recommend checking out the other flags available in the mix test command. We use flags such as --stale and --cover on a daily basis.

---

8.   https://hexdocs.pm/ex_unit/ExUnit.html
9.   https://hexdocs.pm/mix/Mix.Tasks.Test.html

The testing philosophy is equally important to the tooling. Elixir developers put a strong emphasis on concurrent tests. ExUnit lets you run a group of tests concurrently by simply passing the async: true option when defining your test cases. Frameworks such as Phoenix build on those capabilities, allowing you to run tests concurrently even when your application needs to talk to the database.[10]

Avoid Mocking Libraries

Another important testing philosophy is that the Elixir community prefers to avoid mocking libraries that dynamically change the code under test.[11] For example, if you need to communicate to external services, tools such as Bypass[12] let you to run a web API on the same VM as your tests. This API can be controlled by your tests through composed external responses. This way your tests fully exercise the code that integrates with the third-party service, from your business logic to the HTTP client. Bypass has been invaluable to test the integration with external systems at Bleacher Report and icanmakeitbetter.

On the other hand, if you really need to define a mock in your application, you can use Mox.[13] That library is an option that enforces explicit contracts in your code while still allowing tests to run concurrently.

As you get into Elixir, those practices and philosophies will become clearer through the documentation and the tooling. If you are using individual frameworks such as Nerves and Phoenix, those ecosystems will help point you in the right direction as well.

With that basic introduction out of the way, let's move on to other useful testing tools. In the next section, we'll show you how to capture a basic metric for test health: coverage.

Measuring Test Coverage with Excoveralls

In this chapter, we've focused not just on automation tools but measurement tools. One such measurement is test coverage. Code coverage doesn't measure the quality of your tests. It measures how much of your system your tests execute. As your team adopts Elixir, it's easy for code to creep into the codebase without tests. With a coverage tool, you can objectively measure how much of your code that's exercised by at least one test. Just as importantly,

---

10. https://hexdocs.pm/ecto/Ecto.Adapters.SQL.Sandbox.html
11. http://blog.plataformatec.com.br/2015/10/mocks-and-explicit-contracts/
12. https://github.com/PSPDFKit-labs/bypass
13. https://github.com/plataformatec/mox

you can use it to see whether any individual line of code in the system has supporting tests.

Test coverage is a good rubric by which to measure the overall health and stability of an application. With high test coverage, we can be confident when we refactor or add new features. It helps eliminate regression and other bugs. Ultimately, if you have meaningful tests, it's a testament to the code doing what it says it does.

Excoveralls[14] is a library that measures test coverage, sending a report to the command line, to HTML, or to external services. For our purposes, let's focus on the command-line and HTML output options.

To use Excoveralls add ex_coveralls to the deps function in mix.exs:

```
ensuring_code_consistency/belief_structure/mix_2.exs
defp deps do
  [
    {:credo, "~> 0.8.8", only: [:dev], runtime: false},
    {:dialyxir, "~> 0.5", only: [:dev], runtime: false},
    {:excoveralls, "~> 0.7.4", only: [:test], runtime: false},
    {:ex_doc, "~> 0.18", only: [:dev], runtime: false},
    {:inch_ex, "~> 0.5", only: [:dev, :test], runtime: false}
  ]
end
```

You also need to add the test_coverage tuple to the project function. The test_coverage configuration is a mechanism to configure the tool and options for how you want to test your application. The default is a wrapper around cover[15] that ships as part of Erlang/OTP.

Now, open up mix.exs and fill out the preferred_cli_env to use with coveralls. preferred_cli_env allows you to set the preferred environment to run command-line tasks:

```
ensuring_code_consistency/belief_structure/mix_2.exs
def project do
  [
    app: :belief_structure,
    preferred_cli_env: [
      "coveralls": :test,
      "coveralls.detail": :test,
      "coveralls.post": :test,
      "coveralls.html": :test,
    ],
    test_coverage: [tool: ExCoveralls],
```

---

14. https://github.com/parroty/excoveralls
15. http://erlang.org/doc/man/cover.html

Now just run mix coveralls:

```
----------------
COV     FILE                               LINES RELEVANT   MISSED
 66.7% lib/belief_structure.ex                18        3        1
  0.0% lib/belief_structure/hexify.ex         11        2        2
[TOTAL]  40.0%
----------------
```

If you run mix coveralls.detail you'll get a command-line output of each file with the covered lines highlighted in green. Like mix coveralls.detail, mix coveralls.html outputs to cover/excoveralls.html.

These detailed reports can help to up test coverage or, from a reviewer's point of view, make it easy to see how the code-to-be-committed fits in with the rest of the application and how well it's tested.

As with InchEx, you can decide how much coverage you want to maintain. The icanmakeitbetter team maintains full 100% coverage, except for ignored files that work on external interfaces. At Bleacher Report, the team does not require full coverage, but does measure it. They choose to invest in code quality in other ways. You'll need to figure out what makes sense for your team and stick with the approach that works best for you.

Bureaucrat

Many of the tools available directly in Elixir, such as ExUnit and documentation, focus on modules and functions. ExUnit is a great tool for unit testing. ExDoc is excellent for generating documentation from your modules and functions, with guides covering the remaining functionality.

However, as developers tackle particular domains, such as the domain of web applications with Phoenix, the need for more specific tools arises. So before finishing the testing section, we are going to cover two tools that are specific to web applications, exploring them in the context of Phoenix. If you are using Elixir for other domains, such as embedded software or data processing, it is likely those domains include their own abstractions, which provide similar benefits.

To get started, let's take a look at a Phoenix controller test:

```
test "GET /posts/:id ", %{conn: conn} do
  response =
    get(conn, "/posts/post-name")
    |> json_response(200)
  assert response.status == 200
```

It's a standard controller test. Every framework has its quirks, and Phoenix is no different. You'll pass in the %{conn: conn} map. This is just syntactic sugar for MyApp.ConnTest.build_conn() which sets up a test connection.

Recall that conn is the data that Phoenix needs to describe the whole life of a connection, from the initial attributes about the URL to intermediate data in an application and eventually to the response and status code. Since response is the output of the set of functions you can assert or refute anything that's related to the request and response cycle. It makes integration tests easy to write and explain to new Elixir developers.

But documenting all of the endpoints and attributes available in our APIs is a constant struggle. Those of us who have coded more than a couple of decades remember excessive comments. Our teachers and mentors would request acres of comments at the top of each method. Over time, some have come to understand that comments can get out of sync with your codebase.

A similar issue occurs with API documentation. The problem is that no matter how vigilant one is in maintaining it, inconsistencies emerge. For someone who writes loads of API docs, it's a time-consuming process, and *errors undermine confidence.*

Enter Bureaucrat,[16] a tool that attempts to solve this discrepancy problem. Bureaucrat is a library that generates API documentation from tests. If you have good API tests, then the API docs are always in sync.

Let's try it out. By now, the steps for integrating a new tool should seem familiar. Add bureaucrat to the deps section in mix.exs and then run mix deps.get. You'll also need to update test/test_helper.exs and modify it like so:

```
Bureaucrat.start
ExUnit.start(formatters: [ExUnit.CLIFormatter, Bureaucrat.Formatter])
```

All this does is start Bureaucrat when you run your tests and adds the Bureaucrat.Formatter module to the list of formatters to run when ExUnit runs. Additionally, you need to modify test/support/conn_case.ex:

```
defmodule MyApp.ConnCase do
  using do
    quote do
      # ... all of the other Phoenix imports omitted
      import Bureaucrat.Helpers
    end
  end
end
```

---

16. https://github.com/api-hogs/bureaucrat

And that's it. All that remains is to tell which tests Bureaucrat should document. Bureaucrat makes it spectacularly easy to generate documentation from tests:

```
test "creates and renders resource when data is valid", %{conn: conn} do
  conn =
    conn
    |> post("/ratings", rating: @valid_attrs)
    |> doc

  assert json_response(conn, 201)["data"]["id"]
  assert Repo.get_by(Rating, @valid_attrs)
end
```

Then run DOC=1 mix test, and it generates your documentation, which should look something like this:

```
Creates and renders resource when data is valid

Request

  • Method: POST
  • Path: /ratings
  • Request headers:

  accept: application/json
  content-type: multipart/mixed; charset: utf-8

  • Request body:

  {
    "rating": {
      "favorite": true,
      "location": "Berkeley, CA",
      "stars": 3
    }
  }

Response

  • Status: 201
  • Response headers:

  content-type: application/json; charset=utf-8
  cache-control: max-age=0, private, must-revalidate
  x-request-id: q5fj1d7dmp0lul68fn3d8hanluct9v71
  location: /ratings/29

  • Response body:

  {
    "data": {
      "favorite": true,
      "id": 29,
      "location": "Berkeley, CA",
      "stars": 3
    }
  }
```

By default, Bureaucrat outputs documentation to web/controllers/README.md but you may also output all documentation to a custom directory like this:

```
Bureaucrat.start(
  writer: Bureaucrat.MarkdownWriter,
  default_path: "doc/APIDOCS.md",
  paths: [],
  env_var: "EXPORT"
)
```

Creating accurate API docs on the fly is invaluable because now as long as there is sufficient test coverage, the relevant documentation is always in sync.

Putting It All Together: Code Reviews

All previous sections in this chapter lead to the code review. Each section reinforces the others and paves the way for meaningful collaboration in the form of code reviews.

Authors have editors, builders have inspections, and judges have appellate courts; even cosmetologists have oversight. Programmers, on the other hand, have none of these things. Although bad code often has serious real-life consequences (such as grounded planes or stolen identities), we don't handle formal reviews very well as an industry. Healthy code needs accountability, and that requires many sets of eyes on the same code. Here's the thing about code reviews, though: good code reviews take effort, and inconsistent code provides friction that multiplies that effort.

Automating Your Consistency Checks

Everything we've written so far builds up to writing the healthiest, most consistent code possible so your reviews can be better and more effective. You don't have to follow all of these techniques, but each one helps prepare a pull request so the reviewer can focus on what's important to you. Putting together the last few sections we can now create an alias in your mix.exs to do all the work for us. You can make your mix file look like this:

```
ensuring_code_consistency/belief_structure/mix_3.exs
def aliases do
  [
    "ensure_consistency": ["test", "dialyzer", "credo --strict", "inch",
                           "coveralls"]
  ]
end
def project do
  [
    app: :belief_structure,
    aliases: aliases(),
```

Now, whenever you run this alias, you'll get all the information a developer needs—from style to documentation to typespecs and test and test coverage—before a code review, after a major refactoring, when hiring a new developer, or before a major release. When these requirements are met, you'll be better prepared for whatever the world throws at you.

You may even decide to run tests, or check for the existence of one or more of these artifacts *each time you commit*. To do so, you can use a continuous integration (CI) server such as Travis-CI,[17] circle-ci,[18] or Jenkins.[19] Another compelling tool is Ebert.[20] This tool automates your review process by running linters such as Credo each time you do a pull request. In the interest of full disclosure, keep in mind that Ebert is a paid service from Plataformatec, the company behind Elixir.

The computer can do the things computers are good at—measuring test coverage, enforcing types, and the tedious job of implementing consistent style. The computer can even automate enforcement of the above. Reviewers can then focus on ensuring that business logic matches your business rules, and the functions do what they are supposed to do. Let's assume you've run your consistency check, with a CI server or by hand. The next step is to get a set of experienced eyes on that code.

Performing Code Reviews

The best way for new programmers to learn is to start coding—but that's not enough. Coders need oversight just like code does. Without good mentoring and proper reviews, simply writing code just reinforces bad habits. Good mentoring that can augment code reviews instead breaks bad habits before they start and reinforces good behaviors.

How you do code reviews is up to you. Sometimes, two developers can pair, with the author walking the reviewer through the most critical details. Other times, team leads might review code from a formal pull request, or a senior developer might simply read through a commit summary. You can use many different approaches to get to the same place. The important thing is that your development process builds in accountability and oversight so real people read code as soon as it is ready. Keep these concepts in mind as you decide what's best for you:

---

17. https://travis-ci.org/
18. https://circleci.com/
19. https://jenkins.io/
20. https://ebertapp.io/

- Larger and more inexperienced teams need more communication.

- Larger teams need more formal mechanisms to enforce reviews.

- Reviews are one of the most important ways to ramp up inexperienced developers quickly.

- All teams need regular reviews.

Once you've decided how to perform your reviews, your next decision is how to provide feedback. A quick word of advice: code reviews don't impact all programmers in the same way. Stay gentle and kind. Refrain from making judgments about people, and avoid biting humor. In this context, such comments often prove more toxic than you expect.

Even if your reviews are verbal, it's best to come out of each review with a tangible punch list. Your punch list may be an informal text file, but tickets work best. You can even combine many tasks in a single ticket if the requests aren't too sweeping. This approach allows you to formalize follow-up with the tools you already have on hand.

Wrapping Up

This chapter took a look at code consistency. More than a dry list of dos and don'ts, we focused instead on how to build a process with a series of automated measurements to ensure a lasting, healthy codebase. These techniques and tools are not mandates. Each team must decide which ones to adopt and which to ignore based on experience, code complexity, and the makeup of the team.

We started with coding standards. Elixir's code formatter enforces a consistent style and the Credo linter helps to measure code quality. We then moved on to types. Typespecs help make your intentions clear and Dialyzer uses them with other clues in the language to find bugs and stylistic inconsistencies. Documentation tools help establish metrics for the health of your system and build more effective documentation.

We spent a good amount of time on tests. Elixir's testing philosophy is different, with a focus on concurrency and eschewing dynamic mocks and stubs in favor of tools such as Bypass and Mox. Measurement tools such as Coveralls measure coverage as a basic metric for code health and Bureaucrat builds documentation for external interfaces.

All of these concepts build toward better code reviews. Automating these elements led to code reviews that could focus on the application domain rather than tediously pointing out lacking tests, inconsistent style, or imperfect documentation. This was a lot to cover, but we're ready to stop talking about coding standards and consistency, and start talking about implementation. In the next chapter, we'll discuss how to integrate with legacy systems and manage your dependencies. You're almost through Part I.

## CHAPTER 4

Legacy Systems and Dependencies

If you're considering Elixir and you have legacy code, your head is likely swimming with risk factors, plans, and contingencies. You may even be considering Elixir for the exact purpose of replacing a legacy system. Migrating some small aspect of your system is hard. Migrating an application in another language complicates simpler migrations by changing not just your language but the set of libraries and tools you've come to depend on. In this chapter, we'll show you some approaches that will help you mitigate that risk.

On the other hand, if you are using Elixir to start a brand-new business or project, you may be wondering how to keep the code you are writing today from becoming legacy. We have bad news and good news. The bad news is that the code you wrote today is already legacy code. You will have to maintain, evolve, and support it. That's OK. The good news is that a lot can be done to make this maintenance a pleasant experience.

This book is about adopting Elixir *to write maintainable applications*. Making tomorrow's legacy code beautiful is something we can work on proactively and continuously, but our applications do not exist in a vacuum. They also have dependencies, even some that may be out of our control. If you are not careful, any *dependency* may become a legacy system to replace.

A complete discussion of legacy systems and dependencies could fill a book of its own. Therefore we will focus on three main topics that are actively debated in the Elixir community. The first one is how to replace a legacy web application gradually with Elixir. Then we will talk about umbrella projects as an alternative to manage dependencies by your team. The third topic will cover how to manage *code* dependencies. We won't discuss how to handle external dependencies, like third-party APIs, nor how to choose other parts of your stack that you depend on, such as the operating system and the database.

That's a pretty full list, so let's get started.

Replacing a Legacy Web App

You may have heard this old joke: the only way to move a mountain is one stone at a time. Legacy application migrations are nearly impossible to handle all at once. You have to break the problem into manageable pieces to even have a chance. Over the course of this section, we'll walk you through this process. The resources available to you and the size of your platform certainly has an effect on how long this process will take, but the process will remain the same. There's a political element and a technical one.

The political element involves setting expectations and managing risk. Throughout this book, we stress the importance of setting expectations. Programming is more than 1s and 0s. Successful programmers communicate.

The technical element is isolating small bits of the application to migrate, step by step. With a little time and effort, you can have a common web API that has two back ends, one for your legacy system and one for the new. Then, you can flip the switch, either all at once or one subsystem at a time.

Where you begin depends on a number of factors, including your company's architecture and urgency. Let's start with architecture, of which we'll consider two general types: monolithic and service-oriented architecture (SOA). Many companies with scaling and code maintenance issues use a monolith of some sort. Monoliths are large systems written as a single project with little to no boundaries between its components. They are often hard to understand and maintain due to their size and the coupling they promote between components. Even worse, such large applications often take a long time to boot, followed by a long-running test suite, both undermining the development feedback cycle. Since monoliths are the hardest one to manage, we'll assume your legacy system is a monolith.

Most organizations who adopt service-oriented architectures do so because they've been through the pain of managing a monolith. SOA is composed of many services that communicate via a protocol, such as HTTP+JSON or Apache Thrift. Replacing a service is a matter of looking at the Elixir ecosystem for libraries that implement said protocol and then replacing the problematic services by others implemented in Elixir while keeping the same API. One of the benefits of SOA is exactly the replaceability of subsystems and that's what we get here.

Here is the plan. We will start with a case study from Bleacher Report on how they migrated their eight-year-old monolith gradually, discussing how they mitigated risk and their approach to incremental APIs. Luckily for us, the Elixir ecosystem has grown considerably since Bleacher Report took this effort and tools built specifically for interfacing with legacy systems have surfaced. After that, we will explore one of them called Terraform.

When Bleacher chose to adopt Elixir, their system as a single application was eight years old. Their monolith was designed as a desktop-first experience, and now the majority of the company's traffic comes from mobile devices. Their business grew as they added the capability to follow individual teams and players. With the advent of the smartphone, notifications alerted users to breaking news and events, driving their traffic higher.

The problems that haunted their system were scaling and serving personalized content on demand. You've read about their attempts to cache or add servers. After that, it was clear they had to introduce a new technology, as they had reached the limits of their existing stack. They had to break up the monolith.

Around this time they forged their agreement with key stakeholders. The potential risk was enormous. The team decided to build their core content streams in a language that had only recently reached 1.0 (in 2014) and use Phoenix, a framework that was about a year away from 1.0. That was the core of their business.

The team drew the boundaries around this first Elixir service. The service would fetch a user's subscriptions and built content streams for each subscription. As they built the service, they also had to change the legacy application to request the service using an HTTP client. Eventually the service would serve as the single source of truth for the rest of Bleacher Report. Today, mobile applications and the front end access the service directly without passing through the legacy application.

Once the team came up with the app boundaries, the next problem was deciding who should work on it. They wanted to balance two concerns. They identified leaders who were the primary Elixir advocates. They also needed to mix in enough business experience to solve the problem, so they identified the developers who wrote or supported the legacy code. That combination gave them both domain knowledge and enough Elixir chops to solve the critical problem.

It was high-risk, high-precision surgery with a small and confident team. The sports giant decided to replace a core part of their system but one very limited in scope. Doing too much or getting too many people involved would have increased risk even further, and that's the last thing they wanted.

Once a prototype was ready, they didn't deploy it to production right away. Instead, they ranked content streams roughly by *ascending* popularity to proxy to the new Elixir service.

They used less popular streams to test how the service performed. If a stream were to fail, they'd prefer to draw the ire from Olympic equestrian fans in a non-Olympic year than World Cup soccer fans at the peak of the tournament. They built a simple app to direct requests based on a static file, routing streams to either the Elixir servers or the existing legacy ones. As Bleacher Report has roughly 70,000 content streams, this approach was quite cumbersome. It did work though and it allowed both the development team and business side stakeholders to develop confidence until they completely removed the stop-gap.

That was the basic rubric that the team used to port its first critical legacy component to Elixir. To summarize:

- They isolated the part of the legacy system that was failing the most.
- They built a team just large enough to solve the problem.
- They included both Elixir skill and legacy domain experience.
- They tested their prototype in production gradually until they had enough confidence to fully depend on it.

With their first victory in hands, the technical team was ready to push forward and migrate other critical components to Elixir. They chose the strangler vine[1] technique to move forward. The strangler vine means you build new pieces of a large application over months or even years using a new technology until the old system just dies and is subsumed. It was deliberate and incremental. Steady, iterative progress will win over time.

Three years after they started, they're still porting the last few bits of the legacy system, partially because the urgency isn't as great. Some of the stragglers aren't traffic-dependent services and others are internal tools around the edges of their system. Now their performance is better, their teams are more productive, their customers are happier, and their software is easier to extend.

In the next section, we will add some technical depth by exploring the Terraform project and show how some of the techniques used by Bleacher Report translate to code.

---

1.   https://www.martinfowler.com/bliki/StranglerApplication.html

Terraform and API Evolution

As Bleacher Report took their first steps in replacing a legacy web application, one of their initial challenges was visualizing how to go from a single application to potentially many without disrupting the service. They opted for an approach where the new service was completely decoupled from the legacy application but the legacy application had to be changed to talk to this new system via an HTTP client. This worked well in their case, as the functionality they were isolating was quite focused. While a good chunk of their system would depend on this new service, the service in itself depended on little else.

You may not be so lucky. Depending on your application, you may be hard pressed to find a subsystem that does not depend on other core components, such as authentication. For this reason, many companies choose the authentication service to be the first to be replaced or extracted from the legacy system. This can get quite complex, as you need both old and new code to have the same logic when it comes to encryption of passwords and generation of tokens.

In this section, you will explore one particular approach to migrating legacy web applications. You'll replace a legacy application with Lauren Tan and Dan McClain's Terraform library.[2] Terraforming is the act of transforming a planet so as to resemble the earth, especially so that it can support human life. The Terraform library allows you to wrap endpoints of your web application and replace them with an Elixir alternative. That allows you to change your "planet" as smoothly as possible by keeping the overall web API the same while you work in small increments, replacing a single API at a time. Terraform handles the rest. You don't need to change all of your endpoints at once because Terraform proxies unhandled legacy requests and hands them off to the old system.

Lauren's blog post "Rise from the Ashes"[3] walks you through the Terraform basics.

Let's take a look at Lauren's example application[4] for a Terraform primer. Like any other dependency, the first step is to add it to the mix.exs file in your projects:

---

2. https://github.com/poteto/terraform/
3. https://medium.com/@sugarpirate/rise-from-the-ashes-incremental-apis-with-phoenix-b08cd66bd142
4. https://github.com/poteto/reverse_proxy

```
defp deps do
  [
    ...#omitted
    {:terraform, "~> 1.0.1"}
  ]
end
```

Next, we need to define both a terraformer and a client. A terraformer matches on the incoming request and proxies it to the legacy application. In the reverse proxy example, the terraformer matches all GET requests and raises a Not Implemented Yet exception otherwise. Let's go through this module bit by bit:[5]

```
defmodule ReverseProxy.Terraformers.Giphy do
  use Plug.Router
  require Logger
  alias ReverseProxy.Clients.Giphy

  @host Application.fetch_env!(:reverse_proxy, :giphy)[:host]

  plug :match
  plug :dispatch
```

The external API URL in this case is Giphy. plug :match and plug :dispatch are the building blocks of a Plug.Router.[6] This router tells Plug to first match on a route and then dispatch the request. Let's see the routes next:

```
# match specific path
get "/v1/hello-world", do: send_resp(conn, 200, "Hello world")

# catch all `get`s
get _ do
  %{
    method: "GET",
    request_path: request_path,
    params: params,
    req_headers: req_headers
  } = conn
  # logging omitted
  res = Giphy.get!(request_path, req_headers, [params: Map.to_list(params)])
```

This section of the module defines what routes terraformer proxies to the external service. Remember, a proxy is simply a service that forwards one request to some third party. This example handles /v1/hello-world locally, and hands other requests to the general catch-all get _ do. Any request that falls through to this catch-all will proxy to Giphy, returning hilarious and insightful gifs.

---

5. https://github.com/poteto/reverse_proxy/blob/master/lib/reverse_proxy/terraformers/giphy.ex
6. https://hexdocs.pm/plug/Plug.Router.html

Next, we should handle non-get requests, like this:

```
match _, do: raise "Not implemented yet"
defp send_response( { :ok, conn,
    %{headers: headers, status_code: status_code, body: body}}) do
  conn = %{conn | resp_headers: headers}
  send_resp(conn, status_code, body)
end
```

The second catch-all `match` handles any non-GET routes. A private function handles and formats the response from the external API. Terraform provides an elegant way to handle incremental API development both in its flexibility and in its simplicity, server side.

Let's take a look at the client now:[7]

```
defmodule ReverseProxy.Clients.Giphy do
  use HTTPoison.Base

  @host Application.fetch_env!(:reverse_proxy, :giphy)[:host]
  @secret Application.fetch_env!(:reverse_proxy, :giphy)[:secret]

  def process_url(url) do
    @host <> url
  end
  def process_request_headers(headers) do
    headers
    |> List.keyreplace("accept", 0, {"accept", "application/json"})
    |> List.keydelete("host", 0)
  end
end
```

Beautiful. This example shows simple layering of functional APIs. The client uses an HTML client called HTTPoison[8] to do much of the heavy lifting. HTTPoison.Base enables Giphy, our custom client. With Terraform, you need to define process_url/1 and handle the response.

Finally, add the transformer in web/router.ex like so:

```
use Terraform,
  terraformer: ReverseProxy.Terraformers.Giphy
```

That's all there is to it. Now you can start porting all of your code route by route as needed, eventually phasing out the legacy system completely. There is a slight overhead in the response time but it's minimal. You can see the results of Lauren's load test in the blog post referenced earlier.

---

7. https://github.com/poteto/reverse_proxy/blob/master/lib/reverse_proxy/clients/giphy.ex
8. https://github.com/edgurgel/httpoison

Now that we've taken Terraform for a spin, it's time to see how it came to be. Let's see what Lauren has to say about the library migrating legacy systems:

Ben: *What prompted you to write Terraform? Was it for work or personal projects?*

Lauren: *It started out as a toy library to see if it would even be possible. You can already do reverse proxying in something like Nginx, but I was curious to see if it would be possible to do so in an idiomatic way for Phoenix apps that aren't behind Nginx, HAProxy, or something similar. I also wanted the solution to be simple to implement and allow teams to quickly start porting smaller endpoints into Phoenix.*

Ben: *What have been some of the difficulties associated with migrating legacy apps to Elixir/Phoenix?*

Lauren: *At my previous company, I worked on a project where we were asked by a client to rewrite their Node.js API with Elixir and Phoenix. This was before I wrote the Terraform plug with Dan McClain (my colleague at the time). The number one challenge was that the rewrite was up against a moving target, as the Node.js API was still in active feature development. They didn't have a very comprehensive test suite either, so this was another difficulty. We also couldn't ship the Phoenix application until it achieved feature parity with the production API. This was quite frustrating! In fact, I would say that this was one of the primary frustrations that led us to write the Terraform plug.*

Ben: *How have you gone about identifying which legacy systems to replace?*

Lauren: *I generally advise against rewrites unless there is a compelling reason to do so. In most cases, I believe people will cite factors like performance and maintainability as motivating factors for rewrites, but I think that you can very likely solve those problems by paying off technical debt in your current technology rather than going into a full rewrite.*

To me, a rewrite only makes sense if the benefits greatly outweigh the cost, and that the new language/platform is something that the development team can quickly ramp up on and be productive.

Elixir is a really great choice if your legacy system has constraints/requirements that make it difficult to maintain in the current language. For example, there are fault-tolerance libraries in various languages, and probably none of them can do as good of a job as an Erlang/Elixir-based system while staying maintainable. If the legacy application is frequently failing and negatively affecting the business, then switching to Erlang/Elixir could make sense. It might also be that your legacy system needs to be able to handle a large number of concurrent WebSocket connections. Then Phoenix becomes a very compelling choice.

I would definitely also factor in the skillset of the development team and whether they would be able to rapidly become proficient in Elixir and usage of OTP.

Ben: *Any unexpected difficulties you've encountered when porting legacy systems to new Elixir apps?*

> *Lauren:* *None that are unexpected so far. I am exploring ways to integrate Elixir web applications and microservices into Netflix, and the primary challenge is being able to effectively use the suite of tools that we already have on our platform. The good news is that this is very possible, so I'm excited to see what I can come up with in a few months.*

As with most of the best tools, Lauren created Terraform to satisfy a specific need. Given this context you can see how the proxy approach evolved and how it allows you to port legacy systems with an incremental strategy that moves one endpoint at a time.

Moving Incremental Releases into Production

Once you've decided on an approach to incrementally migrate your application and chosen the technology to go with it you can begin to think about your release strategy. Whether or not you decide to use a service like Terraform, you will begin to migrate your legacy system piece by piece. You will incrementally release new versions to production as you phase the old system out.

Imagine you've finished working on a new version, and you're ready to deploy it. You've load-tested it sufficiently and feel fairly confident that it should perform as expected. You're confident that you've uncovered all of the mysteries the legacy app contains. Then you put it into production, and error reports start rolling in.

There's a better approach to sanity checking your application before it goes live. It works like this. You build a throw-away staging server that will run your code just as it would on a production server, but with copied data. You plan to throw away the results and mine the error logs and reports for information about bugs.

Let's look at the approach in more detail. You'll proxy the requests you are receiving in production to staging servers. Elixir's lightweight independent processes let us test each new service much more safely than you could in the legacy system. In the Task module, there's a start/1 function. start/1 is essentially a fire-and-forget function. As the docs say,[9] you should only use start/1 if you have "no interest in the returned result."

Here's how this process plays out. A user makes a request to the server. If the duplexing is inactive, the staging server never receives a request. When duplexing is active, we use Task.start/1 to make a non-blocking request with the same parameters to the staging server. This approach works equally well with monoliths and smaller services.

---

9. https://hexdocs.pm/elixir/Task.html#start/1

You can probably see where this is going. Let's add this functionality to the Terraform example from the previous section. Let's make sure that all requests to the legacy system also include a request to the staging system. We are using Terraform but this technique could work with other libraries as well. Open up the ReverseProxy.Clients.Giphy file again, specifically the process_url/1 function:

```
@host Application.fetch_env!(:reverse_proxy, :giphy)[:host]

def process_url(url) do
  @host <> url
end
```

We can use Task.start/1 and set another attribute called proxy_host to point to the staging environment:

```
@host Application.fetch_env!(:reverse_proxy, :giphy)[:host]
@stag_host Application.fetch_env!(:reverse_proxy, :stag_giphy)[:host]

def process_url(url) do
  Task.start(fn -> proxy_request_to_stag(url) end)
  @host <> url
end

defp proxy_request_to_stag(url) do
  @stag_host <> url
  # make request
end
```

Now there's a non-blocking fire-and-forget request that the application sends off to the staging environment. It doesn't have any noticeable effect on performance, and you can gauge how your app performs with real traffic. Since Task.start/1 returns nothing, you'll need some monitoring and logging on the staging servers to verify that the expected amount of traffic is flowing through the app. Fortunately, we cover that technique in detail in Chapter 10, *Making Your App Production Ready*, on page 193.

Eddie Dombrowski, an engineer at Bleacher Report, came up with the initial idea and the Bleacher Report team has had great success with this strategy. They use the proxy technique whenever they launch any major service, practically eliminating launch-related bugs. We've seen many others that had the same experience.

So far we've seen strategies for migrating an existing application. That's only half the battle. Now, let's examine how to keep it from becoming a monolith just like the one you're are replacing. That's our next topic.

Umbrella Projects: Between Monoliths and Services

Over time, we've come to understand that clean lines between independent services make more maintainable software. Think about using modules to organize code. Beginning programmers often throw all functions into a single module. More experienced programmers learn to group related functions into modules, better defining the responsibilities of each. Modules improve even more when you take the time to define which functions are private and which are public because that practice better defines your module's API, and helps you control the interactions between modules.

Breaking your applications into well-defined modules leads to code that's easier to understand, test, and maintain. Umbrella projects work in the same way. A monolith is like the first few apps you built as a programmer, with all of the functions in the same place. An umbrella helps you better delineate the individual responsibilities of the major parts of your application and then formalize the communications between them.

Now that we've built the intuition, let's formalize the definition some. Many negative traits characterize monoliths:

- Monoliths force coupling across components with poorly specified boundaries, making the application hard to evolve, maintain, and understand.

- Monoliths often have large codebases, leading to long compilation times, a slow boot process, and long-running test suites which overall mean slow feedback cycles.

- You can only scale a monolith in one direction, as you are unable to scale each component independently.

- Organizing multiple teams around a monolith requires coordination across development efforts and deployment.

We are not saying all monoliths are plagued by these issues but many are. One alternative to monoliths is to build an architecture around services or microservices that communicates via your protocol of choice. You can develop those services independently and deploy them in complete isolation. Choosing such architecture will require a very different set of skills from your engineering teams and introduce its own set of complexities.

Others argue for a mixed approach called "Monolith First,"[10] where you start with a monolith and migrate to services once you have a better understanding

---

10. https://martinfowler.com/bliki/MonolithFirst.html

of your domain and of the solution. At this point, it is painfully clear that there is no silver bullet and our goal with this section is not to present one. Instead, you'll find an approach between monoliths and service-oriented approaches.

Elixir provides an alternative called *umbrella projects.* An umbrella project hosts many applications that you can develop together but test and deploy separately, *provided there are no conflicting dependencies between them.* Umbrella projects tackle some of the development, testing, and deployment woes associated with monoliths by defining clearly delineated boundaries between applications when you're working on the details. It also allows developers to run the entire application when you're working on the interfaces between each app in the umbrella.

Monoliths, SOA, and Umbrellas

If you have ever read about or used SOAs, you may be wondering how SOA services compare to umbrellas. Let's break them down.

Monoliths are single-tier applications that combine data, user interface, and control logic into a single application. Elixir umbrellas are separate applications that live in the same repository and share common resources like configuration and dependencies. SOA services are completely independent services that are built separately and share nothing but well-defined interfaces.

If monoliths are single, tightly coupled applications, SOA and Elixir umbrellas are two strategies for decoupling them. SOAs provide complete independence. You can develop and deploy each app independently, with no potential dependency entanglements. You can use Elixir to build SOAs. Umbrellas are an alternative to manage large applications without resorting to SOA. You get some decoupling between the components of the umbrella but they do not yield the same development independence and deployment isolation that SOAs do.

Building an Umbrella Example

Let's create an umbrella project with two applications inside. Go to your command line and type the following:

```
$ mix new my_umbrella --umbrella
```

This command creates a new umbrella project. Different from regular Elixir projects, the umbrella project does not have a lib directory but rather an apps one. Now run this:

```
$ cd my_umbrella/apps
$ mix new app_1
$ mix new app_2
```

That's it, you created two applications in the apps directory. Now, you can see the full power of umbrellas. You can access, compile, and test each of those applications individually. You can also run the application altogether when you're trying to work on integrations between the components. Let's go back to the umbrella project root and do it all at once:

```
$ cd ..
$ mix test
```

All Elixir systems are built of multiple applications, typically packaged as OTP servers. Applications are responsible for packaging your code. The Elixir programming language itself is an application that is part of all Elixir systems. Each application has its own initialization and shutdown logic and can be started and stopped as a unit.

Elixir applications are naturally isolated and decoupled. The applications app_1 and app_2 we have created are very similar to any other Elixir application, except for four lines of code that can be found in their mix.exs configuration:

```
build_path: "../../_build",
config_path: "../../config/config.exs",
deps_path: "../../deps",
lockfile: "../../mix.lock",
```

Those four lines of code add some coupling between app_1 and app_2. The first two say that they use the same configurations, the last two say they use the same dependencies. This coupling means any dependency shared by app_1 and app_2 have to use the exact same version with the exact same configurations. If there is a new version of a dependency used by both, you can't update app_1 without also updating app_2. app_1 and app_2 also can't use the same dependency with slightly different configurations. If you are running into those scenarios, then you will have to break those applications into their own projects.

This coupling only applies to dependencies and configurations; app_1 and app_2 are still isolated. They can be compiled, tested, and deployed separately. If app_1 depends on app_2, it needs to be explicitly added as a dependency in app_1's mix.exs file:

```
defp deps do
  [
    {:app_2, in_umbrella: true}
  ]
end
```

By explicitly listing the dependencies between the umbrella's applications, we start to outline the boundaries between them. It also guarantees our applications won't have cyclic dependencies. If app_1 depends on app_2 which in turns depend on app_1, you will run into compilation errors.

Dividing Applications

Now that you have some of the theory behind umbrellas, let's get a bit more concrete. One approach is to have several different web applications, each using Phoenix for its own presentation layer. One application is stable but the other is in active development. Now imagine the Phoenix team releases a new version. You can't move the currently developed app to the new Phoenix version without also updating the stable one.

In other words, you get independence between the apps that are part of the umbrella but they are tied to the same dependencies. This guarantees a smooth development experience in your umbrella projects. It means switching between applications in an umbrella won't require you to fetch new dependencies nor will it require you to recompile your codebase. The downside is that you'll need to evolve them together.

Another approach is to use umbrellas for code organization purposes. This is the method introduced in Phoenix v1.3. Imagine part of your codebase needs to talk to an external API, another needs to talk to a database, and so forth. You can develop each of those concerns as separate applications and have one other application that is responsible for the "web" presentation, taking care of HTTP, HTML, JSON, GraphQL, or what have you. In this scenario, you never really wanted to deploy those components independently, but you may still use umbrella projects to break a big application into manageable chunks.

In practice, you may end up with a hybrid approach. Using this strategy, you'll build a mixture of independent services and apps created for code organization purposes. For example, one umbrella project may be made of four apps:

- domain: This is the app that talks to your data store and holds most of your business logic

- cms: A small app that runs your homepage, a blog, and other marketing-related concerns

- web: An app that interfaces with cms and domain and presents them over HTTP

- event_processor: An app that consumes events out of RabbitMQ (or similar) and acts on them, often sending new data to the domain app

The domain and cms apps just shown could have been a single application. However, since the CMS is used by the marketing team and completely isolated from the business logic, we created them as separate components. As your system grows, you may even break the domain application apart, extracting concerns such as payments and authentication to separate apps, each with their own storage.

On the other side, web and event_processor are completely independent services, so we develop them as such, but build and deploy them together for convenience.

One question that comes with umbrella projects is whether to introduce a new application to the umbrella. Our advice is to not overthink this decision and create new apps when they are built on different infrastructure, such as different data sources, and when there are clear domain segmentations, such as a CMS for your marketing team. Once you get familiar with breaking your app apart in broad strokes, you will become more confident with handling more complex relationships, should it become necessary.

The reality is that every application will one day become a legacy application. You can control whether that legacy system will be easy to maintain and modify or not. By building systems in isolated pieces, you will ensure that future maintenance will be much more incremental, and thus less invasive. With Elixir, you have a choice. You can build every application as a separate project, as you'd typically do for a SOA. Alternatively, if you have applications that you'll frequently run together, ones that share common services, you can optionally use an umbrella.

Umbrella projects provide an alternative for those who have been burned by monoliths but are worried about the complexity associated with SOAs. Contrary to monoliths, umbrella projects allow developers to define their own boundaries through applications. Like monoliths, all of the code in your umbrellas needs to be built on the same set of dependencies and configuration. If your goal is to build truly independent and isolated subsystems, each with their own technological stack, then services are the way to go.

Applications inside an umbrella may *depend* on each other but often we must depend on code that we didn't write. That's the subject of the next section.

Managing Third-Party Dependencies

At its roots, dealing with legacy systems means dealing with dependencies, each with its own set of potential problems. You'll have to understand whether your dependencies are healthy, poorly maintained, or abandoned altogether. Every application depends on other libraries and each dependency may depend on libraries of its own, often requiring specific versions. Developers need a way to manage these dependency trees so each language has a reliable way to list dependencies, compute the right versions that fit together, and work with the result.

Elixir has a package manager called Hex.[11] Adding Hex dependencies to a project is quite easy but it does not mean it should be done carelessly.

Any dependency becomes fully married to your application, for better or for worse. You may need to get support for it or even debug it yourself. In extreme scenarios, a dependency can eventually become fully unmaintained, forcing you to to either maintain or replace it. While you don't need to worry about the most prominent projects in the community being abandoned, thinking about each added dependency carefully is a helpful exercise. We offer the following advice:

- Before adding a dependency to your project, take a look at its codebase and ask yourself "Would I be able to maintain this library if I had to?" Look for documentation and especially for a test suite.

- Is the functionality that you need complex enough to warrant bringing in an external library, which often comes with its own set of features? Sometimes a little strategic copying is better than adding a full dependency.

- See if the library is maintained. Be forewarned: a lack of activity does not mean the code is unmaintained—sometimes a library is simply complete.

- See if the project has a license you can work with.

- If the project is very active, check if it maintains a CHANGELOG so you have a clear path when updating versions.

After you add a dependency, eventually you will have to update them. The simplest way to get a real-time status of your libraries is the `mix hex.outdated` command. From the root of your application, run the following command:

```
$ mix hex.outdated
```

You should see something like the following:

```
Dependency          Current  Latest  Update possible
benchfella          0.3.4    0.3.5   Yes
bypass              0.7.0    0.8.1   Yes
cowboy              1.0.4    1.1.2   No
credo               0.6.1    0.8.5   No
decimal             1.3.1    1.4.0   No
```

---

11. https://hex.pm/

```
earmark                1.1.1    1.2.3    No
ex_doc                 0.17.1   0.17.1
excoveralls            0.6.5    0.7.2    No
gettext                0.13.1   0.13.1
httpoison              0.11.2   0.13.0   No
inch_ex                0.5.6    0.5.6
logger_file_backend    0.0.10   0.0.10
phoenix                1.2.4    1.3.0    No
phoenix_ecto           3.2.3    3.2.3
phoenix_live_reload    1.0.8    1.0.8
phoenix_pubsub         1.0.2    1.0.2
plug_logger_json       0.3.1    0.4.0    No
postgrex               0.13.3   0.13.3
```

```
A green version in latest means you have the latest version of a
given package. Update possible indicates if your current requirement
matches the latest version. Run `mix hex.outdated APP` to see
requirements for a specific dependency.
```

You can get more information about upgrading a particular package by giving its name to mix hex.outdated:

```
$ mix hex.outdated phoenix
```

```
There is newer version of the dependency available 1.3.0 > 1.2.4!
```

```
Source                 Requirement
mix.exs                ~> 1.2.4
phoenix_live_reload    ~> 1.0 or ~> 1.2-rc
```

```
A green requirement means that it matches the latest version.
```

If you decide to update a dependency such as Phoenix, set a moment aside to read its CHANGELOG, assess the risks behind the update, and estimate the efforts the update would entail.

While it is important to keep your dependencies relatively up to date, your team also needs to deliver value to your clients so you will need to find a balance between upgrading too frequently and never upgrading.

The only time an update is strictly necessary is when there is a security release or the version you are currently running on has a critical bug. Luckily, Hex also includes a task called mix hex.audit that let us know whenever a package is retired. Let's see how to audit Hex dependencies. For example, Distillery v1.3.3[12] had a package retired because important functionality was broken. Say your project depended on Distillery 1.3.3, a dependency for building deployment releases. Running mix hex.audit would give you:

---

12. https://hex.pm/packages/distillery/1.3.3

```
$ mix hex.audit
Dependency  Version  Retirement reason
distillery  1.3.3    (other) Custom commands are broken in this release
Found retired packages
```

If there are retired packages, mix hex.audit will exit with a non-zero status, which can be useful if you want to integrate the command in your continuous integration pipeline.

Finally, if you like to live on the leading edge and give valuable feedback to the community and the projects you use, you can run beta versions and release candidates in staging and even use the duplexing technique we learned in *Moving Incremental Releases into Production*, on page 69 to test upcoming releases.

Wrapping Up

In this chapter we focused on legacy code. We spent most of our time working through tips and techniques for moving larger applications but we also assessed Elixir dependencies.

The migration of any large application is a problem with both technology and people. Understanding the risk factors and getting buy-in from the beginning are critical elements. The application you move might be composed of independent services or a few monoliths. Moving a monolith means isolating different elements and moving them one section at a time.

Terraform is a library that eases monolith migrations by allowing a team to move a few endpoints at a time. The toolset uses a proxy technique. Each new request is either processed in the new system or sent to the old server for processing. Sometimes, within the transition period, it makes sense to send the requests to both new servers and old for a period of time to test the services on a staging environment and catch errors.

Migrating monoliths is especially hard, so we spent some time working on techniques to prevent new codebases from becoming monoliths. The umbrella approach is not quite a full services architecture, but it is an incremental movement in that direction. Umbrella projects allow a project with related dependencies to be developed, deployed, tested, and maintained separately. Carefully considering dependencies is another element of creating beautiful, maintainable code. Hex has some mix tasks that can help with that effort called mix hex.outdated and mix hex.audit. They can both assist a team in maintaining a viable, healthy set of dependencies.

Now that we've got a plan in place, it's time to move to the next part of the book where we'll start the process of developing with Elixir.

Part II

Development

Every plan looks great in the beginning, but no plan survives contact with the enemy. In this section, you'll explore the techniques you'll need to succeed once you start coding in a new language. Since many teams will come from backgrounds with object-oriented languages, we'll show you how to think about organizing your Elixir project, and how to reason through the different concepts you'll find in this functional, concurrent language. You'll explore the design techniques that build the correct boundaries in your system and keep your code adaptable and extensible. You'll then grapple with some of the tricky details that make the effective design and implementation of distributed systems so difficult. Finally, you'll explore some tools that will help you integrate with applications that you can't or shouldn't move to Elixir.

## CHAPTER 5

Making the Functional Transition

You've made the business case for Elixir, and started shaping your team with the right building blocks for personal growth and consistency. You have read the getting started guide, consulted the documentation, and reviewed some of the many books available, yet something is still missing. That's only natural.

If you and your team are familiar with Elixir and functional programming, you might skip ahead to the next chapter but we know from our research that a fair number of our readers are not quite comfortable with Elixir. Here's what we mean. If you've ever watched a non-native speaker learn any spoken language, you probably saw them borrow native language concepts that didn't quite fit. On this team, José is famous for his English puns, but occasionally he'll try one that has us all scratching our heads.

Learning Elixir is like that. The basics take time, and even after establishing the fundamentals, questions will remain in the journey from apprentice to master. Object-oriented developers adopting functional languages tend to try to reinvent object-oriented concepts in them. It's common for such users to have questions:

- If you are coming from an object-oriented background, what does it take to properly design applications in a functional and concurrent programming language like Elixir?

- When are modules and functions enough and when should we resort to processes?

- What's a GenServer, and why is it one of the most prevalent Elixir abstractions?

- What role does Supervisor play in building applications?

Each of these concepts is new to teams who code object-oriented applications that only dabble in concurrency. In this chapter, we will talk about these questions and more. We will cover higher level concepts and abstractions. Internalizing these foundational concepts will speed your adoption curve tremendously. Along the way, you will see examples that will provide a mental framework that lets you put your newly acquired knowledge to use. We expect that you are already familiar with Elixir data types such as lists, tuples, and maps. You will also need to know about abstractions such as tasks and agents.

Let's go beyond the basics. We want to help you apply foundational Elixir concepts in the context of the complex applications you'll encounter in the real world. Let's start with one of the most fundamental concepts of functional programming languages: immutability.

Elixir vs. Mutable Objects

Since Elixir is a functional programming language, it does not have objects. The language also has a strong focus on immutability. In Elixir we *transform* data rather than *mutate* it.

Said another way: *OO changes. FP copies.*

While this difference may be subtle and might even seem inefficient, it's transformational. Many of Elixir's most important benefits flow directly from this design decision. In this section, we're going to look at what those benefits might be, and why they matter to you. Let's take that apart.

Understanding Mutation

Mutable objects bundle three concerns that are distinct in Elixir: state, behavior, and time. Take this example:

```
dictionary.store("key", "value")
```

If this were like most object-oriented programs, dictionary would be an object holding a dictionary with multiple keys and values, probably in the form of a hash. That object would provide a store method that changes the hash *in place*. It's this in-place change that we call a mutation.

In object-oriented languages, mutations represent time because the value of the object will depend on when you access it. If you access that dictionary after a mutation, you get the new version and the old version no longer exists. Such changes are very hard to track, especially when more than one client uses the same piece of code. Adding more objects often introduces more moving parts, with little visibility on how those parts change through time; adding concurrency makes reasoning about such code nearly impossible.

Elixir decouples these three concepts. Data structures are immutable and represent state. Modules define our behavior. Processes send and receive messages, embodying the concept of time.

The previous code would be written in Elixir as:

```
new_map = Map.put(map, "key", "value")
```

map is the data and Map.put/3 is a function defined in the Map module that receives three arguments. Map.put/3 never mutates the map; it always returns a new one. map will never change so for this code:

```
value1 = Map.get(map, "key")
# ...
# Some other code
# ...
value2 = Map.get(map, "key")
```

value1 and value2 *will always be the same* unless map is reassigned to another value somewhere between the two calls. And even if you rebind the map variable, the underlying map does not change. The variable is just pointing somewhere new.

Now you have a guarantee. The map referenced by the variable map will never change, even if some other code is holding a reference to the same map, and *that* guarantee makes all of the difference in the world. We pass the map around confident in the fact that no other code can modify it.

If you want to intentionally violate this guarantee, you'll need to reach for another abstraction, the process. We're going to hold a tiny bit of state in another process, an agent, and we'll communicate with that process as needed. Consider this counter:

```
{:ok, pid} = Agent.start_link(fn -> 0 end)
value1 = Agent.get(pid, fn x -> x end)
Agent.update(pid, fn x -> x + 1 end)
value2 = Agent.get(pid, fn x -> x end)
```

In this example, calling Agent.get/2 with the exact same arguments may give you different results. This arrangement lets you save state using separate processes. Since you can only communicate with a process via explicit messages, Elixir allows developers to reason about how their application state changes over time. *In effect, processes such as agents isolate state change with the explicit, formal set of rules governing message passing.*

If you wanted to, you could use agents, or files, or any other stateful abstraction as mutable variables, and completely undo Elixir's stateless advantages. In fact, many beginners fall into this trap. Good languages sometimes let you run with scissors. Elixir's important decision in this regard is to keep these choices explicit. An agent *feels* like a more serious commitment than a mutable variable because it *is* a more serious level of commitment.

While time adds complexity to our applications, functional programming is about making the complex parts of our system explicit. By modeling state changes with processes and message-passing, we make our software easier to understand, simpler to write, and much more stable.

Elixir as an Object-Oriented Language

You may have heard that Elixir processes are objects, according to Dr. Alan Kay's definition of "object-oriented programming." In an email discussion with Stefan Ram,[a] Kay coined the term object-oriented programming and says "OOP to me means only messaging, local retention and protection and hiding of state-process, and extreme late-binding of all things."

While Elixir processes do neatly fit that description, we think the comparison may cause more confusion than insight, as processes should not be used as a code design tool in the same way objects are used in most object-oriented programming languages.

---

a. http://www.purl.org/stefan_ram/pub/doc_kay_oop_en

Immutability and Memory

The pipe operator |> is one of the first constructs Elixir developers learn, as it embodies transformation and the decoupling between data and behavior. When we pipe between functions, it receives all data it needs as input and returns all relevant information as output. There's never hidden or mutated data. Each pipe is a standalone transformation with an explicit contract.

When writing your business logic, you may use Ecto[1] changesets to handle data casting and validation:

```elixir
def changeset(user, params \\ %{}) do
  user
  |> cast(params, [:name, :email, :age])
  |> validate_required([:name, :email])
  |> validate_format(:email, ~r/@/)
  |> validate_inclusion(:age, 18..120)
  |> unique_constraint(:email)
end
```

---

1. https://github.com/elixir-ecto/ecto

Each function along the way transforms the changeset. You may be asking yourself about the cost of immutability. Many developers assume that each time you change a map or a struct, Elixir creates a whole new one in memory. That's not true.

Elixir represents a map with multiple elements as a tree in memory. Adding, putting, or deleting an element requires changing only the path to that element on the tree. All other elements in the map are shared between the old map and newly transformed map. Let's explore how that sharing works with a list example.

Elixir represents lists internally as *cons cells*. Each cons cell is a simple data structure with two elements in the [left | right] form.

Lists are nested cons cells. The list [1, 2, 3] expressed with cons cells is [1 | [2 | [3 | []]]]. In memory, it would be represented like this:

```
[1 | •]
        ↘
    [2 | •]
            ↘
        [3 | •]
                ↘
                []
```

Let's see what happens when we create a new list from an old one. Consider this code:

```
iex> list = [1, 2, 3]
[1, 2, 3]
iex> first = [4 | list]
[4, 1, 2, 3]
iex> second = [5 | list]
[5, 1, 2, 3]
```

Elixir *does not need to create two full copies*. It simply needs to create two new cons cells, one with 4 and list and another with 5 and list, like this:

```
[4 | •]
        ↘
        [1 | •]
      ↗       ↘
[5 | •]     [2 | •]
                    ↘
                [3 | •]
                        ↘
                        []
```

That's why prepending to lists is *always* fast, while appending is slow. Prepending enables sharing, appending requires us to copy the whole list since we need to change the last cons cell to point somewhere else.

The exact transformation mechanisms and costs depend on the data structure, and we'll not go into them here. What's important is that *immutability is exactly what makes this kind of transformation efficient*, because the VM knows the data underneath *is not going to change*. For example, if you have a tuple with three elements, {:one, 2, "three"}, in memory you have a tuple container that points to :one, 2, and "three". If you change the second element of the tuple, you get a new tuple, but it will still point to the same :one and "three" exactly because, even if another piece of the code is holding a reference to the old tuple, no one can mutate any of its contents.

This immutability contract gives Elixir tremendous freedom. Think about this simple function:

```
def one_two_three do
  [1, 2, 3]
end
```

Other languages that support mutability would likely need to return a separate copy of the list upon each invocation because each client could mutate the list. Elixir doesn't have that restriction. Each time you invoke that function, you'll get the *same exact list in the same exact memory address* because nobody will ever change it.

Immutability makes our software easier to understand and also introduces simplifications at the compiler level that make it easier to share data throughout.

There's a cost, though. In some situations immutability may have performance implications. Even though the language relies on advanced techniques such as sharing, a piece of code needing to execute millions of operations per second on the same data structure may generate an unnecessary amount of garbage. In such cases, you may need to resort to the mutable components available in Elixir, such as ETS or the process dictionary.

However, it is worth pointing out that in our 10 years of collective experience working with Elixir, we recall such performance-centric optimization was necessary only once, when implementing a data-processing engine.

Data and Behavior

By separating data and behavior, Elixir allows developers to focus on the shape of the data. The code is more explicit than languages that don't do so, and explicit code makes its intentions clear. Consider this OO code:

```
URI.parse(url).path.split("/").last
```

Each `.` makes it hard to track the source of each method. You might ask yourself "Where does split("/") come from?" Maybe it is a String method, or maybe there is a Path object in there somewhere. You just don't know.

Contrast that example with this one in Elixir, where each operation along the way is explicitly named:

```
URI.parse(url).path
|> String.split("/")
|> List.last
```

Granted, the Elixir version is more verbose. In exchange, you and your editor know exactly where each function comes from. The use of the pipe operator clarifies each step in the transformation. Each step transforms the data but never mutates it.

Polymorphism

Sometimes, adopting a new language means letting go of features that you've grown to depend on. Even though Elixir decouples the concepts of data, behavior, and time, you still may argue in favor of other OO concepts like polymorphism. For example, in the previous section, we wrote this code:

```
URI.parse(url).path.split("/").last
```

We argued that .split("/").last may be a source of confusion since we don't know where methods like split come from. You might counter "It's not a bug; it's a feature." In some situations, you don't actually care which object has the function; you only care that it knows how to split("/"). That's polymorphism.

It's our position that *polymorphism is an essential mechanism for designing applications.* You can't build good software without it, but if you're not careful, you'll complicate your code and doom future developers to a special kind of hell. Bad polymorphism can obscure your intentions and hide critical concepts. Use polymorphism with the same care and wisdom you use to treat mutable state.

Polymorphism in Elixir happens in two forms. The first form is pattern matching with function heads or case. Take this example:

```elixir
def split(contents, path) when is_list(contents) do
  contents
  |> List.to_string
  |> split(path)
  |> Enum.map(&String.to_charlist/1)
end

def split(contents, path) when is_binary(contents) do
  String.split(contents, path)
end
```

This code can handle lists, strings, or any other case we consider upfront when implementing the split/2 function. With pattern matching, *you organize code around the task, not the type.* Use pattern matching when you know all scenarios up front. Once the code is compiled, you cannot extend it without changing the code again.

Pattern matching is what Bleacher Report used when designing their content-type system outlined in *Functions Transform Data,* on page 23:

```elixir
def changeset(post, content_type, params) do
  data
  |> cast(params, @required_fields)
  |> cast_content_type(content_type, params)
  # other general validations
end

defp cast_content_type(audio, "audio", params) do
  validate_extension(audio, :url, [:mp3])
end
defp cast_content_type(video, "video", params) do
  validate_extension(video, :url, [:mp4])
end
```

Adding a new content type to their application consisted of implementing a new function clause in cast_content_type that matches on the new value. Pattern matching was essential in helping them make the transition from their object-oriented mindset to functional concepts.

At other times we want polymorphism to be extensible as in many object-oriented languages. You may want to say "I don't care what this argument might be as long as it satisfies my contract." Rather than using pattern matching, Elixir uses protocols to handle this form of polymorphism.

Let's say you wanted to split more than strings or lists. You could define a Splittable protocol, like this:

```
defprotocol Splittable do
  def split(data, pattern)
end
```

Each desired data structure would then implement the protocol. You can define a Protocol at any time. Your application can define a new protocol and retroactively implement it for all the built-in data types that are part of Elixir. Alternatively, you can create your own data structures and implement the protocols provided by any library or the Elixir language itself, such as:

- Enumerable is used by the Enum module to enumerate collections, such as in Enum.map/2.

- String.Chars is used by to_string/1 to convert a data type with a valid string representation.

- And many others.

Protocols associate data and behavior in an opt-in fashion, exactly when you need it.

Agents and Tasks

Processes play a crucial role in Elixir. We have seen how processes model state changes. Processes are also used to enable concurrency and provide fault tolerance.

Elixir provides two abstractions, called agents and tasks, that are specializations of those use cases. Agents and tasks are supervised processes. An agent[2] is a process that handles *state*. An agent is perfect for keeping some shared state that is accessed by multiple processes in your application. Earlier in this chapter we implemented a counter using agents.

A task[3] is about supervised *behavior*. For example, to do two things concurrently, use Task.async/1 to spawn each task and Task.await/1 to wait for the result, like this:

```
task1 = Task.async(fn -> do_some_work() end)
task2 = Task.async(fn -> do_more_work() end)
Task.await(task1)
Task.await(task2)
```

We start two tasks concurrently and wait for both to finish. The Task.async function makes a couple of assumptions. By default, if do_some_work() or

---

2. https://hexdocs.pm/elixir/Agent.html
3. https://hexdocs.pm/elixir/Task.html

do_more_work() fail, the process that called them will fail too. That's an explicit design choice: the async and await combination helps you add concurrency to sequential code without changing the code semantics. So if the previous code would fail if any of those functions failed, the concurrent code will fail too. That's normally what you want.

The Task module also provides a wide range of APIs when those assumptions aren't enough. The Task API can give you explicit control over how long to wait for a task to terminate, via Task.yield/2, or when to shut it down. You can use the Task module to control timeouts or determine how failure may affect the system.

As specialized solutions, agents and tasks are simple and readable, but sometimes processes need to juggle state, concurrency, and fault tolerance at the same time, so agents and tasks might not be enough. In such cases, we need full-blown processes without restrictions and those often take the shape of GenServers.

The Generic Server

One of the most important abstractions for both the Elixir and Erlang ecosystems is called OTP, and the heart of OTP is the generic server. It's an abstraction that you'll use to wrap up critical features as application services, represent state using processes, and use built-in supervision to make those features reliable. As you saw in *Elixir vs. Mutable Objects*, on page 82, Elixir leans heavily on processes to make the notions of state, behavior, and time explicit. In this section, we'll focus on OTP, a critical abstraction providing common services many processes need, such as supervision.

In the following sections, we want to shine a light on GenServer and discuss cases of use and misuse, relaying some stories from the field and greater Elixir community. To do so, we'll walk you through enough foundational concepts so that you can appreciate the nuanced conclusions that follow.

The GenServer's Story

If you're like many new Elixir developers, the terms OTP and GenServer may immediately send you into a trance like a fraternity student after a big party at that 8 a.m. calculus class. We're going to build the intuition for a generic server from the ground up.

The essence of OTP is not complex, but it is important. You're going to need these concepts as you make your way through this book and throughout your Elixir programming career. When we're done with this section, you'll understand the essence of how you might use recursion, concurrency, and supervision to build lightweight services that do all kinds of things.

Take this very simple Counter. It receives messages to increment its state and allows other processes to request its value, like this:

```
making_fun_transition/counter_1.ex
defmodule Counter do
  def start_link(initial_value) do
    {:ok, spawn_link(__MODULE__, :loop, [initial_value])}
  end

  def loop(counter) do
    receive do
      {:read, caller} ->
        send(caller, {:counter, counter})
        loop(counter)
      :bump ->
        loop(counter + 1)
    end
  end
end
```

That example uses some basic Elixir constructs to start a process with the start_link function using spawn_link. Then, you'll see a recursive function called loop that responds to two messages. The first returns the value of our counter, and recursively calls loop. The second bumps the counter and calls loop. Think of loop as a long-lived function, and counter as the state for one invocation of that function.

This program uses the foundational pattern underneath *all* OTP programs. Our small server receives messages, some that require a reply, such as {:read, caller}, and some that do not. Now let's add the client API to the same module that will effectively send messages to the server:

```
making_fun_transition/counter_2.ex
defmodule Counter do
  def read(counter) do
    send(counter, {:read, self()})
    receive do
      {:counter, counter} -> {:ok, counter}
    end
  end

  def bump(counter) do
    send counter, :bump
  end
```

The previous code may not look offensive but it has some major flaws. For example, let's see what happens to read/1 when the counter is no longer running. Run iex counter.ex and then try this:

```
iex> {:ok, counter} = Counter.start_link(0)
{:ok, #PID<0.56.0>}
iex> Counter.read(counter)
{:ok, 0}
iex> Process.unlink(counter)
true
iex> Process.exit(counter, :kill)
true
iex> Counter.read(counter)
# you'll be here a while.
```

We started a counter, read its value, then removed the link between the IEx process and the counter process so we can kill the counter without terminating the shell. Then we called read again. This time, the counter blocks indefinitely, because it will never get a reply.

You could add a typical five-second timeout, but that's wasteful. Furthermore, a single timeout doesn't necessarily imply a dead server. Maybe the client didn't wait long enough or maybe the server was temporarily busy. In both cases, you may end up with unwanted replies. For a more robust service, you'll need to take some steps to remedy this problem:

- Add a timeout, and exit in case the timeout is reached. The exit will work as a back-pressure mechanism because a timeout typically implies the server is busy. Users can catch the exit if they want to at their own peril.

- Change read to handle a dead process by monitoring the counter before each invocation and handling a DOWN message.

- Identify each request with the unique reference returned from the monitor call.

Let's do those things now:

making_fun_transition/counter_3.ex
```
def read(counter, timeout \\ 5000) do
  ref = Process.monitor(counter)
  send counter, {:read, {self(), ref}}
  receive do
    {^ref, counter} ->
      Process.demonitor(ref, [:flush])
      {:ok, counter}
    {:DOWN, ^ref, _, _, reason} ->
      exit(reason)
  after
    timeout -> exit(:timeout)
  end
end
```

Let's also change the loop function to match on the reference received in the :read message and include the same reference in the reply:

```
making_fun_transition/counter_3.ex
def loop(counter) do
  receive do
    {:read, {caller, ref}} ->
      send(caller, {ref, counter})
      loop(counter)
    :bump ->
      loop(counter + 1)
  end
end
```

If you look closely, you'll find each of our three previous improvements. The after clause for receive addresses the timeout, the monitor request monitors each invocation, and the receive clauses now pass the reference returned by the monitor.

Keep in mind that changing this Counter in a larger application isn't enough. You'd need to change *all of our services like this*, because each service needs these features, or something like them. Furthermore, you've not yet addressed the loop implementation, which has issues of its own:

- The loop/1 function only reads certain messages out of its inbox. Unexpected messages will wait forever on its inbox, leaking memory.

- The counter process is hard to debug, and the existing implementation has no hooks for retrieving useful runtime information.

- You'll need to bring down the counter in production to update the code, destroying the state.

Once you've addressed all of these requirements, it is easy to see why processes are a powerful primitive but not enough for building your applications. You might suggest that we encapsulate those solutions in a single place. That's a better idea. Let's build a module to handle all of these concerns.

Call this module Boat. After all, a wise man once said that a boat is a hole in the water to pour time and money into. If you don't like that name, you could choose MoneyPit or TimePit. At this point, you're probably thinking that a wiser man once said that other people's boats are way better than your own. Let's get someone to write that module for us and call it OtherPeoplesBoats. You're in luck. They already did, and called it the GenServer.

A GenServer is a great abstraction that encapsulates the generic concerns for managing state, concurrency, and fault tolerance. For example, in a GenServer, we can find both GenServer.call/3 and GenServer.cast/3, which encapsulate the behavior found in the previous read/2 and bump/1 functions. It's exactly these concepts that make the design of the Erlang VM so elegant. The basic primitives such as processes, monitors, links, and exit signals provide all of the components necessary for building the concurrent, fault-tolerant and distributed applications the language is known for.

Gen stands for generic, and generic is beautiful and dangerous. These simple, open concepts leave a wide open field for exploration—and venturing into that space without a guide can hurt you. While it may be hard for us to outline all of the use cases for a GenServer, we can certainly provide a few examples and discuss some patterns and anti-patterns along the way.

Use GenServer as a Coordinator

In the previous section we have peeked at all of the concerns a GenServer handles for us when we attempted to implement a mutable counter. At the same time, we have also shown how we can implement a very simple counter with agents in four lines of code. Behind the scenes, agents are implemented with GenServers. Therefore, if we want to use a GenServer, we need more than just mutable state. One such example is when we need a process to coordinate the action of multiple other processes.

In a concurrent system, coordinating the allocation and release of resources is sometimes demanding. You may have heard that Elixir developers rarely rely on try/catch or try/rescue. In many cases, it's cleaner to use tuples and pattern matching because operations such as File.read/1 return {:ok, contents} or {:error, reason} instead of failing with an exception. There's more to the story, though.

try and catch or rescue are just not enough when processes are involved. If a process terminates due to another linked process, you're done. You can't catch, after, or rescue across processes. Check this out:

```
iex> try do
...>   Task.async(fn -> raise "oops" end) |> Task.await()
...> after
...>   IO.puts "this will never be printed"
...> end
** (EXIT from #PID<0.84.0>) an exception was raised:
    ** (RuntimeError) oops
```

For cases like this one, the correct solution is to implement a process that keeps the state for different processes running in the system and do the proper clean-up action. In other words, we need a minimal coordinating process, a little state, and fault tolerance for proper clean-ups. A GenServer fits perfectly.

Imagine you need to accumulate or compute some data to upload to an external service. You have already determined the most efficient way of doing so is by writing the data to disk and then letting the operating system do the work of uploading the file. You plan to remove the file once the upload completes. You no longer need the file on disk and it must be removed.

This solution won't work:

```
{:ok, file} = File.open!("path/to/temp/file")
write_to_file(file, data)
File.close(file)
```

because write_to_file/2 might fail so the file won't be removed from disk. try/after won't save you.

GenServer comes to the rescue. It can work as an allocator of file system paths. Every time you need a temporary file, you will ask the server for a temporary file path. The server will generate one and monitor the calling process. When the caller terminates, the server can automatically remove the file.

Let's get started and set up a GenServer with a start link and an allocate API:

```
making_fun_transition/path_allocator_1.ex
defmodule PathAllocator do
  use GenServer

  # Store the name in a module attribute for readability
  @name PathAllocator

  def start_link(tmp_dir) when is_binary(tmp_dir) do
    GenServer.start_link(__MODULE__, tmp_dir, name: @name)
  end

  def allocate do
    GenServer.call(@name, :allocate)
  end
```

GenServer.start_link will invoke the init callback which we define next. The callback receives the temporary directory, which it returns as part of its state, alongside an empty map:

```
making_fun_transition/path_allocator_1.ex
def init(tmp_dir) do
  {:ok, {tmp_dir, %{}}}
end
```

Next, we implement handle_call, which contains the allocation logic. For each path allocated, we monitor the process that owns the path. Monitoring a process returns a unique reference ref which we will store in the map alongside the path we have just generated:

making_fun_transition/path_allocator_1.ex

```
def handle_call(:allocate, {pid, _}, {tmp_dir, refs}) do
  path = Path.join(tmp_dir, generate_random_filename())
  ref  = Process.monitor(pid)
  refs = Map.put(refs, ref, path)
  {:reply, path, {tmp_dir, refs}}
end

defp generate_random_filename do
  Base.url_encode64(:crypto.strong_rand_bytes(48))
end
```

Now our server will receive a message whenever a monitored process terminates. The last step is to match on this message in the handle_info callback and
remove the path associated to the message:

making_fun_transition/path_allocator_1.ex

```
  def handle_info({:DOWN, ref, _, _, _}, {tmp_dir, refs}) do
    {path, refs} = Map.pop(refs, ref)
    File.rm(path)
    {:noreply, {tmp_dir, refs}}
  end
end
```

And that's it. You can start the allocator with PathAllocator.start_link(System.tmp_dir)
and get a new path at any time with PathAllocator.allocate().

This structure is fairly common for a GenServer that needs to coordinate or
clean up after other processes. The goal is to monitor a process, store the
monitoring reference, match on the dying process, and then do your work.

That's a positive example. Let's take a look at a negative one.

Don't Use GenServers for Code Organization

We just saw an example that plays to all of the GenServer strengths. GenServer
is a beautiful abstraction, and like anything good in the hands of an inexperienced developer, it's prone to overuse. Let's look at some of its properties.
A GenServer:

- Encapsulates a shared service.
- Holds state.
- Allows concurrent access to shared resources.
- Handles supervision to take care of normal and abnormal startup and
  cleanup.

These are the problems a GenServer is built to solve. The previous problem needed
all four of these characteristics, so a GenServer was an excellent fit. When you
need to organize code, you don't need a full GenServer. You need a module.

Here's the point: if you see the characteristics that remind you of GenServers, use a GenServer. If you don't, don't. In particular, don't use a GenServer to layer or organize your code. For example, imagine you wanted to write a Calculator module. You could use a GenServer to build your API, like this:

```
def add(a, b) do
  GenServer.call(__MODULE__, {:add, a, b})
end

def handle_call({:add, a, b}, _from, state) do
  {:reply, a + b, state}
end

def handle_call({:subtract, a, b}, _from, state) do
  {:reply, a - b, state}
end

...
```

You've built a codebase that loses the essence of a calculator in all of the noise. Worse yet, you've introduced a potential bottleneck into your application. Any piece of code that needs to use the calculator now needs to go through a main calculator process.

A calculator is all about *functions*. To build it, use *a module holding functions*. Group those into *modules*. You don't need anything else.

Sadly, we'd be lying to you if we said we've never seen this exact pattern in production. A new developer team started building their Phoenix applications. They had always heard GenServers could be treated like microservices but even tinier. This "wisdom" led them to push all of their database access control to GenServers. They even built a DSL making it easier to put their implementation behind a GenServer. At the end of the day, they had code like this:

```
defmodule MyApp.PostsService do
  use MyApp.Services

  defcall all() do
    MyApp.DatabaseRepository.all(Post)
  end
end
```

where defcall would define both the client and server API which eventually invoked MyApp.DatabaseRepository.all(Post). One month later, they had enough built to put a prototype into production and they started benchmarking it. The performance was abysmal. Under high-enough load, some pages took 3 seconds to render because *they built a bottleneck where none existed*. They defeated Ecto connection pools because all access happened through a single process.

In essence, they made it easy to *create global, mutable variables in Elixir*. They essentially crippled the single biggest advantage of functional languages, for no gain whatsoever.

Once they converted their code back to functions, the problem disappeared. They achieved better performance with much simpler code.

Although this example used GenServers, it applies to processes in general. *Use processes to model runtime properties, such as mutable state, concurrency, and failures, but never for code organization.*

Supervisors

Most new Elixir developers tend to think of supervisors in terms of fault tolerance because they provide the restart strategies that are the essential part of building reliable systems. Supervisors are so much more. They form the backbone of Elixir applications.

Ultimately, supervisors are responsible for how our processes start and shut down, whether an application is crashing and restarting or simply starting. Restarting of processes is optional, while starting and stopping them is essential. Let's explore startup flow by addressing a bug in our PathAllocator implementation defined in *Use GenServer as a Coordinator*, on page 94.

Starting a supervisor is a matter of defining all of its *child specifications* and then calling start_link. A child specification specifies exactly how the supervisor starts a child process, when and how many times to restart it, and how to shut it down. For a complete reference on child specifications, consult the Elixir documentation for Supervisors.[4]

We can start the PathAllocator example in *Use GenServer as a Coordinator*, on page 94 under a supervisor by defining a list of children, where each element is a tuple with the module name as first element and the argument given to start_link as second argument, like this:

```
children = [
  {PathAllocator, System.tmp_dir}
]

Supervisor.start_link(children, strategy: :one_for_one)
```

Upon startup, a supervisor starts all of its children in the order they're defined. Similarly, upon shutdown, the supervisor terminates all of its children in the

---

4. https://hexdocs.pm/elixir/Supervisor.html

reverse order. The initialization logic is in the init/1 function, but we haven't defined the termination logic.

Whenever a supervisor restarts its children or the node shuts down, PathAllocator's supervisor is going to send it an exit signal. By default, that exit signal will terminate the PathAllocator, regardless if it has processed all messages in its inbox or not, leaving spurious paths behind.

Let's address this bug by cleaning up all files in the refs map on terminate. The first step is to trap exits with Process.flag(:trap_exit, true) on init, like this:

making_fun_transition/path_allocator_2.ex
```
def init(tmp_dir) do
  Process.flag(:trap_exit, true)
  {:ok, {tmp_dir, %{}}}
end
```

By trapping exits, if any external process causes the allocator to exit, the allocator won't shut down immediately. Instead, it will run the terminate/2 callback. Next, we can write the termination logic, like this:

making_fun_transition/path_allocator_2.ex
```
def terminate(_reason, {_tmp_dir, refs}) do
  for {_, path} <- refs do
    File.rm(path)
  end
  :ok
end
```

The logic is dead simple. We simply remove every file in refs. This change guarantees PathAllocator will clean up all entries on shutdown or even when a bug causes part of your application to restart.

This example highlights the importance of proper termination of supervision trees in our applications. Once the supervisor sends the exit shutdown signal to the worker, the worker has 5 seconds to terminate, by default. If a given process requires more time to shutdown, you can specify the shutdown time when defining the process child specification.

Be careful, though. terminate/2 won't happen in extreme scenarios, such as a spilled beer or a machine shutdown, so be defensive. For example, our PathAllocator's init function could remove all files from the given directory to ensure a fresh start.

When we run an Elixir system in production, starting up a system is a matter of starting all applications and their supervision trees. Shutting a system down consists of stopping all applications and their supervisors trees in the reverse order. Each child in a supervision tree has its own start and stop specification, giving us full control on how our system boots and terminates.

Whenever our system is up and running, it is important to think about the guarantees such a structure provides. If you are working on an application that talks to a database, its supervision tree probably starts a process that connects to the database.

```
children = [
  # ... some children ...
  {StorageConnection, username: "josé", password: "password123"},
  # ... more children ...
]
```

At this point, you have a guarantee that, if your application boots, it has a connection to a working database. The flip side is also useful. If the database is not available, then your application will not boot at all.

For some applications, the lack of a database connection indeed means that the application should not be online. For others, this choice has disastrous consequences, as other parts of the system could be running even without a database. In those cases, you will need to use a different strategy, such as starting the connection outside of the initialization process with the help of functions such as Supervisor.start_child/2.

At the end of the day, supervisors go beyond fault tolerance and provide our systems with guarantees around starting up and shutting down. For an overview on how applications are started and stopped as part of a system, see the Application module documentation.[5] For further discussion on the supervisor guarantees, we recommend Fred Hébert's article "It's All About the Guarantees."[6]

Wrapping Up

In this chapter, we noted that object-oriented developers learning Elixir tend to use object-oriented concepts because that's what they know, and we examined the most popular ones. Adopting Elixir means more than learning its idioms and syntax. To get the most out of it, you'll need to understand its basic abstractions.

We started by examining how to think about mutable state. When you've made the transition, you'll see how the concepts of behavior, state, and time

---

5.   https://hexdocs.pm/elixir/Application.html
6.   https://ferd.ca/it-s-about-the-guarantees.html

go from something implicit and tightly coupled to much more explicit concepts. Just using stronger, higher-order abstractions such as processes and concurrency raise mutable state to a more serious level, where it belongs.

Next, we talked about polymorphism. Where most object-oriented developers reach for inheritance first, Elixir developers tend to use pattern matching when dealing with a known set of variables. To support unknown services in an API or application, you can use protocols. Taken together, these two provide all of the power of inheritance and a more complete list of options for organizing code.

Finally, we introduced Agents, Tasks, and GenServers. We used agents to model state with processes, and tasks to model behaviors. Then we looked at the GenServer abstraction to do both at once. You learned to use processes to:

- Model state accessed by multiple processes.
- Run multiple tasks concurrently.
- Gracefully handle clean startup and exit concerns.
- Communicate between servers (to be discussed in a future chapter).

We learned that applications that require most of these services are ideal targets for OTP, but those that don't should reach for simpler abstractions like modules and functions first. Then, we looked at some examples for each.

Next, we learned the GenServer is your go-to abstraction when you need to tackle state, concurrency, and fault tolerance all at once. If you don't need those things, don't use a GenServer. Understanding when a GenServer fits and how to leverage agents and tasks will take you far in your Elixir journey.

Lastly, we learned that beyond reliability, supervisors define how our system starts and shuts down as a whole. Elixir takes full advantage to provide guarantees for services your application depends on.

In the next chapter, we'll make a shift toward deeper technical advice. As you begin your Elixir journey, you'll have some tools available to you that you might not have had on your previous platform, tools that should make you think about organization and architecture in a different way. Among other topics, we'll discuss the different alternatives you'll have for persisting data and evaluate strategies for sending remote messages. We're turning up the intensity so it's no time to slow down. Turn the page and we'll get started!

## CHAPTER 6

Distributed Elixir

Most programmers think of distributed systems as black magic, at once mysterious, valuable, and extraordinarily sensitive. They're not far from wrong, but nearly all systems have distributed elements—every mobile application that reaches a server to exchange information, a load balanced web server, each new car navigation system that is part of a network, an application that communicates with a database, even simple web servers that connect to a social network for authentication. As programming requirements change, languages have to change with them.

The fact of the matter is that distributed systems are hard. Elixir doesn't make them easy. It merely tries to make things a bit easier by offering tools, abstractions, and guarantees in the form of messages, nodes, and more. They help greatly when you do the difficult work of reasoning through the inevitable design constraints.

Take a simple database such as PostgreSQL. You might reach for it by default, but that choice brings assumptions. When you adopt your database as your sole source of truth, your choice impacts your response times. Every time you need new information from the database, your request will go over the network, and that takes time. Your database can also become a bottleneck (although a database used correctly will perform quite well despite popular folklore).

More to the point, if the database goes offline, in the best-case scenario it will be unable to accept writes or even be completely unusable. That's the crux of distributed systems design. Communication between working nodes is only a small part of the problem. It's usually availability and resilience rather than performance that drive us to distributed systems. Handling the unexpected is the heart of excellent distributed systems design. In essence, you need to get comfortable entertaining the question "What happens if I kill this?"

Rather than give you incomplete chapters that deliver a poor attempt at a complete anthology of distributed systems, we'll explore Elixir's constructs for distribution and how to leverage them for building systems you wouldn't have considered otherwise. Like the other chapters in this book, this one will help you put core concepts in place and tell you where to find more. Then, when the time comes, you'll be ready to go in depth on your own.

Remote Message Passing

Throughout this book, we've been addressing your Elixir adoption one layer at a time. We started with functions and walked through how to organize code and think functionally. Next, we moved into concurrency. In Elixir, the fundamental constructs for concurrency are processes, and the OTP abstraction built upon them. We talked about building layered applications and a structure for sending messages between them.

Next, we'll introduce the concept of nodes. A node is an abstract group of processes. They may be running on the same machine or different ones. When you're using Elixir, *you send messages between remote processes and local processes in exactly the same way.* That means processes form the foundation of distributed applications. Elixir uses the same send/2 function for sending messages to processes running on the same node or on a separate node over the network. Throughout this chapter, we're going to set up some nodes and do exactly that.

To start a node, you need to start it with a name. The name may be short, allowing connections only from the same machine, or long, allowing connections over the network. In both cases, nodes can only communicate if they share the same *cookie*. It is not a browser cookie; it is a unique identifier stored as an atom. You can find this cookie at ~/.erlang.cookie. Erlang creates one automatically when you start a named node, or you can pass the --cookie flag when starting the VM to specify your own. Keep in mind data sent between nodes is not encrypted out of the box. The security implications of running distributed Erlang in production are discussed in *Security Guidelines*, on page 166.

Start a new IEx session and give the node a short name of chip. You'll only be able to access this node by name from other nodes running on the same machine, like this:

```
$ iex --sname chip
iex(chip@macbook)> node()
:"chip@macbook"
```

Now, start another node, named dale:

```
$ iex --sname dale
iex(dale@macbook)> Node.list()
[]
iex(dale@macbook)> Node.connect(:"chip@macbook")
true
iex(dale@macbook)> Node.list()
[:"chip@macbook"]
```

Your two nodes are now connected. Remember the examples here will likely have different node names when running on your machine and you need to adjust it accordingly.

When connected, Elixir maintains an open TCP connection between the nodes. If more nodes join the network, they'll hold direct connections to each other. We call such a network a *fully meshed network*. If the TCP connection between two nodes drops or the node becomes unresponsive, those two nodes will then disconnect. You can do so explicitly via Node.disconnect, like this:

```
$ iex --sname dale
iex(dale@macbook)> Node.disconnect(:"chip@macbook")
true
iex(dale@macbook)> Node.list()
[]
```

To send a message from a process running in chip to a process running in dale, you need to be able to identify and find processes across nodes. One option is to give the process a local name and ask the node to send a message to a process running locally with a given name.

Back in chip@macbook, give the IEx process the name of :my_iex:

```
iex(chip@macbook)> Process.register(self(), :my_iex)
true
```

Now in dale@macbook, let's send a message to node chip, asking it to deliver that message to a local process named :my_iex:

```
iex(dale@macbook)> send {:my_iex, :"chip@macbook"}, :hello_from_dale
:hello_from_dale
```

Elixir used the tuple {process_name, node_name} to (a) open a connection to node chip@macbook if one does not yet exist, (b) serialize, and (c) send the message. The first point deserves special attention. Elixir will always attempt to connect the two nodes when sending remote messages, even if they've been explicitly disconnected.

Back on chip@macbook, you can run flush() and verify the IEx process has indeed received a message and the nodes are connected once again, like this:

```
iex(chip@macbook)> flush()
:hello_from_dale
:ok
iex(chip@macbook)> Node.list()
[:"dale@macbook"]
```

So, you can send messages across nodes. You can monitor processes across nodes too. Back in dale@macbook, monitor the :my_iex process running on chip@macbook:

```
iex(dale@macbook)> Process.monitor({:my_iex, :"chip@macbook"})
#Reference<0.0.4.113>
```

Now, if you terminate the chip@macbook node, the IEx session running on dale@macbook will receive a :DOWN message with a :noconnection reason, like this:

```
iex(dale@macbook)> flush()
{:DOWN,
  #Reference<0.0.4.124>,
  :process,
  {:my_iex, :"chip@macbook"},
  :noconnection}
```

The same primitives we use for building concurrent and fault-tolerant applications are also available for building distributed systems. None of this behavior is specific to Elixir; it is all part of the Erlang runtime. But don't let that fool you. Network communication brings a whole new set of trade-offs to consider.

For instance, in order to exchange messages between processes in these examples, you named the IEx process running on chip@macbook. To uniquely name a process, you need to use a *process registry*. The process registry used here is a *local process registry*. We'll talk more about them in *Finding Processes*, on page 112 so we'll just give you a quick working definition now.

A local process registry is straightforward to implement but it's limited in capabilities. For example, to check if a process exists on a given node, you'll always need to use the network to ask that node if the process is alive. Furthermore, a *local process registry* only guarantees uniqueness locally, but a *distributed process registry* must guarantee that a name is unique across the whole cluster.

Different process registries will choose different trade-offs and those choices will impact the design of your applications. To understand how this affects your systems, you'll need to understand *state*, *persistence*, and *replication*.

Persistence Strategies

In the previous chapters, you learned about Elixir's excellent tools for reasoning about state. In this chapter, we've begun to explore some of the abstractions for building distributed systems. At this point, you may be wondering, when to use Elixir abstractions and when to instead rely on off-the-shelf solutions. Sometimes the lines between creating a database and a GenServer may blur.

You are not alone. The team at Plataformatec heard similar questions, from the community and different clients around the world. Those conversations often involved different technologies, ranging from databases to messaging systems. To address such questions, the first topic Plataformatec engineers would bring up was about *persistence*.

To frame any persistence application, you need to answer one question first: "Can you afford to lose the data?" Often, an application's data is essential, and losing it is catastrophic, but sometimes, such as in a cache, the data is disposable. We call such data *ephemeral* or *ephemeral state*.

If you can't afford to lose data, your choice is usually easy. Don't reinvent the wheel; choose a database that fits your constraints.

Dealing with Ephemeral Data

If the data is ephemeral, you're in for a treat. Elixir is great at dealing with such problems. In such cases, you can likely keep the information in memory, and use all of the tooling Elixir provides. Let's view a classic example of ephemeral state.

Imagine that you want to show how many users are connected to your application right now. Every time a new connection arrives, you start monitoring that connection process and increase the connection counter. Once you receive a notification that the connection process no longer exists, you decrease the counter.

If the server crashes, you lose the state of however many connections were in that server, but you don't care, because all connections were dropped anyway when the server crashed!

If you have a single server or you are only interested in counting the connections per server, then you can go have a beer, or a Shirley Temple, with a smug "mission–accomplished" grin. However, if you would rather show how many users are connected across all servers in the cluster then you need to find a mechanism to *replicate* the data across servers, and your work has only begun.

The choice of replication depends on how much precision you require. It is likely you want only a rough estimate of connected users. In this case, you can likely have each server report to each other how many users are connected locally in a given time interval, such as every 15 seconds. The data won't be precise because over that time interval, users could have come or gone, but you have a reasonable interval for updates.

However, if you need an exact count, the periodic solution falls apart. Keeping all servers in sync will likely be too expensive. You could implement a consensus protocol but that is not a straightforward task. In those cases, an off-the-shelf solution such as a database might be a better choice.

We may have started and ended this discussion telling you to use a database, but the devil is in the details between those extremes. That's where Elixir shines. Throughout this chapter, we'll discuss different trade-offs and show that they do not only impact the choice of external tools, such as PostgreSQL, Redis, or RabbitMQ, but also the tools within the Erlang VM for tracking processes.

Still, one scenario trumps all others in terms of simplicity: read-only data, which we'll see next.

Case Study: Moz with a Database-Free Architecture

One of the biggest problems with keeping data in memory is what to do when it changes. Dealing with large amounts of mutable in-memory data leads to all of the same challenges as handling mutable data in a database or file system. You'll need to persist changes, back up the data, replicate it, and solve all of those problems that mutability causes, but on a different scale. If you're fortunate enough to be working with clean, unchanging data, you won't have to deal with any of those problems, and a database-free architecture can open up exciting possibilities.

Such is the case with Moz. This company takes historical digital marketing and SEO data and offers timely, actionable analysis on numerous search marketing dimensions. Recently Moz started a comprehensive overhaul of their back-end architecture in order to improve the performance and user experience of their applications while satisfying their clients with timely releases of important features.

In an article describing their implementation,[1] some of the "limiting factors were non-scalability, non-standard use of MySQL, and concurrency limitations in Ruby." As their feature set grew and they accumulated more data, they became more and more limited due to their database architecture. Even if they had hundreds of weeks of data stored, they could only show the last 12 weeks and at limited depth.

Here's the interesting part. Since their system dealt with historical data, they didn't have a mutability problem. Sure, the datasets for customers grew, but past data never changed. They decided to forgo their sharded MySQL architecture to use a database-free solution with Elixir.

In their new system, instead of storing their dataset on MySQL, they store the data as serialized data structures using the mechanism provided by the Erlang VM, composed of :erlang.term_to_binary/1 and :erlang.binary_to_term/1. Their application fetches the raw data from S3, converts it to indexed Elixir data structures, and persists it on a network share. When a given client wants to analyze some information, they fetch the indexed data from the network share, deserialize it, and keep it in memory while the user navigates the application. Working with the data in-memory by using Elixir functions like map, filter, and group is much more efficient than going over the network to reach the database.

The new solution provides 20 times faster response times and greatly improves the user experience. Indexing is 30 times faster and uses 63 times less disk space. The new architecture allows them to effectively remove the 12-week limitation, showing up to 156 weeks in some of their active campaigns.

Myron Marston is one of the developers that implemented the system described in this case study and we had the opportunity to ask him some questions about Elixir and its usage inside Moz:

> **José:** *Why did Moz choose Elixir?*
>
> **Myron:** *As a team, we were looking to build our next generation of services in something besides Ruby, having run into some maintainability and performance problems with our Ruby applications. Given the multi-core servers our code runs on, we wanted something that made it easy to take advantage of all those cores. We also found the immutable data structures and explicit state management of a functional language appealing.*
>
> *Elixir met all of our criteria. A couple of us had played around with Elixir and Phoenix and were very impressed with how productive we were, particularly given that we were newcomers, and how easy it was to get good performance. Moreover, in spite of it being such a new language, Elixir's use of the Erlang VM meant that its runtime*

---

1. https://moz.com/devblog/moz-analytics-db-free/

had a long, proven track record. Finally, we were extremely impressed with how easy it was to create abstractions that worked correctly in a concurrent environment. Unlike a more imperative language like Ruby, where you'd have to do careful synchronization to make something threadsafe, in Elixir, we've found we arrive at concurrency-safe abstractions naturally.

José: In what capacity are you using Elixir?

Myron: The Moz Pro Platform team is the only one at Moz using Elixir. Six of us on the team are using Elixir as the primary language across three production systems. One of those in particular is quite a large codebase, having seen continuous development since July 2015. In other languages we probably would have felt the need to split the project into multiple systems, but with Elixir's umbrella apps, we've found an elegant way to decompose the app into smaller components while keeping it all part of one system.

José: What was your biggest concern when you first considered using Elixir?

Myron: No one on the team had ever run an Erlang or Elixir system in production before. With any language runtime, you're going to run into unanticipated hiccups in production, and it's typical to rely on people with pre-existing knowledge of the technology for troubleshooting help. Embarking on a major architecture project without this domain expertise on the team was a risk.

José: How has your company benefited from Elixir?

Myron: We've seen benefits in several areas:

Maintainability We've found Elixir systems to be very easy to maintain, and our velocity has been very consistent over nearly two years of continuous development.

Reliability Our Elixir services have been much more reliable than our Ruby services ever were. In particular, our on-call rotation receives a small fraction of the pages with the new Elixir system compared to the old Ruby-based one. In addition, the only outage we've ever experienced from this application had nothing to do with our Elixir code (our Storage Area Network ran out of space)!

Performance As detailed in our blog post, we saw a 20x performance improvement from moving to Elixir.

Ease of deployment Early on, we encountered challenges deploying Elixir apps as we adjusted to significant differences from Capistrano. Having acclimated to Erlang release process we now find deployment a breeze. We build our production releases as part of our CI on TravisCI, which facilitates a rapid, three-step deploy process that fetches the release from S3, unpackages it, and starts it.

Lower cost Our Elixir services take much less hardware than our Ruby services did.

Unlocked features Rebuilding a service in Elixir allowed us to unlock key features that our product team wanted, as detailed in our blog post.

To be fair, many of these benefits are as much about the architecture we chose for the new system as it is for Elixir itself, but in many ways, Elixir is the enabling factor that allowed us to choose that architecture. A language like Ruby with a Global Interpreter Lock (GIL) would not have supported the style of architecture we've gone with.

José: *Have you had hiccups or roadblocks along the way? How did you overcome them?*

Myron: *One of our early challenges was related to how we handle production configuration. Mix config works well but isn't suitable for credentials and other runtime config values, especially when we use an external service (Travis) for our CI. We wound up creating our own RuntimeConfig library that allows us to put config in an external JSON file. The path to the JSON file is then injected via an environment variable.*

For most of our other hiccups and roadblocks, the Elixir community was there to support us. We've received help from members of the community on IRC, from the mailing list, and on the Elixir forum. One recent example was when we were trying to troubleshoot GenServer timeouts, and you helped us out.[2]

José: *Any other comment?*

Myron: *Elixir was an optimal fit for our team here at Moz. In addition to the myriad technical benefits and operational improvements we realized in our migration to the Elixir ecosystem, we were delighted to find a community that echoed Moz's values. Elixir's mission and its code of conduct describe a community that is friendly and welcoming; happy and helpful. Our own TAGFEE code[3] similarly promotes openness and generosity in all we do. As our team of engineers from varying backgrounds and levels of experience embarked on this project, they found in Elixir both a technology and a community that were an ideal match.*

One of the most important aspects of their solution is the decoupling between the writing and reading of the data. They still certainly have an infrastructure for collecting all of those events, but their Elixir backend does not care about it. This particular technique has nothing to do with language! It's easy to manage static data in memory because it will never change. In a hard crash, the user request just goes to another node, which simply loads the indexed data. Nothing is lost. And if they need to add new features that require extracting different insights from the data, they can just reindex it.

Elixir helped them maximize their database-free design by giving them abstractions to reason about state. The app can create separate processes and keep information about different clients isolated. When busy, the system purges the oldest data first to make room for new requests.

---

2.   https://elixirforum.com/t/troubleshooting-a-slow-genserver/3939

3.   https://moz.com/about/tagfee

Finding Processes

When building distributed systems with Elixir, naming and grouping processes is fundamental. A process registry lets you uniquely name a process. A process group lets you group processes based on a property or on a shared attribute.

Process registries and process groups store mutable information. After all, a registry can name a processes, assign it to a group, or destroy that information at any time. However, process data is still ephemeral. Once a process is dead, its name or group don't matter. If an asteroid strikes your data center, all name and group information will be lost, but all processes will be gone too.

For process registries and process groups, you don't need to worry about persistence, but you *do* need to discuss the trade-offs between local and distributed storage, and the strategies for replicating data.

Process Registries

A process registry lets you uniquely name a process.

There are two kinds of registries: *local registries* store the names of processes that belong to the current machine, and *distributed registries* store the names of processes across the whole cluster. Let's explore some of the registries and their trade-offs, focusing on the registries that are part of Erlang and Elixir standard libraries.

The Local atom-Based Registry

The atom registry is a tool that binds an atom to a process. In a previous chapter, we defined a PathAllocator which started like this:

```elixir
defmodule PathAllocator do
  @name PathAllocator

  def start_link(tmp_dir) when is_binary(tmp_dir) do
    GenServer.start_link(__MODULE__, tmp_dir, name: @name)
  end

  ...
end
```

When Elixir starts a process and gives it an atom name, such as PathAllocator, it uses the *local* registry from the Erlang VM. By convention, Elixir names those processes by the module defining them to simplify introspection and debugging.

Since the registry is local, node A can't see if there's a process named PathAllocator on node B, but node A *can ask* node B to send a message to local process named PathAllocator.

The atom registry supports only atom names. Because atoms are not garbage collected, you should never use the atom registry to register dynamically named processes! That would lead to a memory leak. Use the atom registry when you know the name at compilation time.

Beginning with version v1.4.0,[4] if you want to dynamically register non-atom names locally, you can use the local, highly scalable Registry module[5] that ships as part of the Elixir standard library.

Both the built-in atom-based registry and the Registry module are local. If you want to uniquely identify a processes in a cluster, you can use OTP's :global registry.[6] Check out its documentation for examples and a full reference. Here we'll focus only on the design decisions and trade-offs taken by the :global module.

The :global Registry

:global is a distributed registry with atomic registrations so a global process named :my_iex will be visible to all nodes at the same time. Each node keeps its own copy of registered processes so there's no central storage and the translation of a name to a PID is always fast. Each node can answer without resorting to communication if there is a process named :my_iex or not.

The downside of this approach is that registration becomes more expensive as the number of nodes grows. If you have 10 nodes, registering a single process requires coordination across all nodes. If one of these nodes is unresponsive, it may block the registration for many seconds, until the node is back up or other nodes mark the unresponsive node as offline.

Those design decisions imply that :global may also not suit you well if you want to dynamically register names, as the rate of registrations become quite limited when the number of nodes grows. The :global registry is best used when you need to identify processes that must always be running from the moment the system starts. Its limitations are well known and documented; for more information, see the paper "Evaluating Scalable Distributed Erlang for Scalability and Reliability"[7] by N. Chechina, K. MacKenzie, et. al.

For example, if you are building a multiplayer game, you may need to identify where each player is connected in your cluster. Players can join the game at any time at a pace so fast that the built-in :global registry may not provide the

---

4.   http://elixir-lang.org/blog/2017/01/05/elixir-v1-4-0-released/
5.   https://hexdocs.pm/elixir/Registry.html
6.   http://erlang.org/doc/man/global.html
7.   http://ieeexplore.ieee.org/document/7820204/?reload=true

throughput necessary. In such cases, you can try alternatives provided by the community, such as Syn,[8] or use a third-party data store for the user tracking.

Process Groups

While process registries allow you to uniquely identify a process, a process group allows us to group processes under a given topic or property. Like registries, process groups may be local or distributed.

Let's briefly explore the process group implementations available in the standard libraries and ecosystem.

The Registry Module

Elixir's Registry module[9] has two modes of operation. When configured to use unique keys, it works as a process registry, storing a unique entry for each key. When you choose duplicate keys, it stores multiple entries under each single key, and it effectively works as a process group. It's all about the data structures you choose. In the former, a key maps on to a value; in the latter, a key maps to a list of values.

Let's see an example with duplicate keys. First, start the registry:

```
iex> Registry.start_link(:duplicate, MyProcessGroup)
{:ok, #PID<0.65.0>}
```

"hello" has no worker processes:

```
iex> Registry.lookup(MyProcessGroup, "workers")
[]
```

Now, register the same process twice, with different properties, and then perform another lookup:

```
iex> {:ok, _} = Registry.register(MyProcessGroup, "workers", :high_priority)
iex> {:ok, _} = Registry.register(MyProcessGroup, "workers", :low_priority)
iex> Registry.lookup(MyProcessGroup, "workers")
[{#PID<0.59.0>, :high_priority}, {#PID<0.59.0>, :low_priority}]
```

Registry.register always registers the current process and expects the registry name, the key (which is the group name), and some property of the registration.

Registry implements a *local process group*. Curiously, you can send a message to all processes in a cluster that belong to a given group by using the local atom-based registry and a local process group:

---

8.   https://github.com/ostinelli/syn
9.   https://hexdocs.pm/elixir/Registry.html

1. On every node, start a GenServer named MyPubSub and a process group named MyProcessGroup using the Registry module.

2. Each process interested in joining the group "workers" registers itself under their local MyProcessGroup.

3. To broadcast a message to all workers in the whole cluster, you get a list of all nodes, using Node.list, and use send/2 to send a message to the MyPubSub process running on each node, as we did in the "Remote Message Passing" section. Being a GenServer, MyPubSub will receive the message on its handle_info/2 callback and proceed to broadcast the message to the local "workers" group using the Registry API.

That's effectively how distributed pubsub works in Phoenix.PubSub. See the Registry documentation[10] for more use cases and the complete API reference.

The :pg2 Module

The :pg2 module[11] provides a distributed process group implementation. Using :pg2, you can create groups and processes may join and leave those groups at any time.

Though you could implement a distributed PubSub using the Registry module, other operations may be expensive to perform using only local tools. Say you wanted to both broadcast messages and know how many of your cluster's processes are in the "workers" group. One solution would be to message each node and ask their local count, which they would message back. That's going to be inefficient.

:pg2 is like :global. Joining a group happens atomically across the whole cluster. Each node keeps its own copy of available groups so there's no central storage. Fetching all of a group's processes in the cluster is always fast because it's a local request. The downside is the same as in :global. Joining becomes more expensive as the number of nodes grows, so you should use :pg2 to identify group services only at startup time. Avoid :pg2 for dynamic registrations.

As usual, the community has filled in the blanks with their own solutions. Phoenix implements Phoenix.PubSub and also a presence mechanism called Phoenix.Presence. Behind the scenes, it uses a distributed process group implementation called Phoenix.Tracker.[12] Each process joins a Phoenix.Tracker group locally, and nodes in the cluster periodically exchange group information.

---

10. http://erlang.org/doc/man/registry.html
11. http://erlang.org/doc/man/pg2.html
12. https://hexdocs.pm/phoenix_pubsub/Phoenix.Tracker.html

This solution trades instant visibility for availability and performance. We say such a system is *eventually consistent.*

This trade-off is completely reasonable for Phoenix Presence. If a user connects to node A, users connected to node B can easily wait a few seconds to see node A user. You'll need to decide if this kind of trade-off works for your application.

That's all of the tools we want to cover here. If you don't find what you're looking for here, check out the other tools in your ecosystem.

Cache and ETS

Moz fetched all of their data up front using a databaseless strategy. Another company called Ministry of Games kept mutable data in-memory and persisted it to the database at specific moments and time intervals.[13] Those are great examples of leveraging the power of Elixir to design optimal solutions.

You can also leverage the tooling provided by the VM machine on simpler problems, such as caching. A cache allows you to store the result of a computation and re-use it several times, perhaps by multiple entities. Caches are a classic example of ephemeral data. If you lose the cache, you can just rebuild it again.

In Elixir, when you need to store shared data across multiple processes, you can use ETS,[14] which is the Erlang Term Storage. ETS provides a high-level mechanism for storing data in-memory, and it's often the tool of choice for caches. For example, Ecto uses ETS to cache the compilation of Ecto queries, leading to great performance. Then each application needs to compile its query once. There's one ETS table per node, and a single Elixir node scales very well, so ETS makes a highly efficient cache.

If you can build the cache cheaply and you have multiple instances of the Erlang VM deployed across multiple servers, it's better for each instance to have its own cache rather than using some network cache. We call such a cache *local.* Remember: accessing the data stored in-memory is orders of magnitude faster than using any external service. That's why Elixir developers rarely resort to Redis or Memcached. ETS, or ETS abstraction such as con_cache,[15] is almost always a better solution.

If a local ETS cache is not enough, developers can use the tools described in this chapter to provide more sophisticated solutions. For example, imagine

---

13. https://www.infoq.com/presentations/building-scalable
14. http://erlang.org/doc/man/ets.html
15. https://github.com/sasa1977/con_cache

that building the cache is slightly expensive and, if another node in the network has already built the cache, you would rather get a copy of the cache than rebuild it. You can use a process group implementation to keep a list of processes across your cluster that hold certain caches. When you need to access the cache and the list of caches is not empty, you can ask one of those processes to send the cache to you.

In the worst-case scenario, where computing of the cache on demand is infeasible, you may want to resort to a more robust solution that builds the cache in the background and updates a *global* storage, such as a database or even S3, in a solution quite similar to the Moz application.

Message Delivery Guarantees

Good developers often associate certain words with particular pitfalls or techniques for avoiding them. Large dataset aggregation suggests the map-reduce pattern; immutability may suggest functional languages. In this section, we'll build another association. Whenever you consider events, you should also consider message delivery guarantees.

Consider a simple welcome email that you might want to send each time a user creates an account. You could do so asynchronously with the Task module, but if the client fails or the server abruptly terminates, the email won't be sent. Maybe you are willing to live with the consequences—if the email contained the user confirmation token, they can always request a new one later. In such cases, we provide *at-most-once delivery*. The email may be sent or not.

Maybe you're not willing to drop the email, because losing it could impact adoption. This means you need a persistence mechanism. If the node responsible for sending the email catches on fire, another node needs to pick this job up. Once persistence becomes part of the equation, don't reinvent the wheel. Use a third-party solution designed for the problem, such as RabbitMQ.

Once we add persistence, we can explore other delivery guarantees. In the email case, the best we can do is *at-least-once delivery*. For example, imagine that when the user creates an account, we store a job on RabbitMQ. A worker in your cluster picks up that job and sends the email, but while sending the email, an error happens. Was the email sent or not really?

Due to how emails work, we can't quite answer this question. So the best strategy is to consider the job as failed and try again. Maybe the user will receive the email twice but they will hardly lose sleep over it.

At-least-once delivery is not enough in certain cases. For example, when billing a credit card, you surely don't want to bill it twice. We need *exactly-once delivery*. It happens that, when communicating over the network, it is quite hard to guarantee exactly-once delivery. Imagine you send a message to an external server and it does not reply in 30 seconds. Does it mean it failed? Or does it mean it is busy and your message will be processed eventually? How long should you wait then?

If you need exactly-once delivery, the safest bet you can make is to guarantee that your messages are idempotent: if messages are idempotent, sending multiple messages won't further affect the status of the system. In the billing case, this can be done by generating unique numbers for each transaction. When you message the billing service, you can include a unique ID. If the request fails, you send the same request, with the same unique ID. If the server has already seen and processed that unique ID, it can reply back that all is OK. If the server has not seen the ID, then it knows it has work to do.

Homogeneous vs. Heterogeneous Systems

Thanks to Erlang, Elixir excels at building homogeneous systems, which are systems where all nodes are running exactly the same code. In this section, we explore the alternative. Two completely different codebases that use a common communication protocol is a *heterogeneous system*. Typically, you won't build one with Erlang/Elixir for a number of reasons:

- The Erlang distribution keeps a fully meshed network. Fully meshed systems means any node can talk to any other node in the system. In such a system, nodes having nothing in common may end up directly connected. For example, if system B needs to talk to systems A and C, systems A and C will end up connecting by default. The runtime supports hidden nodes but that will require more work on your end.

- Many of the tools we've talked about so far are hard to customize for heterogeneous systems. For example, when a process joins a group, :pg2 adds it to all nodes in the cluster. In case of heterogeneous systems, that means system A would end up receiving process group updates from the processes running in system B, simply because they have been connected via the Erlang distribution.

- We need to not only consider Elixir limitations, but also the availability of tooling and other design constraints. For example, if system A wants to talk to system B, there are probably many nodes in system B that are able to fulfill system A requests. In such case, which node to choose? Which process? You may end up reimplementing load balancing.

At the end of the day, if you are interested in building heterogeneous systems, you may also be interested in mixing and matching systems that are written in different languages. Sticking to distributed Erlang means you are limited in terms of choices. You can only use platforms that implement distributed Erlang protocols.

When confronted with such choices, many teams decide to use HTTP and JSON for communicating between systems. We find this can be a verbose, inefficient, and unproductive method for system communication. We would recommend relying on middleware solutions, such as messaging systems, for the communication between those different systems. Messaging systems may come with the benefit of adding persistence, which will help guarantee messages exchanged between systems won't be lost.

We stress the importance of using existing solutions, however pedestrian, because they are often the best tool for the job. Here is an anecdote of junior and senior developers exploring persistence possibilities:

Junior: "We don't need a database. We are going to store everything in a GenServer."

Senior: "Great! Can you afford to lose data?"

Junior: "No... but we could do backups at certain intervals. And we have two instances."

Senior: "Are you going to partition the data and direct the access accordingly?"

Junior: "Hm. Maybe we can replicate the data between nodes?"

Senior: "Congratulations; you've just invented a database!"

This team ended up storing their data in PostgreSQL. A couple weeks later the service was up and running in production, with no surprises—just high uptime and happy users.

We are not saying you always need a database, but neither are we saying you should always ditch your database. And as you saw throughout this chapter, your choice is not strictly binary, either.

Sometimes the choice depends on data locality. For cache systems, we can compute the information locally and optionally rely on an ad-hoc communication system for sharing the cache in a cluster. A database or a shared storage should only be used as a last resort for caches that are expensive to build.

Other systems, such as Phoenix.Presence, keep only ephemeral data: the users connected to your system right now. Each node running Phoenix.Presence replicates the information they have based on a time interval. There is no need for an external storage, data is replicated between nodes directly.

Finally, we saw some systems prefer to keep mutable data in-memory but persist the latest version of the data to a shared storage every 3 minutes or when the user reaches particular check points. The huge majority of the time, you will not observe any data loss, but when things go bad, no more than the last 3 minutes of the user's progress will be lost.

Remember, one size does not fit all. You can explore the many tools the VM provides to find your best design. That's enough for now. It's time to wrap up.

Wrapping Up

In this chapter, we looked at bringing distributed applications into the mix. While the Erlang patterns implemented in Elixir make solving such problems easier, the nuances can take years of experience to get right. The best way to learn is to try and fail (or follow the wisdom others have acquired during their own attempts). You've seen a broad collection of advice and experience based on years of experience with Plataformatec and the customers they've encountered.

We started the discussion with distributed message passing. You learned that Elixir uses the same abstractions to send local messages and messages across nodes. Along the way, we built a sample app using nothing but the console, and saw how to monitor nodes just as you would processes.

Next, we looked into managing persistence, state, and replication. We looked at a family of problems that don't have to worry about changing state, opening up a broad array of potential solutions. We examined a database-free architecture created by the Moz team and looked at the trade-offs that made such a solution possible. Later, we talked about the trade-offs that might lead you to use a database instead.

We then moved on to the topic of finding processes in a distributed system. We looked at three basic solutions: the local registry, the global registry, and process groups.

We discussed caches as simple in-memory key-value pairs. We learned that ETS tables are perfect abstractions for caching data, and saw how to build such a system. We wrapped up the chapter with brief discussions of message delivery guarantees and a small discussion of homogeneous versus heterogeneous systems.

We understand that our treatment of distributed systems is far from complete. People can and have spent whole careers studying individual topics that we've covered in a few short paragraphs. The best we can do is to show you what's out there, and point you in the right direction.

In the next chapter, we'll finish up our development discussion. We'll focus on integrating with code written in other languages. A bunch of exciting things are happening in these areas. To find out for yourself, just turn the page!

## CHAPTER 7

Integrating with External Code

So far we have been talking about scenarios where Elixir and the Erlang VM really shine. The combination of a couple of years of explosive growth and Erlang's decades' long history will serve you well when you need to integrate with the tens of thousands of available packages and libraries written in both Erlang and Elixir.

We're not blind, though. Elixir has its limitations. For example:

Serious math Statistical libraries and the like can be slow because the VM was not designed for number crunching. If your application depends on computing statistics, executing numerical methods, or finances, you may find the VM lacking.

Solutions built on top of matrices The naïve implementation of matrices in Elixir would use lists of lists, which are not an efficient representation of multidimensional matrices. Also, the lack of mutability would make modifying large matrices expensive and lead to excessive copying regardless of the data structure your implementation uses.

Shared memory parallel algorithms Engineers designed certain families of algorithms for parallel computing with shared memory in mind. Graph algorithms, such as minimum spanning tree, are hard to implement efficiently using the shared-nothing concurrency that Elixir provides.

Command-line applications The VM takes about 0.3s from startup to shutdown on modern hardware, so Elixir may not be as good as some other scripting languages or languages that build native executables. After all, Erlang was designed for long-running systems. Plus, every command-line application needs to ship with the VM, unless the command-line application is for Elixir developers.

Existing non-Elixir libraries You may find that you need to interface with libraries native to languages like C or C++ that are already implemented.

That's not a comprehensive list. You'll doubtless find your own set of problems that Elixir is not ideally suited to solve. Most of the time, you'll probably be willing to live with trade-offs. For example, when it comes to mutability, concurrency, and list handling, Elixir's approach has performance implications based on the types of problems you're solving. We're not talking about these kinds of trade-offs.

We're talking about times when Elixir would cripple a single aspect of a critically important problem, such as heavy statistics on large datasets or grinding through huge machine learning scenarios. If Elixir fits *most* of your requirements, you don't have to abandon it just to satisfy that final 5% of your application. There are some excellent integration options available to you. When Elixir and the Erlang VM aren't good enough, you can solve such problems in other languages and technologies, and integrate them with your Elixir codebase.

In this chapter, we'll show you some of the mechanisms you can use to do so. We'll look at some integration options and write some basic code. Let's get started.

Lay of the Land

You may use three main strategies to integrate with external code. Each strategy has a different level of coupling. With the tightest coupling first, here they are:

- Strategy 1: Your application can share the same memory address space. Think of it as a function running in the same OS process. You can load the external code inside the VM that is running your Elixir code. This is implemented in the Erlang VM using the so-called native implemented functions (NIFs).

- Strategy 2: Your code can invoke the external code as a separate program on the same machine. Think of this strategy as a different OS process, but running on the same machine. In Elixir, we do so by using ports.

- Strategy 3: You can communicate with the external code over the network. This strategy is a different OS process, different machine. Rather than using generic solutions such as HTTP APIs or message queues, we are interested in exploring solutions that are specific to the Erlang VM. We will communicate with external systems using the Erlang distribution protocol.

In this chapter, we will explore solutions to each of those problems. We're not aiming for complete solutions. Instead, we'll focus on a quick exploration allowing us to examine the trade-offs of each solution. Let's look at each strategy in more detail.

Strategy 1: Native Implemented Functions (NIFs)

Native implemented functions, or NIFs, allow developers to load external code into the same memory address space as the Erlang VM. Your code can integrate quite closely with functions implemented in other languages. While such tight integration may seem appealing because of the obvious performance benefits, you need to be careful. This power comes at a price. If you've ever had a bad experience with a roommate, you know exactly what we mean. NIFs may be clean, but they do not necessarily share the same founding principles we do in ElixirLand. We must think of NIFs as unsafe. In particular:

- A crash in a native function will crash the whole VM, not just one process.

- A native function can cause internal VM inconsistencies, leading to crashes or unexpected behavior.

- They may interfere with Elixir's scheduling. A native function doing lengthy work can block other processes from running, causing inconsistent performance, high memory usage, and poor load balancing. We'll learn more a little later.

In other words, NIFs are dangerous. Treat them as such.

A Short Example

Let's build a quick example of using NIFs within Elixir. The steps are straightforward. We're going to create a project, build an Elixir module that loads a NIF, build our C NIF, then build it all and run it. Let's start a new project:

```
mix new elixir_nif
```

The main responsibility of the Elixir code is to define a template for functions that'll be replaced when the C code is loaded by the VM. Open up lib/elixir_nif.ex:

```
external_code/elixir_nif/lib/elixir_nif.ex
defmodule ElixirNif do
  @on_load :load_nif

  def load_nif do
    nif = Application.app_dir(:elixir_nif, "priv/elixir_nif")
    :ok = :erlang.load_nif(String.to_charlist(nif), 0)
  end
```

```
  def hello do
    "Hello from Elixir"
  end
end
```

The @on_load :load_nif annotation tells the VM to execute the load_nif/0 function. Timing is important. As soon as the VM loads the ElixirNif module into memory, the @on_load directive will fire the load_nif function. It will happen at compile time and also the first time the VM references ElixirNif on startup.

The load_nif/0 function will look for an .so or .dll file in the priv/elixir_nif directory. load_nif/0 must return :ok. Otherwise, the module won't successfully load.

This C code replaces the hello/0 function defined in Elixir with a hello function implemented in C. If you want, you can provide a default implementation in Elixir, and use a C implementation if it's available. If you prefer, you can code defensively by raising in the Elixir definition, like this:

```
def hello do
  raise "NIF could not be loaded"
end
```

Finally, the C code in c_src/elixir_nif.c will define a hello function that receives 0 arguments and instructs the VM to load it into ElixirNif.hello/0, like this:

```
external_code/elixir_nif/c_src/elixir_nif.c
#include "string.h"
#include "erl_nif.h"

static ERL_NIF_TERM hello(ErlNifEnv* env,
                          int argc,
                          const ERL_NIF_TERM argv[]) {
  ErlNifBinary *output_binary;
  enif_alloc_binary(sizeof "Hello from C", output_binary);
  strcpy(output_binary->data, "Hello from C");
  return enif_make_binary(env, output_binary);
}

static ErlNifFunc nif_funcs[] = {
    {"hello", 0, hello},
};

ERL_NIF_INIT(Elixir.ElixirNif, nif_funcs, NULL, NULL, NULL, NULL)
```

At the top, our erl_nif.h header contains the structs, macros, and definitions used in the snippet. You can find the full reference in the Erlang documentation.[1]

---

1. http://erlang.org/doc/man/erl_nif.html

The hello function allocates a new ErlNifBinary C struct, copies the C string "Hello from C" into its data and builds an Elixir binary with enif_make_binary. At the end of the file, we call the ERL_NIF_INIT macro with Elixir.ElixirNif, our complete module name, followed by the functions we want to replace in that module. When you're working with Erlang, remember to prefix all Elixir modules with Elixir.

After we define the C function, we need to compile the C code into a shared library with the proper flags. First, we need to find the Erlang installation and the path to its C header files, like this:

```
$ elixir -e "IO.puts :code.root_dir()"
/usr/local/Cellar/erlang/18.1/lib/erlang
```

That command will vary based on your operating system, but you get the idea. The result is the Erlang install path. Inside that directory, you'll find a directory that looks something like erts-x.y, such as erts-9.2. That directory will have an include directory inside, where you will find the erl_nif.h file. Whew.

Now, we can compile our C library. First, make sure the priv directory exists, which is where we will write the compiled artifacts. We'll show the versions for a few different operating systems, but you may need to tweak them for your environment and your Erlang installation.

On Linux:

```
gcc -o priv/elixir_nif.so -shared -fpic \
    -I/usr/local/erlang/18.1/lib/erlang/erts-9.2/include \
    c_src/elixir_nif.c
```

Remember, you'll have to replace the -I with the path you found previously. The flags -shared and -fpic tell GCC to build a shared library with position-independent code, meaning the code does not expect to be loaded into a specific memory address.

On macOS, we need to specify two extra flags and the correct path for -I, like this:

```
gcc -o priv/elixir_nif.so -shared -fpic -dynamiclib \
  -undefined dynamic_lookup \
  -I/usr/local/Cellar/erlang/18.1/lib/erlang/erts-9.2/include \
  c_src/elixir_nif.c
```

Remember to type the previous on one line. And on Windows, on one line:

```
cl /IERTS_INCLUDE_PATH=C:\erlang\18.1\lib\erlang\erts-9.2\include
   /LD /MD /Fe priv\elixir_nif.so src\elixir_nif.c
```

In practice, you'll probably not compile any of your C code by hand. You'll use Makefiles.[2] Once you create your Makefile, you can invoke it directly from Mix with Elixir Make.[3]

To learn more, you can look at existing projects like the ones below to learn how to organize your C code:

- https://github.com/riverrun/comeonin
- https://github.com/antipax/nifsy
- https://github.com/devinus/markdown

Finally, the Erlang VM documentation also contains tutorials on writing NIFs[4] and includes a reference manual,[5] linked earlier in this section. Before we wrap this section up, we need to dive into a couple of details.

Preemption and Dirty Schedulers

Elixir processes use *preemptive multitasking*. Each process gets a discrete number of *reductions* which are the basic building blocks that make up our programs. When a process runs its allocation of reductions, the Elixir VM preempts it to allow the next process to run its allocated reductions. That's an important design choice that allows the VM to provide predictable latency.

Unfortunately, NIFs are not preempted by the virtual machine. If a NIF requires 1 second to run, it will run for the whole second, without giving any other VM processes the opportunity to run. As you might expect, this is a problem. The official recommendation from the OTP team is to not perform operations that take longer than one millisecond in a NIF.

This time limitation can be quite restrictive. Code that requires more than one millisecond to run requires adjustments. You may need to build in the ability to stop mid-processing and yield the control back to the VM, and that means your C programs get more complicated, and more likely to crash—which brings down the whole VM.

Luckily, to solve this problem, the folks at Basho teamed up with the OTP team to provide a feature called dirty schedulers. Here's how they work.

For every core, the BEAM virtual machine starts a thread that runs a scheduler. By default, there are as many schedulers as cores, each running in its

---

2. https://en.wikipedia.org/wiki/Makefile
3. http://github.com/elixir-lang/elixir_make
4. http://erlang.org/doc/tutorial/nif.html
5. http://erlang.org/doc/man/erl_nif.html

own thread. Those schedulers are the ones responsible for scheduling which VM process or port (to be discussed in the next section) will run next.

You can get the total number of schedulers by calling :erlang.system_info(:schedulers). You can fetch the number of online schedulers, or the schedulers currently running, by calling :erlang.system_info(:schedulers_online). You can configure the number of schedulers only during the VM startup, but you can turn schedulers on and off with :erlang.system_flag(:schedulers_online, number_of_schedulers_online).

Because NIFs run in the scheduler's processes, long-running NIFs means blocking the scheduler, and that's *bad*. Erlang recently introduced a separate group of schedulers, ones designed especially for running NIFs. These so-called *dirty schedulers* were introduced as an experimental feature in Erlang 18. To enable them, compile Erlang from source with the flag --enable-dirty-schedulers. The feature became official by Erlang 20.

We divide dirty schedulers into two categories: I/O bound and CPU bound. Similar to schedulers, we have one CPU-bound dirty scheduler per core. The VM also starts ten threads as I/O-bound dirty schedulers. If you compile Erlang with the dirty schedulers flag, you should see the dirty schedulers information when starting up IEx:

```
Erlang/OTP 19 [erts-8.0] [source] [64-bit] [smp:4:4] [ds:4:4:10]
               [async-threads:10] [hipe] [kernel-poll:false]

Interactive Elixir (1.5.2) - press Ctrl+C to exit (type h() ENTER for help)
```

The [ds:4:4:10] says dirty schedulers is enabled, with four dirty CPU schedulers, where all four of them are online, followed by ten dirty I/O schedulers.

Your C code will choose which dirty scheduler to use when you build your ErlNifFunc structs. If you specify a dirty scheduler, the NIF will no longer run in the primary scheduler but in one of the specified dirty schedulers, like this:

```
static ErlNifFunc nif_funcs[] = {
    {"hello", 0, hello, ERL_NIF_DIRTY_JOB_CPU_BOUND},
};
```

You can choose between ERL_NIF_DIRTY_JOB_CPU_BOUND or ERL_NIF_DIRTY_JOB_IO_BOUND. For more information on dirty schedulers, consult Erlang's reference documentation.[6] There's also an excellent video from ElixirConf 2017 called "Well-Behaved Native Implemented Functions for Elixir" by Andrew Bennett.[7] For a reference implementation, check the Nifsy project.[8]

---

6. http://erlang.org/doc/man/erl_nif.html
7. https://www.youtube.com/watch?v=FYQcn9zcZVA
8. https://github.com/antipax/nifsy

To summarize, NIFs allow very tightly integrated C code. You can get great performance if you're careful, and spotty concurrency, inconsistent data, and instability if you're not.

Strategy 2: Communicating via I/O with Ports

Ports provide a safer alternative to integrate with external software. Each port starts the third-party software as a separate process in the operating system. If that port terminates, your Elixir code gets a message, and you can act accordingly. A segmentation fault in the external port won't bring your Elixir system down.

It is possible that you've already spawned ports in your Elixir applications, like this:

```
System.cmd("elixir", ["-e", "IO.puts 21 * 2"])
{"42\n", 0}
```

This command finds the elixir executable in your operating system and invokes it passing the command-line arguments -e, for code evaluation, and the contents IO.puts 21 * 2. Then System.cmd returns the result written to the standard output, which is "42\n" and the status code, which is 0, indicating success. Similar to processes, ports are built on top of asynchronous communication. System.cmd hides this communication behind a synchronous command that blocks only the current process until the executable exits.

If you need to integrate with a third-party program, you should consider ports before resorting to NIFs. Ports put stability and reliability before performance—and you should as well, unless you really need the numbers.

Sometimes, external code is a crucial part of your architecture and may even play a central role. If you're using Nerves, the core Elixir framework for embedded systems, you're using ports. Let's see how Nerves leverages ports for building embedded systems and how Le Tote is using those systems in production.

A Case Study: Nerves and Le Tote

Nerves[9] is a framework to craft and deploy bulletproof embedded software in Elixir. When you write embedded software, you need to communicate with all kinds of peripheral devices, such as displays to show status, buttons to customize automations, Wi-Fi board to communicate with other devices, RFID

---

9. http://nerves-project.org/

readers to read identity chips, and the like. Assembling all the drivers and software to integrate with those devices is an error-prone and riddling process.

The Nerves creators saw this is as a perfect opportunity to use Elixir and OTP. Instead of building custom operating systems that try to tie this all together, they decided to let Elixir control them. Their application spawns a process that communicates with the Wi-Fi board or a barcode scanner, and if something goes wrong with those devices, Elixir can restart it. Elixir thrives in that environment because it was built to solve such problems.

Nerves offloads the burden of managing those devices from the embedded operating system. This strategy has certain specialized requirements. For example, a bug in the RFID reader should not bring your system down so all the communication with the RFID reader must happen through ports. As with the rest of the Elixir ecosystem, Nerves reliability depends on active supervision. When the process controlling the port dies, the supervisor will take action, such as a restart.

he Nerves team follow this guideline almost religiously. All integration happens through ports. Even when they need to write C code to expose new capabilities, they write the C program and communicate with it through a port.

Bringing Elixir's fault-tolerance and developer productivity principles to embedded software proved to be a successful combination. Nerves is capable of automating the whole process of packaging and deploying embedded systems. During development, it can even push code to the device over the wire.

Charlie Bowman is the CTO at Le Tote, a forward-thinking fashion rental company that is attacking embedded systems development, a branch of our industry that badly needs retooling. Le Tote is betting on using Nerves and embedded systems to provide a much more automated experience for their warehouse, which is critical for the fashion rental business.

> **Ben:** *Why did you choose Elixir?*

> **Charlie:** *We were rethinking our entire warehouse management system (WMS) and Elixir offered the best solution to our problem. One reason for the WMS rethink was due to our desire to move from a barcode-based system to RFID. We wanted to create custom hardware and software solutions that maintained a constant connection to the cloud-based application so that we could have real-time inventory data in the warehouse. Phoenix channels was perfect for this on the software side. We also started creating custom hardware devices to be used, and Nerves allowed us to quickly develop custom firmware to be used on these devices. These customer hardware devices running Nerves allowed us to create a perfectly optimized solution to our problem.*

Ben: *What was your biggest concern when you first considered using Elixir?*

Charlie: *My lack of experience was my biggest concern. This was my first time making a decision for a given technology that I was not at least somewhat experienced in. My background was in OOP, specifically Ruby, so the thought of moving to a functional system based on OTP was a big leap for me. It took some time for me to wrap my head around Elixir processes and GenServers.*

Ben: *How has your company benefited from Elixir?*

Charlie: *Far and away the biggest benefit from moving to Elixir has been the team we've been able to assemble. Passionate and experienced engineers have already started making the move to Elixir because it keeps so many things they love about modern programming (expressive languages, MVC frameworks, rapid development) while offering proven strategies for concurrency and fault tolerance. From a purely technical point of view, Elixir, Phoenix, and Nerves all offer rapid development and fault tolerance, both of which are absolutely critical when writing software that is used by hundreds of people in a warehouse that requires near perfect uptime.*

In short, Elixir and ports allowed Le Tote to revamp their entire warehouse management system. Le Tote is at the forefront of the coming automation revolution. They're solving problems with cutting-edge technology in Nerves, and they're even creating the technology as they go along.

We like to share this story because developers have this dangerous habit of valuing performance above everything else. Nerves and Elixir help to balance the scales by focusing on reliability. When it comes to external systems, ports are the way to go. Let's code an example.

All-Caps I/O Program

In this section we are going to implement an all-caps I/O program in Elixir and interact with it using ports. The program is going to read lines from the standard input, upper case them, and then write them to the standard output. In practice you'll use ports to interact with software written in all kinds of languages except Elixir itself. Using Elixir here is enough to learn how it all works.

This time, we'll work with two script files instead of creating a full Elixir project, one to provide the all-caps implementation and the other to run it. Let's start with all_caps.exs:

external_code/port_1/all_caps.exs
```
for line <- IO.stream(:stdio, :line) do
  IO.write String.upcase(line)
end
```

Run it with elixir all_caps.exs. Give it a try:

```
$ elixir all_caps.exs
hello
HELLO
```

Hitting Ctrl+D closes the I/O device, terminating the I/O loop and the software. Our second script will open up a port to use the all_caps.exs program. Crack open program.exs and key this in:

external_code/port_1/program.exs
```
port = Port.open({:spawn, "elixir all_caps.exs"}, [:binary])

send port, {self(), {:command, "hello\n"}}
receive do
  {^port, {:data, data}} ->
    IO.puts "Got: #{data}"
end

send port, {self(), :close}
receive do
  {^port, :closed} ->
    IO.puts "Closed"
end
```

You can run it like this:

```
$ elixir program.exs
Got: HELLO

Closed
```

The program opens up a port by spawning elixir all_caps.exs and configures it to return binaries. Then, we send messages to the port, using send/2, *just as if it were an Elixir process!* We can also get data from the port, which is "hello\n" in all caps. Finally we issue a message to close the port and wait for its termination.

Don't lose sight of what's happening here. You're taking an application, potentially written in a different language, and you're interacting with it *just as if it were written in Elixir*. With this technique, your ability to organize and layer your code is limited only by the interface you can build in the external language.

If you want, you can access a port using the Port API. The functions in the Port module are synchronous. Let's rewrite program.exs to use the Port API:

```
external_code/port_1/program_command.exs
port = Port.open({:spawn, "elixir all_caps.exs"}, [:binary])

Port.command(port, "hello\n")
receive do
  {^port, {:data, data}} ->
    IO.puts "Got: #{data}"
end

Port.close(port)
IO.puts "Closed"
```

Refer to the Port module documentation[10] for a description of all messages sent to and received by ports as well as the Port module API.

Before we wrap up our discussion about ports, there are some details we should discuss. First, we'll discuss packets, which are helpful when you're working with communication protocols. Next, we'll talk about shutting down port applications cleanly, and what to look out for in case you don't.

Packets

When you open a port, you'll use the Port.open/2 function, which accepts a wide range of options. In the all-caps program we used the :binary option to receive string data from a port, but we could have easily used a list. Here are some useful options you can use, alone or together:

- :exit_status will send a status message on termination. Sometimes, you don't need to use the output of a program. You just need to know if it was successful.

- :cd starts the port with the given current working directory.

- :args passes a list of arguments to the port. For example, we could have started the port as Port.open({:spawn, "elixir"}, args: ["all_caps.exs"]).

- :env executes the port program with additional environment variables.

- :nouse_stdio uses file descriptions 3 and 4 for communication instead of the standard io for communication. Use this option when the software writes messages you don't want in the standard output.

The Port module documentation has many other options. In this section, we will explore one other option, called the :packet option.

The trouble with our all_caps.exs software is that we have no control over the size of the messages we receive. For example, if we attempt to upcase a long

---

10. https://hexdocs.pm/elixir/Port.html

message, the response may be split over multiple port messages. If your goal is to keep the port open and send it multiple messages, over and over again, it becomes hard to know when a response for a given message is complete.

The `packets` option instructs the port to automatically include a number of bytes: 1, 2, or 4, at the beginning of every message with the message length. In fact, we must precede all messages with the length as well. This way we know exactly how long each message is and the `Port` module takes care of only delivering us the response when it is complete. We are also no longer restricted to finish each command with a new line.

Let's use a packet of 4 bytes for the length encoding. To do so, we'll change all_caps.exs to read only the first four bytes, containing exactly 32 bits. Then, we'll decode those bytes into an integer containing the message length. When we write the message back, we'll need to compute its length and place it as the leading 32 bits. Here's the new, improved all_caps.exs:

external_code/port_2/all_caps.exs
```
for length_binary <- IO.stream(:stdio, 4) do
  <<length::32>> = length_binary
  all_caps = length |> IO.read() |> String.upcase()
  IO.write <<byte_size(all_caps)::32, all_caps::binary>>
end
```

Our program.exs also requires only one small adjustment, passing the `packet: 4` option when the port is open. We will use this opportunity to include a more complex example:

external_code/port_2/program.exs
```
port = Port.open({:spawn, "elixir all_caps.exs"}, [:binary, packet: 4])

Port.command(port, "command without newline")
receive do
  {^port, {:data, data}} ->
    IO.puts "Got: #{data}"
end
Port.close(port)
IO.puts "Closed"
```

Now let's run it:

```
$ elixir program.exs
Got: COMMAND WITHOUT NEWLINE
Closed
```

As you can see, the program converted our message all at once, though it contained a newline.

All Caps and Unicode

When converting all_caps.exs to use packets, notice we receive the message length, convert the message to all caps, and then compute a new message length. However, you may be wondering: won't the returned message have the same length as the incoming message?

The answer might surprise you. Since the String module works on Unicode, it will upcase not only ASCII characters, but also many other characters. One such character is the Latin ligature ﬀ, represented by the codepoint FB00, which occupies 3 bytes. When converted to uppercase, ﬀ becomes FF, which is the ASCII letter F twice, represented by the codepoint 0046, which takes 2 bytes!

So, the answer is "The returned messages will not necessarily have the same length."

Next, we'll cover a common ports concern. You will want to take measures to make sure your processes terminate cleanly.

Termination and Zombie Processes

In this section, we want to cover a common trap. The termination of the Elixir software that starts a port *will not guarantee the termination of the port itself.* Instead, the port's standard I/O device is closed. That's what your port should use to decide what to terminate!

We didn't have to worry about this edge case in any of the previous examples because our all_caps.exs file streams the I/O device, and that stream automatically stops when we close the standard input, causing Elixir to terminate.

However, not all software you'll want to use from a port will read from standard input, so there is a chance they won't terminate when the standard input closes. That can lead to *zombie processes* when your ports terminate abruptly.

Luckily, there are many solutions available. For example, the Elixir documentation for the Port module[11] includes a section on Zombie processes with a bash script you can use to wrap ports that don't listen on the standard input.

Our last ports topic will help you build common, shared resources to handle common tasks.

Pools

While you can start as many ports as you want from Elixir, your memory may not love you for it. For example, imagine that you are building a web

---

11. https://hexdocs.pm/elixir/Port.html

application that needs to start a port for each request of an export action. If that port process takes about 20MB, 100 concurrent requests to that page means 100 ports, which will take around 2GB. There's a better way.

If you are expecting concurrent usage of your ports and you want to limit the amount of ports started, we recommend the same strategy that many databases and message queues use: pooling. You can use libraries such as poolboy[12] to start a certain amount of processes, each with its own port, and limit the number of ports to a number you can configure at startup. This strategy trades raw concurrency for predictable growth and performance.

We've covered NIFs and ports. It's time to cover our lone distributed strategy: the Erlang distribution protocol.

Strategy 3: The Erlang Distribution Protocol

On our spectrum, the strategies have moved from very tight integration within the same process to looser coupling between processes. Both of these techniques integrate systems that reside on the same machine. This last technique will introduce distribution between machines.

In Chapter 6, *Distributed Elixir*, on page 103, we introduced the Erlang distribution protocol which Elixir uses to communicate between nodes. There's no reason to limit its use to the Erlang VM. As long as a language or a platform implements the distribution protocol, you can use that language to communicate with Erlang nodes.

Implementing the Erlang distribution protocol is not easy because it requires the ability to serialize and deserialize Erlang data structures into binaries, and the capability to communicate with Erlang's Port Mapper Daemon (EPMD). Luckily, OTP itself ships with the implementation of the distribution protocol for C and Java, called ErlInterface and JInterface, respectively. Those interfaces provide another mechanism for Elixir developers to leverage the wide range of libraries in those ecosystems.

The EchoServer Class

Let's take a look at an example. We'll build an EchoServer in Java. The EchoServer will register itself as a node on EPMD and start a message box which will receive messages from other nodes. We'll create our simple Java program, set our class path so Java can find our Erlang integration, compile our service, start it, and then access it from the Elixir shell.

---

12. https://github.com/devinus/poolboy

Let's get started. Create a file named EchoServer.java, and key this in:

external_code/distributed_erlang/EchoServer.java

```java
import com.ericsson.otp.erlang.*;

public class EchoServer {
  public static void main(String[] args) throws Exception {
    OtpNode node = new OtpNode("java");
    OtpMbox mbox = node.createMbox("echo");

    while (true) {
      OtpErlangTuple message = (OtpErlangTuple) mbox.receive();
      OtpErlangPid from = (OtpErlangPid) message.elementAt(0);
      OtpErlangObject[] reply = new OtpErlangObject[2];
      reply[0] = mbox.self();
      reply[1] = message.elementAt(1);
      mbox.send(from, new OtpErlangTuple(reply));
    }
  }
}
```

We give our Java node the name :java and register the inbox as :echo. After our method creates the message box, we enter a loop waiting for messages to arrive on the inbox. The new messages will have the format {elixir_pid, contents}. We can then extract the PID, the contents, and send a message back in the format of {java_pid, contents}, where java_pid is the PID for the Java message box.

In order to compile our EchoServer class, we need to invoke javac with the OtpErlang.jar in the classpath. To find the JAR file, first find the root of your Erlang installation:

```
$ elixir -e "IO.puts :code.root_dir()"
/usr/local/Cellar/erlang/18.1/lib/erlang
```

You'll find the JAR file at lib/jinterface-x.y/priv/OtpErlang.jar, starting from the Erlang root directory we previously found. Note though some Erlang distributions may not include the .jar files unless explicitly instructed to do so during installation.

We can compile the EchoServer like this (but all on one line):

```
javac -classpath "/usr/local/Cellar/erlang/18.1/lib/erlang/lib/
                   jinterface-1.6/priv/OtpErlang.jar" EchoServer.java
```

Now, everything is compiled. It's time to take it for a spin.

Running EchoServer

We'll use the java command, just as you'd expect. Start the server like this (keeping it all on one line):

```
java -classpath ".:/usr/local/Cellar/erlang/18.1/lib/erlang/lib/
                 jinterface-1.6/priv/OtpErlang.jar" EchoServer
```

We can verify the server is running on EPMD, like this:

```
$ epmd -names
epmd: up and running on port 4369 with data:
name java at port 62257
```

The Java node will use the same cookie as Erlang nodes, which by default is stored in ~/.erlang.cookie. That means we can connect to the Java node directly from IEx, like this:

```
$ iex --sname elixir
Interactive Elixir (1.6.0) - press Ctrl+C to exit (type h() ENTER for help)
iex(elixir@macbook)1> Node.connect(:"java@macbook")
true
iex(elixir@macbook)2> send {:echo, :"java@macbook"}, {self(), "hello"}
{#PID<0.62.0>, "hello"}
iex(elixir@macbook)3> flush()
{#PID<8579.1.0>, "hello"}
:ok
```

In this quick snippet, we connected to the Java node, sent it a message, and got our echo message back. Your local names will likely be different than java@macbook and elixir@macbook, so you'll need to adjust the examples here accordingly.

If you want to know more, check out the documentation on both Jinterface[13] and Erl_Interface[14] for more information about these Java and C interfaces.

Remember, communication between nodes is not encrypted, though you'll need a cookie to join the conversation. Overall, the pitfalls of using the Erlang distribution protocol for communicating with Java, C, or other languages are the same ones you'll encounter when building heterogeneous systems on top of the Erlang distribution (refer back to *Homogeneous vs. Heterogeneous Systems*, on page 118 for more information).

If you need to run multiple Java nodes, you will have to decide how to load balance them from Elixir, and that's a demanding problem to solve. You'll also probably need to reimplement part of your infrastructure, and that implementation will probably limit you to languages in the Erlang family. Considering these severe trade-offs, it is more likely that you will end up building an API based on web standards or use a messaging system. Still, if

---

13. http://erlang.org/doc/apps/jinterface/jinterface_users_guide.html
14. http://erlang.org/doc/tutorial/erl_interface.html

you are in a situation where the Erlang distribution is sufficient, you have enough to get started.

Wrapping Up

There you have it. In this chapter, we explored three strategies for integrating external code:

- Strategy 1: Native implemented functions (NIFs) allow developers to load code into the same memory space address as the Erlang VM. It is the most performant option but also potentially unstable and insecure. A crash on a NIF can bring the whole node down and long-running calls can cause the VM to misbehave, but dirty schedulers can mitigate some of the disadvantages.

- Strategy 2: Ports run on the same machine as the Erlang VM node, but in a different process. They use I/O for communication. Ports are generally the best option to consider for integration, as it does not contain any of the safety implications behind NIFs nor the overhead behind the Erlang distribution protocol.

- Strategy 3: The Erlang distribution protocol allows other platforms to piggyback on Erlang VM's ability to communicate between nodes to allow integration with other languages. It has the same downsides of using the Erlang distribution for heterogeneous systems (as it is effectively a heterogeneous system).

In the unlikely scenario none of these strategies suit you, there are many other options we haven't explored here. These are beyond the scope of this book, but we will point them out for further exploration:

- The Interoperability tutorial[15] provided by the OTP team covers the solutions reviewed here as well as other topics we haven't discussed, such as linked-in drivers.

- Projects such as Porcelain[16] and erlexec[17] are built on top of ports to provide a different set of APIs and conveniences.

- The erlport project[18] provides integration with languages like Ruby and Python.

---

15. http://erlang.org/doc/tutorial/introduction.html
16. https://github.com/alco/porcelain
17. https://github.com/saleyn/erlexec
18. https://github.com/hdima/erlport

- Finally, projects such as Rustler[19] provide a safe bridge for creating NIFs in Rust.

That wraps up Part II, *Development*, on page 79. We explored building clean code based on clean abstractions, and how to instrument and measure results so it stays beautiful and easy to implement. Then we worked through integration strategies for other nodes and external libraries.

Next, we'll introduce Part III, *Production*, on page 143. In it, you'll learn how to deploy code, make it fast, and make the measurements you need to keep it running fast and smooth. We're hitting the home stretch, so turn the page!

---

19. https://github.com/hansihe/rustler

Part III

Production

In this final part, you will learn how people are thinking about deployment. It usually takes a little time to develop good automated systems for deploying when working with new languages, and Elixir is no exception. Now that the details are coming together, you'll find out how teams handle that challenge today. You'll also learn to measure your system and assess its performance so you can get the most out of Elixir. In addition, we'll cover the tools you'll need to trace running systems, understand crash reports, and establish good alerting and logging practices, ensuring your team is ready and gets notified when problems do occur.

## CHAPTER 8

Coordinating Deployments

A common story we've heard from Elixir newcomers is that deployment was particularly challenging. If you're going to successfully adopt any new language, you need to be able to get that beautiful, powerful code onto production servers, but that's not enough. You need to do so reliably, without downtime, and with the ability to gracefully recover should things go wrong.

To illustrate this point, meet Tetiana Dushenkivska. She's a Ruby developer who adopted Elixir early on and was the keynote speaker at ElixirConf Europe 2017. She mastered Elixir concepts when we had one-tenth of the available learning resources that we do today:

Bruce: *How was your first encounter with Elixir?*

Tetiana: *I was happily working with Ruby, when a colleague shared his finding, Elixir. At first, I didn't get too excited. I was thinking: "Those languages and frameworks keep popping up and I don't have time right now to learn another language." Regardless of that thought, I still took a quick look. At first glance it looked much like Ruby, but soon enough I started to understand that maybe it looks like Ruby, but it doesn't behave like Ruby. The more I read about Elixir, however, the more I wanted to keep learning about it. The first thing to motivate me to start building something in Elixir was the ability to do things concurrently. Then I thought: "Oh, this language looks VERY interesting, I should definitely learn more about it."*

Bruce: *How did you move forward from there?*

Tetiana: *Programming Elixir by Dave Thomas was my introduction to Elixir, together with the official getting started guide on the website.*

The concept of functional languages resonated quickly with me. When I was studying electronic engineering at university I learned about signals and how they're transformed from one shape to another. Functional programming is somewhat similar. A signal is like data in functional programming which when put through some filters, or functions in Elixir, results in a new signal. You can't rebind a signal.

You just have an input signal and when it comes out of the black box it's a new signal. And every time we pass the same input to the black box, we get the same output.

Bruce: *Have you had hiccups or roadblocks along the way? How did you overcome them?*

Tetiana: *I would say deployment was hard. There are lots of ways to "build releases" and it took a bit of time to research and find a way that would work for me. Thankfully, the Elixir community is a great place to ask questions. Michał Muskała pointed me in the right direction, which helped me solve the deploying applications challenge.*

The Elixir community is doing a great job helping people who are stuck, to solve their problems. I am glad that people who have learned something are happy to share their knowledge, so that everyone else can learn faster.

Tetiana is not alone. For new languages, the deployment story almost always takes time to crystallize. We've heard story after story from happy early adopters of many emerging languages identifying deployment as a pain point. The same is true with Elixir.

Even so, we're starting to see some overarching strategies and contenders begin to surface in the deployment space. In this chapter, you'll learn about these emerging technologies. Elixir developers are moving beyond the Mix tool for deployment, and they're formally defining releases using tools such as Distillery. Then, rather than focusing on hot-code-swapping, they're using a technique called blue-green deployments. We'll walk you through how these tools and techniques work. That's what we'll focus on, but there are a few topics we won't cover.

In this chapter, we won't discuss any particular stack. We won't give you specific recipes for deploying to Heroku or using Docker containers, automating with Chef, or managing your cluster with Kubernetes. In fact, we've seen all of those options being successfully used to run Elixir systems. Instead of giving a way-too-thin blow by blow for each option out there or anointing a winner when the market has yet to decide, we're going to focus on the Elixir bits. After all, this book is called *Adopting Elixir*. Let's get to it.

Deploying with Mix

The emergence of deployment tools within git and Elixir's basic tooling makes it pretty simple to stand up a dead-simple deployment strategy for a single machine. The easiest way to run an Elixir application in production is by fetching or pushing the source code to your servers and calling:

```
$ MIX_ENV=prod mix run --no-halt
```

mix run will compile and start the current application and all of its dependencies. --no-halt guarantees Elixir won't terminate just after the application is booted. Phoenix is similar. Instead of mix run --no-halt, you will execute mix phx.server, still setting the Mix environment to "prod".

MIX_ENV=prod ensures your application is running in the production environment with the relevant configurations. One of those configurations is the :start_permanent option, which you will find in your mix.exs file:

```
start_permanent: Mix.env == :prod
```

Each application runs as :temporary or :permanent. If a permanent application shuts down, it automatically causes the whole VM to shut down too, so something else can restart it.

Here's the problem :permanent was designed to solve. Say you were to start a Phoenix application without setting :start_permanent. Suppose its top-level supervisor has to restart its children multiple times in a short period due to a fault. If the supervisor exceeds the amount of restarts allowed in a timeframe, it terminates, causing your application to also terminate. If your application has not been set to permanent, the remaining applications will continue running without your Phoenix app, so you can't accept any more requests. In development, that's likely fine, but in production, you want to shut the VM down so something else can restart it cleanly.

If you are using a Platform-as-a-Service (PaaS) offering such as Heroku for your deployment, it's likely using mix run or a similar task for starting your applications. The advantage of using Mix in production is that you can rely on the same tooling that you use for your development. All you need is the source code. It is an option that works well for very simple deployments.

As soon as you want to leverage some of the more advanced capabilities that the VM offers you, this approach starts to fall apart. That's what we will do now. We will add some nuts and bolts to our Mix deployment and show it quickly becomes unmanageable.

The –no-compile Flag

Our first modification will add support for a multi-server deployment. We'll compile once and push that code to each server.

Mix was designed primarily as a development tool. When you execute the mix run task, Mix checks to see whether your code requires compilation. Since you're deploying to multiple servers, you may want to compile your application only once and not per server. One option is to have a build machine that exists specifically to build the deployment artifact. When done, the build machine can push the artifact to your production servers or your production servers can fetch it directly from the build machine. Let's see how to construct this artifact with Mix.

On your build machine, you'd run:

```
$ MIX_ENV=prod mix compile
```

And in production:

```
$ MIX_ENV=prod mix run --no-halt
```

Mix works by tracking the modification times of source files and of the generated beam files. There's a problem with this approach. Moving your files changes your modification times, so the mix run task notices the changed times and recompiles, defeating the whole purpose of the build server!

There's a simple fix. You can pass the --no-compile flag when starting in production, like this:

```
$ MIX_ENV=prod mix run --no-halt --no-compile
```

It is one small change, but the first of many. There's more work to do.

The –no-deps-check Flag

There's another Mix downside. It requires the whole source code tree and its dependencies in production, so if you have git dependencies, Mix will require git on the production server. To solve this problem, you'd pass the --no-deps-check flag to disable dependency checking.

On your build machine, you would run:

```
$ MIX_ENV=prod mix compile
$ rm -rf deps/*/.git
```

And in production:

```
$ MIX_ENV=prod mix run --no-halt --no-compile --no-deps-check
```

The previous command still requires dependency source code but does allow removal of any version control metadata from our dependencies. That in turn reduces the size of your production artifacts. The problem is solved, but wait, there's more.

VM Configuration

On production, you'll often want to fine-tune both Elixir and the VM. You can handle some of this tuning in the config/config.exs file. For example, you can choose the proper Logger level by setting:

```
config :logger, :level, :warn
```

That change will show log entries at the :warn level of severity or stronger. That's not the only configuration you'll encounter because some configuration happens when the VM boots.

For example, many applications may want to tweak +K and +A flags for production. +K true enables kernel pooling, which provides an OS-specific I/O event notification system. +A increases the async thread pool, which is a group of threads started by the VM responsible for all of the I/O work done by your code. By default the async pool has 10 threads, but if you are doing a lot of I/O, you likely want to increase that count to about 8 threads per core. If you have 8 cores, 64 threads is a better starting point.

Unfortunately the mix run command can't receive VM configurations because you need to specify those commands when the VM starts. The solution is to invoke mix through elixir, like this:

```
$ MIX_ENV=prod elixir --erl "+K true +A 16" -S \
>   mix run --no-halt --no-compile --no-deps-check
```

By using the elixir command-line script, you've eliminated the problem. You can simply pass VM commands with the --erl flag, using the -S flag to instruct elixir to run the mix command available in your system. Those aren't the only flags to consider, though. If you want to run distributed Erlang, you'll need still more flags.

This kind of application startup complexity is common for running all but the simplest applications. You can try to juggle startup parameters in this way, but you'd be playing with fire because it's an error-prone approach.

In case you're not yet convinced, let's continue pushing the boundaries and see how far we can go.

run_erl and heart

Erlang is more than the standard library and virtual machine. As you might expect after thirty years of history, it ships with many tools for successfully running Erlang in production. Two of those tools are run_erl and heart.

Managing Shared I/O

run_erl[1] helps you manage the standard input and output of a program. The Unix tool redirects all output to log files. For those so inclined, there's a similar Windows tool named start_erl.[2]

run_erl expects a pipe name, the log directory, and the command to execute. *Remember the log directory must be created before you invoke run_erl, otherwise it will silently fail.* Let's give run_erl a try:

```
$ mkdir ./log
$ run_erl ./loop ./log "elixir -e 'Enum.map Stream.interval(1000), &IO.puts/1'"
```

This command runs an Elixir script that prints a number to standard output every second. Assuming you've created a log directory beforehand, you'll see a new file at log/erlang.log.1 with the convenient sequence of logs. run_erl automatically rotates logs every 100KB, keeping the last four files.

In production, run_erl is usually executed with the -daemon flag. Let's give it a try but this time with iex:

```
$ run_erl -daemon ./iex_sample ./log "iex"
```

Here we used run_erl to start iex as a daemon. Notice we have no access to iex though. That's where to_erl comes in.

The first run_erl argument is a named pipe. The pipe lets us interface with any running program via the to_erl tool, like this:

```
$ to_erl ./iex_sample
Attaching to ./iex_sample (^D to exit)

iex(1)> 1 + 2
3
```

to_erl allows us to interact with any system through standard I/O. If you want to shut down the VM, you can invoke System.stop(), which gracefully shuts the Erlang system down, stopping all applications with their respective supervision trees. You can directly invoke System.stop() in your IEx session or send it via to_erl:

```
$ echo "System.stop()" | to_erl ./iex_sample
```

If your application requires specific shutdown instructions, you can send them as well:

---

1. http://erlang.org/doc/man/run_erl.html
2. http://erlang.org/doc/man/start_erl.html

```
$ echo "MyApp.clean_shutdown()" | to_erl ./my_app
```

While run_erl provides logging and log rotation, to_erl can be an excellent tool for debugging live systems. Teams running Elixir in production should definitely account for those tools in their stack. Let's continue to build on our mix run commands, adding run_erl:

```
$ mkdir ./log
$ run_erl -daemon ./my_app ./log \
>    "MIX_ENV=prod iex --erl '+K true +A 16' -S \
>    mix run --no-halt --no-compile --no-deps-check"
```

We are now using iex instead of elixir to boot the app, allowing us to use to_erl and interact with our application at any moment. Note we are nesting single and double quotes. Pay attention. With each step, the blob continues to grow.

Monitoring Heartbeat

heart,[3] another program that ships with Erlang, provides application heartbeat monitoring, restarting it when needed. Start it with the -heart VM flag:

```
$ elixir --erl "-heart" -e "Enum.map Stream.interval(1000), &IO.puts/1" \
heart_beat_kill_pid = 48495
0
1
...
```

Notice the PID of the VM. Now, on another terminal session or using the operating system activity or task manager, kill that process using the next command or your system task manager:

```
$ kill -9 48495
```

Back on the Elixir session, you'll see this:

```
$ elixir --erl "-heart" -e "Enum.map Stream.interval(1000), &IO.puts/1" \
heart_beat_kill_pid = 48495
0
1
...
Killed: 9
heart: Wed May 17 00:38:21 2017: Erlang has closed.
heart: Wed May 17 00:38:21 2017: Would reboot. Terminating.
```

Notice how heart has detected the Erlang VM terminated. Rather than starting a new instance, it said "Would reboot."

---

3. http://erlang.org/doc/man/heart.html

To fix this problem, we need to set the HEART_COMMAND environment variable. In this case, since the initial command is also the command we want heart to execute, set it accordingly:

```
$ export HEART_COMMAND=\
>    "elixir --erl '-heart' -e 'Enum.map Stream.interval(1000), &IO.puts/1'"
```

Now, run the command by evaluating HEART_COMMAND:

```
$ eval $HEART_COMMAND
```

Now when you kill the reported pid, you'll see heart come to life and start a new instance. The new VM will either start counting from 0 again or it will crash:

```
heart: Wed May 17 01:00:22 2017: Erlang has closed.
heart: Wed May 17 01:00:22 2017: Executed "elixir ..." -> 256. Terminating.
heart_beat_kill_pid = 73275
** (ErlangError) Erlang error: :terminated
    (stdlib) :io.put_chars(:standard_io, :unicode, ["1", 10])
    (elixir) lib/enum.ex:1230: anonymous fn/3 in Enum.map/2
    (elixir) lib/enum.ex:1798: anonymous fn/3 in Enum.map/2
    (elixir) lib/stream.ex:1358: Stream.do_unfold/4
    (elixir) lib/enum.ex:1797: Enum.map/2
    (stdlib) erl_eval.erl:669: :erl_eval.do_apply/6
    (elixir) lib/code.ex:176: Code.eval_string/3
```

You might see such an error when the new instance started by heart does not have access to the standard input and output, since the original instance was directly connected to the shell. You can stop heart from restarting the system indefinitely by finding its pid in the operating system and sending it an exit signal.

To permanently solve the issue, ideally you'd have your application write your standard output to disk instead of to the terminal. Since that's exactly what run_erl does, let's tie it all together and use heart to manage your app:

```
$ mkdir ./log
$ export HEART_COMMAND="run_erl -daemon ./my_app ./log \
>    \"MIX_ENV=prod iex --erl '-heart +K true +A 16' -S \
>    mix run --no-halt --no-compile --no-deps-check\""
$ eval $HEART_COMMAND
```

At this point, we were able to add log rotation, a pluggable REPL, and multiple VM configurations to our Mix deployment but our start script has become unmanageable. Let's count the issues:

- Properly handling the escaping of commands with double and single quotes is fragile.

- You would like to be able to take advantage of existing scripts and snippets like this written by others.

- Our Mix deployment still has other intrinsic limitations, such as the need to ship the source code to production and, as we will see next, the inability to control how code is loaded and how applications are started.

Let's stop the madness. For any slightly non-trivial deployment in Elixir, developers should be using releases, which give fine-grained control over the VM boot and encapsulates the usage of tools such as heart and run_erl.

Releases

A release is a self-contained deployment artifact that includes all of your dependencies, including Erlang and Elixir itself. Releases give fine-grained control over how the virtual machine is started. They also provide reliable configuration mechanisms for production systems. When you use this technique, you'll notice several important benefits:

Code preloading

The VM has two mechanisms for loading code: interactive and embedded. By default, it runs in the interactive mode which dynamically loads modules when they are used for the first time. The first time your application calls List.first/1, the VM will find the List module and load it. There's a downside. When you start a new server in production, it may need to load many other modules, causing the first requests to have an unusual spike in response time. Releases run in embedded mode, which loads all available modules upfront, guaranteeing your system is ready to handle requests after booting.

Application configuration

When talking about Mix deployment, we discussed the :start_permanent flag and how it sets all applications to :permanent mode, but sometimes you may not want that setting. Maybe you don't want to restart a given component should it fail. Mix does not provide fine-grained control over your dependencies but releases do. You can control how to start each application or even set up distributed ones.[4]

Multiple releases

Sometimes you must configure the same source code to run in production with different settings than you would use in development. For example,

---

4. http://erlang.org/doc/design_principles/distributed_applications.html

imagine you have both small and large server instances and you've measured optimal configurations for both. You can easily build different releases from the same source code, using different configuration and targeting different capabilities.

Self-contained

A release does not require the source code to be included in your production artifacts. In fact, it does not even require Erlang or Elixir in your servers, as it is capable of including the whole Erlang runtime itself.

Management scripts

Most release tools include a series of scripts that make it straightforward to manage your releases. Those scripts take care of setting up the proper run_erl and heart programs, just as we discussed in the previous section.

A release is a .tar.gz file that must be unpacked on your production servers and then directly executed. Your continuous integration pipeline can build a release, or you may use dedicated build servers. Then your production servers will either download releases from a safe location or have an orchestration tool directly push the release to your machines. We won't discuss the details on how to deliver the .tar.gz package. Instead, we'll focus on how to build it.

Using Distillery

We're going to use a release tool called Distillery.[5] From the readme file:

"Distillery takes your Mix project and produces an Erlang/OTP release, a distilled form of your raw application's components; a single package which can be deployed anywhere, independently of an Erlang/Elixir installation. No dependencies, no hassle."

Let's walk through building a release for a new project using Distillery. First start with mix to set up a new project:

```
$ mix new sample
```

Now open up mix.exs and add :distillery under your dependencies. At the time of writing, v1.5.2 is the latest version, so let's require at least 1.5:

```
def deps do
  [
    {:distillery, "~> 1.5"}
  ]
end
```

---

5. https://github.com/bitwalker/distillery

Now let's fetch dependencies and get started with our release process:

```
$ mix deps.get
$ mix release.init
```

Open up the generated rel/config.exs and look at its contents.

Similar to Mix, releases have different environments. For :dev, Distillery sets dev_mode to true, which supports code reloading for Phoenix and Nerves applications, and sets include_erts to false. ERTS stands for the Erlang Runtime System, which includes the virtual machine and low-level features, such as NIF support. For :prod, we always include the runtime system but skip the source code. For both environments, rel/config.exs also generates a cookie value. Elixir uses the cookie value to authenticate nodes when building distributed Erlang/Elixir clusters.

While Distillery supports cross-compilation by tweaking the :include_erts option, it becomes a very complex topic if your application or any of your dependencies include Erlang NIFs. As you'll recall from *Strategy 1: Native Implemented Functions (NIFs)*, on page 125, NIFs stands for native implemented functions, and they require specific native tools. In such cases, you should build releases in an environment that matches your production target.

Unlike Mix, Distillery supports multiple releases. By default, the rel/config.exs lists a single release, with the same name as the current application:

```
release :sample do
  set version: current_version(:sample)
  set applications: [
    :runtime_tools
  ]
end
```

This release uses the version declared in your mix.exs and lists the :runtime_tools your application needs as extra applications, in addition to the ones already declared in your mix.exs. :runtime_tools contains conveniences to debug and observe production systems. We will explore it in Chapter 10, *Making Your App Production Ready*, on page 193.

You can declare as many releases as you want and give different configurations to each of them. You can also list applications with different requirements. Suppose your project depends on an application called :not_really_important_app. It's not a very important app. If it crashes, you want the VM to continue running. You can specify so in the applications configuration:

```
release :sample do
  set version: current_version(:sample)
  set applications: [
    runtime_tools: :permanent,
    not_really_important_app: :temporary
  ]
end
```

Check out the Distillery documentation[6] for more configuration information.

Once you've specified your releases, you can finally build them by running mix release. Let's do that for production:

```
$ MIX_ENV=prod mix release
==> Assembling release..
==> Building release sample:0.1.0 using environment prod
==> Including ERTS 9.2 from /usr/local/Cellar/erlang/18.1/lib/erlang/erts-9.2
==> Packaging release..
==> Release successfully built!
    You can run it in one of the following ways:
      Interactive: _build/prod/rel/sample/bin/sample console
      Foreground: _build/prod/rel/sample/bin/sample foreground
      Daemon: _build/prod/rel/sample/bin/sample start
```

The whole release is in the _build/prod/rel/sample directory. From there you can either start it by executing a command such as bin/sample start or fetch the .tar.gz file from _build/prod/rel/sample/releases/0.1.0.

Let's do some peeking under the hood to see what we can learn. Under the _build/prod/rel/sample you will find four directories. bin contains scripts for running your release. In practice, those scripts end up executing the scripts for the latest release you'll find in the releases directory. The erts directory contains the Erlang Runtime System while lib contains all applications that are part of the release, all of them properly versioned. If you update your dependencies and build a new release, both old and new versions of your dependencies will be listed there. Finally, the releases directory contains metadata about your releases and everything required to start your system.

Inside _build/prod/rel/sample/releases/0.1.0, we will find many interesting files. sample.rel is the one that effectively describes the release:

```
{release,{"sample","0.1.0"},
        {erts,"9.2"},
        [{kernel,"5.4.1"},
         {stdlib,"3.4.3"},
         {distillery,"1.5.2"},
         {logger,"1.6.0"},
```

---

6.   https://hexdocs.pm/distillery/configuration.html

```
        {compiler,"7.1.4"},
        {elixir,"1.6.0"},
        {sample,"0.1.0"},
        {iex,"1.6.0"},
        {sasl,"3.1.1"},
        {runtime_tools,"1.12.3"}]}.
```

It declares a release, with its name, version, the ERTS version, and all applications that are part of the release. Many of the versions shown here might differ based on the versions of Elixir and Erlang you are using. From the sample.rel file, we build the sample.script file, containing every single instruction the runtime will perform when it boots. Open it up and skim it. Between instructions, you will see the script preloads all modules and applications. From sample.script, a binary sample.boot file is written.

Another important file in your releases is the _build/prod/rel/sample/releases/0.1.0/vm.args file, which includes the arguments that are given to the VM when starting the release:

```
## Name of the node
-name sample@127.0.0.1

## Heartbeat management; auto-restarts VM if it dies or becomes unresponsive
##-heart

## Enable kernel poll and a few async threads
##+K true
##+A 5

## Increase number of concurrent ports/sockets
##-env ERL_MAX_PORTS 4096

## Tweak GC to run more often
##-env ERL_FULLSWEEP_AFTER 10
```

When we first deployed with mix, we used the following command:

```
$ MIX_ENV=prod elixir --erl "+K true +A 16" -S \
>    mix run --no-halt --no-compile --no-deps-check
```

Now you can move the --erl option configuration to the vm.args file, with relevant notes and code comments. You'll likely want to copy the vm.args file to rel/vm.args in the root of your project and specify the release to use a custom vm.args instead:

```
release :sample do
  set version: current_version(:sample)
  set vm_args: "rel/vm.args"
  set applications: [
    :runtime_tools
  ]
end
```

You can see some lovely simplification taking shape here. Now, if you want to enable -heart, simply list it in vm.args, as Distillery scripts take care of setting the HEART_COMMAND environment variable. Similarly, Distillery sets up run_erl and to_erl by default.

Overall, releases provide a more structured mechanism to deploy and configure production systems. After a release is built, keep in mind mix is no longer available. For example, your Ecto and Phoenix applications will need different mechanisms for running migrations and starting servers. Luckily, Distillery's documentation[7] covers those features and more.

Application Configuration

Before we discuss upgrading production systems, we should cover application configuration. Most Elixir developers use config/config.exs to configure their applications and dependencies, but you should remember that Mix loads config/config.exs when building the release. That means environment variables or configuration files you read in config.exs will be available while you build your release, but not in production.

To work around this limitation, many projects like Ecto and Phoenix started to support a special value called {:system, "env"} to allow some dynamic configuration. The problem with this solution is that it works only for certain keys and only for certain applications. Fortunately, Ecto v2.1 and Phoenix v1.3 are moving to a more standardized approach. They'll both move runtime configuration to inside the init callback. Take the following example.

In earlier Ecto versions, if you wanted to dynamically configure the database URL Ecto connects to, you'd do so in your config/config.exs, like this:

```
config :my_app, MyApp.Repo,
  url: {:system, "DATABASE_URL"}
```

While this code effectively moves the configuration to runtime, it is a workaround that works only for the :url option. If you attempt to use the {:system, "env"} format anywhere else, it will likely fail. Furthermore, if you need to dynamically read the database URL from somewhere else rather than the system environment, you're out of luck.

Ecto v2.1 pushes runtime configuration to runtime. Most processes and services should be configured during an init callback. Under Ecto 2.1, the previous code should be moved to the repository:

---

7. https://hexdocs.pm/distillery/

```elixir
defmodule MyApp.Repo do
  use Ecto.Repo, otp_app: :my_app

  def init(_, config) do
    {:ok, Keyword.put(config, :url, System.get_env("DATABASE_URL"))}
  end
end
```

Now if you need to read the database URL from an environment variable, file system, or even an internal service, you just need to change the code accordingly.

At the time of this writing, we believe the Elixir community relies too much on the application environment. Don't get us wrong. This environment is excellent for end-user applications, such as your Phoenix and Nerves projects, but it is a flawed approach for most libraries and frameworks because it is global. For example, imagine using a JSON encoding and decoding library in a project. Many of the dependencies in your project may depend on that same library. If you tried to configure this JSON dependency through the application environment, it would become impossible for each dependency to use that library in a different way, with different configuration requirements.

Instead, most configuration should happen at runtime, by passing options when invoking functions or when starting processes. For example, if you are decoding some JSON payload:

```elixir
JSONDecoding.decode(some_data, option: "foo", another_option: "bar")
```

If instead you are starting a process that connects to the database:

```elixir
SomeDatabase.start_link(username: "...", password: "...")
```

Doing so lets your users configure your application as they wish, be it using a direct value, relying on config/config.exs, reading from System.get_env/1 or from the file system.

Upgrading Code

Now that you've deployed your code to production, eventually you'll need to update your production systems, whether you're using Mix or releases. You may even have heard the Erlang VM is capable of performing *hot code upgrades*. This feature provides the ability to upgrade code live in production without bringing the system down. To do so, you need to build your releases first.

In practice, hot code upgrades are tricky, as they require developers to carefully maintain code and upgrade the state of all changed processes in all running applications. For example, imagine on v1.0 you have a process with a map with keys :first_name and :last_name as state. In v1.1, you decided to merge those keys under a new one called :name. You need to remember to implement the code_change callback and appropriately upgrade the server state. And since the VM cannot upgrade all processes at once, as that would imply the system needs to stop running for a while, you need to carefully identify each group of processes you need to upgrade together, or make sure processes can handle messages from both v1.0 and v1.1, as there will be a period where both versions run at the same time.

As you'll see, the versioning problem is not specific to your Elixir code. As soon as you deploy to more than one server, there will always be a moment when you are upgrading your production systems where the old and new version will coexist. Many teams are familiar with those trade-offs when talking about data and storage. Hot code upgrades have the unfortunate side effect of introducing this problem to your in-memory data too.

For those reasons, we rarely see hot code upgrades used in production. It is easy to understand the benefits of hot code upgrades for old telecommunication systems, where someone is always on the phone, often for very long time periods, and dropping calls is not acceptable. However, most systems running on the web were designed to cope with reconnections. Once you deploy a new version, your server can gracefully move clients to the new one, especially in web applications. In such cases, you can use the load balancer or a reverse proxy to route traffic from old nodes to new nodes transparently.

In this book, we won't cover hot code upgrades and rather focus on blue-green deployments. Hot code upgrades require heavy time investment during development and testing that bring little to no benefit when compared to other solutions. If you are in the rare position where hot code upgrades are a necessity, then we recommend reading more on the Distillery documentation as well as the .relup[8] and .appup[9] manuals.

This, however, does not mean hot code upgrades are useless. Both Phoenix and Nerves frameworks use the module versioning features that power hot code upgrades to perform code reloading in development. Other companies use those features alongside the Erlang distribution to build their own upgrade mechanisms.[10] For most of us, though, blue-green deployments bring all of the benefits we need.

---

8.   http://erlang.org/doc/man/relup.html
9.   http://erlang.org/doc/man/appup.html
10.   http://confreaks.tv/videos/elixirconf2014-otp-in-production-the-nitty-gritty-details-of-game-servers

Blue-Green Deployments

Two decades ago, getting a new server meant literally acquiring or renting new hardware. As a result we would often deploy new versions of our systems to the same machine, mutating our infrastructure as we updated our system.

Today, getting new production machines is only a few clicks away. As the internet grew, automating deployment became a necessity. Downtime or maintenance breaks are no longer acceptable. A spike in requests per second means you need to make new servers available immediately. The virtualization and containerization of software means that setting up new servers can be efficient and automatized. Nowadays autoscaling has become a common offering between cloud services, allowing cloud infrastructures to automatically spawn new servers as deemed necessary.

In the last five years, terms like "immutable server" and "immutable infrastructure" also started to become commonplace. Once a system is created, it is never modified. If there is a new version, you build new containers or new servers. This goes hand in hand with automation, as the operation team is no longer allowed to connect to the server for last-minute tweaks.

You will notice some of those ideas go directly against hot code upgrades. That's fine. Remember, most of us won't benefit from hot code upgrades anyway. But it begs the question: if you can't upgrade your servers live, how do you swap from the old version to the new version with no downtime when upgrading systems?

The idea behind blue-green deployment is that you have two production environments running simultaneously when deploying new versions.[11] Imagine that your system is currently live. You have a load balancer and a group of machines running your application. Let's call this the blue machines group. To deploy a new version, the software is tested and verified on a new group of machines, that's the green one. After the green group is ready, the load balancer starts to send all incoming requests to the green nodes.

For a while, both green and blue nodes will process requests, especially with long-running requests such as file uploads, downloads, and websocket connections. Over time, blue node requests complete and close, so the nodes can come down gracefully.

Blue-green deployments also provide the benefit of fast rollbacks. If errors start to show up as soon as you flip the switch to green, you can rollback to

---

11. https://martinfowler.com/bliki/BlueGreenDeployment.html

blue and carefully debug what went wrong. Another benefit is that your deployment recipes can give your old machines plenty of time to correctly shut down as another group of machines handles new requests. As we will see, this plays well with supervision trees and the runtime ability to perform graceful shutdowns even in the face of asynchronous work.

Since two versions of your application may be running at the same time, this style of deployment requires special care when it comes to communication and data. For example, when writing distributed Elixir applications, blue and green nodes may exchange data. That may be desired but it may also lead to errors. Luckily, this can be solved by generating a new authentication cookie on every deployment, keeping each deployment group fairly isolated.

Unfortunately, matters are slightly more complex when a database is involved. Given both blue and green nodes may be running at the same time, any destructive operation in the database must be carefully planned and rolled out through multiple deployments.

Let's iron out some of those details before moving forward.

Graceful Shutdown

In blue-green deployments, whenever a new version comes up, the load balancer will stop routing traffic to the old version. Only after a couple of minutes or so have passed is it safe to shut those VMs down. While this should be enough time to process all incoming work, sometimes that won't be the case. Let's consider a few examples.

Imagine that some of the incoming requests start new tasks that are responsible for sending emails asynchronously. You want to guarantee that the VM will not shut down before it finishes its tasks.

Supervision trees provide that guarantee. When you invoke System.stop(), the Erlang runtime will stop all running applications in the opposite order they were started within their respective supervision trees, respecting the configured shutdown values for each child. At the beginning of this chapter, we showed you how to pipe System.stop() into the runtime with to_erl. If you are using releases, that's also what bin/sample stop does.

When you build a GenServer, Agent, or other supervised process, you can specify how long the supervisor should wait before shutting down a child:

```elixir
defmodule MyApp.EmailSender do
  use GenServer, shutdown: 5000

  ...
```

You can also override the shutdown value per children when starting the supervisor:

```
children = [
  Supervisor.child_spec(MyApp.EmailSender, shutdown: 5_000)
]

Supervisor.start_link children, strategy: :one_for_one
```

When shutting down the system, the supervisor will send an initial :shutdown exit signal to all children and then wait 5 seconds (the default) for the EmailSender process. Once a child process receives an exit signal, the process terminates immediately unless it is trapping exits. This means the email sender processes must be trapping exits if we do not want them to terminate on :shutdown, as explained in *Use GenServer as a Coordinator*, on page 94. After the initial :shutdown signal, the supervisor will kill any remaining child processes that don't finish in the specified interval (5 seconds, in our example).

The shutdown logic is often important—it guarantees that your application has processed all tasks. You should carefully test all such shutdown logic in your application's test suite.

Other times, your graceful shutdown strategy requires you to explicitly disable some parts of your application. A load balancer can ensure it will no longer send requests to your node but there are other components depending on your application services.

For example, imagine that your application also includes a job-processing component that retrieves messages from RabbitMQ or a database to process them. A new version of the system may generate new kinds of events that the old version does not know how to process. In those cases, it is best to stop pulling messages from RabbitMQ as soon as the new group of nodes is up. If you are using Distillery, you can accomplish this task with custom commands.[12] In this case, a custom command may simply call the appropriate process and instruct it to no longer pull messages in. Keep in mind that in case of rollbacks you will need to do the exact opposite and reenable the job-processing component once again.

Graceful shutdown deals with compatibility of requests and messages. Sometimes, your application will need to deal with other kinds of compatibility, namely, persistent data.

---

12. https://hexdocs.pm/distillery/custom-commands.html

Data Migration

Another concern during blue-green deployments is the role of databases and data compatibility. Imagine you want to rename a table column in the database; for external reasons username has suddenly become name. Your first approach may be to rename all occurrences of username to name in the codebase and then write a SQL script, or a database migration if using Ecto, that renames the username column to name. Upon deployment, either the blue or green system will break. Let's see why.

When deploying, you first want to migrate the database before switching from blue to green. That's because green may use new features that require new tables or columns in the database. However, if you rename a column, blue will attempt to query the database using the old username column, which no longer exists, *even before green goes live*. Once green goes live, everything will work as expected, but not before getting multiple error reports from requests being processed by blue.

That's why *destructive changes to the database must always be carefully planned*. Let's break that harmful migration down into several gentler migrations.

In this case, instead of renaming username to name, you'll first want to add a new name column and prepare the code to read from the name or username columns. You can then deploy this version without any further changes to the database. All writes should still target username.

Once the version that reads from both username and name is up and running successfully, you can change the code to write to the name column and prepare a script that copies data from the old username column to name if name is blank. After you safely convert all of the data, you can deploy a new version that effectively removes username access from the codebase and the username column from the database.

You can see why hot code upgrades are so complicated. Imagine the burden of managing these kinds of details at both the database level *and also for every process in your application*.

You've seen how graceful shutdown and data migration apply to blue-green deployments. It is worth mentioning those issues are not specific to blue-green deployments at all. Destructive changes to the database are dangerous to any deployment pipeline that supports rollbacks. Graceful shutdowns are necessary regardless of your deployment strategy.

Blue-green deployments simply bring those issues to light precisely because they allow us to update systems without downtime while making rollbacks straightforward. If you are building some kind of Platform-as-a-Service application, odds are that you are already using blue-green deployments. With Elixir, you can rely on supervision trees to give you insights on how your application initializes and shuts down, equipping your team with tools and practices that help you tackle such problems.

So far, we've shown you how to build a simple deployment strategy with Mix; we tacked on to that solution until it broke, and we remedied that problem with Distillery releases. Before we close out this chapter, we should talk a bit about distributed Erlang, from an operations perspective.

Distributed Erlang

In Chapter 6, *Distributed Elixir*, on page 103, we discussed distribution from a development and architectural perspective. This time, we will explore it under the operations view, directly tied to the Erlang runtime.

Let's start with a quick summary.

Distributed Erlang works by establishing TCP connections between nodes. Nodes can only successfully establish connections if they share the same cookie. When distributed Erlang starts, it can automatically create a cookie, but we strongly advise teams to generate their own cookies. Once connected, nodes form a fully meshed network, where each node can communicate with all others. By default, the runtime does not encrypt the connection but can be configured to do so.

Nodes keep an open connection between them while both are up and running. Both nodes send a configurable heartbeat (also called ticktime) over the connection. If either node fails to receive a heartbeat in a time interval, the connection is dropped and the nodes disconnected. Since nodes send heartbeats over the same connection as data, you should refrain from sending large amounts of data between them at once, as that would delay the heartbeat message.

Each node has a name and host address. Both :"my_app@node1" and :"my_app @192.168.1.1" are valid node names. The former requires host names to be properly configured in your clusters.

To aid the connection between nodes, Erlang ships with a tool called EPMD, Erlang Port Mapper Daemon.[13] Once a node goes up, it registers its name and

---

13. http://erlang.org/doc/man/epmd.html

port to the EPMD running locally. When a node wants to connect to instance :"my_app@192.168.1.1", it first reaches the EPMD instance running on 192.168.1.1 to fetch all available names and ports. If my_app is one of the available names, it then attempts to connect to the Erlang runtime on the registered port.

Communication with EPMD does not use the cookie for authorization and is not encrypted. This means if the port EPMD runs on is publicly available, an external entity will be able to query EPMD for the list of names and ports. Fortunately, the external entity will only be able to connect to a node if they know the cookie.

The use of EPMD means that distributed Erlang needs two ports for every machine. EPMD by default runs on port 4369. The other port, which is used for connecting Erlang nodes, is randomly assigned. Luckily the range of assigned ports can be configured when starting Elixir under the --erl flag:

```
$ elixir --erl "-kernel inet_dist_listen_min 9100 \
> -kernel inet_dist_listen_max 9200"
```

If you need to use a fixed port, you can set both configurations to the same value. An advantage of using a fixed port is that you no longer need to run EPMD, as the whole goal of EPMD is mapping names to ports, reducing the number of required ports to 1. You can combine this approach with orchestration tools to provide straightforward management of Erlang clusters.

Let's look at how to do so. First, we'll provide general security guidelines. Then, we'll show a distributed Erlang example without EPMD and we'll discuss dynamically setting up clusters.

Security Guidelines

Elixir provides the framework for building safe, secure, and reliable applications, but you'll still need to do your part. Here are the general guidelines for running distributed Erlang:

- Never expose the Erlang distribution ports and EPMD to the public network.

- Never rely on automatic cookies. Generate your own and make sure it is sufficiently large. Distillery automatically takes care of this step.

- If you are running distributed Erlang over a known port, consider disabling epmd (as you'll see next). Given traffic to and from EPMD cannot be encrypted, disabling it may also appease operation teams that do not allow unencrypted services to run, even when the service is not publicly exposed.

- Remember the connection between nodes is not encrypted. If someone can eavesdrop the communication in your cluster or if encryption is required, use TLS.[14] More complete resources are also available.[15]

With that out of the way, let's configure Erlang clusters without EPMD.

Removing EPMD

If your nodes run on a known port, there is no need to run epmd alongside the Erlang VM. We have seen this being handy on two different situations.

In the first situation, all communication had to be encrypted, no questions asked. In the second case, the operations team had to explicitly authorize each port. Sometimes those rules are in place by corporate mandate. You could try to break the rules, but new technology adopters must choose battles wisely. Other times, the rules are there because of external needs, such as in financial institutions or health organizations dealing with patient data.

There are multiple ways to ensure Erlang nodes run on a known port. One option is to choose a fixed port and apply it to all nodes. For this example, we'll choose a slightly more complex mechanism. We'll encode the port in the node name. For example, a node named "example" should now be named "example-9100", where 9100 is the port it is running on. Once you've chosen this mechanism, you can implement a custom EPMD client module that won't invoke EPMD at all. Instead, you can parse the port out of the node name.

Let's start with the EPMD client module. It needs to implement a group of functions, like this:

```
coordinating_deployments/name_and_port.ex
defmodule NameAndPort do
  # The current distribution protocol version.
  @protocol_version 5
```

Our new EPMD client does not have an underlying process, so we return :ignore:

```
coordinating_deployments/name_and_port.ex
def start_link do
  :ignore
end
```

Without EPMD, there is nowhere to register the name and port. We return a "creation" number between 1 and 3 as required by Erlang:

---

14. http://erlang.org/doc/apps/ssl/ssl_distribution.html
15. https://www.erlang-solutions.com/blog/erlang-distribution-over-tls.html

coordinating_deployments/name_and_port.ex
```elixir
def register_node(_name, _port, _version) do
  {:ok, :rand.uniform(3)}
end
```

This implementation will retrieve the port from the node name, and there is no need to contact EPMD:

coordinating_deployments/name_and_port.ex
```elixir
def port_please(name, _ip) do
  shortname = name |> to_string() |> String.split("@") |> hd()

  with [_prefix, port_string] <- String.split(shortname, "-"),
       {port, ""} <- Integer.parse(port_string) do
    {:port, port, @protocol_version}
  else
    _ -> :noport
  end
end
```

There are also no names to fetch without EPMD:

coordinating_deployments/name_and_port.ex
```elixir
  def names(_hostnames) do
    {:error, :no_epmd}
  end
end
```

Write this code to a file and then compile it:

```
$ elixirc name_and_port.ex
```

This command will generate a .beam file at the current directory.

With the new EPMD client in hand, we can start iex using a custom name, port, and our custom client. Note you will need at least Erlang 19.1, as the ability to configure the EPMD client was added in that version:

```
$ iex --sname "example-9100" --erl "-start_epmd false \
> -epmd_module Elixir.NameAndPort  -kernel inet_dist_listen_min 9100 \
> -kernel inet_dist_listen_max 9100"
Interactive Elixir (1.5.0) - press Ctrl+C to exit (type h() ENTER for help)
iex(example-9101@macbook)1>
```

On another terminal, do the same, except we need to use a different name and a matching port:

```
$ iex --sname "example-9101" --erl "-start_epmd false \
> -epmd_module Elixir.NameAndPort  -kernel inet_dist_listen_min 9101 \
> -kernel inet_dist_listen_max 9101"
Interactive Elixir (1.5.0) - press Ctrl+C to exit (type h() ENTER for help)
iex(example-9101@macbook)1>
```

In the last session, we can connect to the first one by running Node.connect(:"example-9100@macbook") and everything should work as expected. Remember your node name won't be precisely :"example-9100@macbook", so change the Node.connect call accordingly.

Although in this example we have defined a file and compiled it by hand, if you are using releases, Mix will take care of compiling the file for you. All you need to do is to move the relevant flags given to --erl to the vm.args file.

Getting rid of EPMD is a fairly straightforward process. If you have fixed ports across all nodes, it can be even simpler. You just need to change the port_please/2 implementation to always return {:port, 9876, @protocol_version}, where 9876 should be replaced by your port of choice. In such cases, the node names are no longer relevant and you can use any name of your choice as long as each one is unique.

Setting Up Clusters

In the previous section, we have explicitly called Node.connect/1 to connect two nodes. Setting up a cluster is simply a matter of calling Node.connect/1 whenever a new node joins the cluster. In the rare cases the list of nodes is static, all you need to do on boot is:

```
Enum.map(list_of_known_nodes, &Node.connect/1)
```

In practice, new nodes may join the cluster at any moment and you need a mechanism to propagate this information throughout the cluster. If you are using a cloud platform like AWS or an orchestration tool such as Kubernetes, it is very likely they expose an API where you can retrieve the IP of all nodes. To dynamically set up a cluster, all you need is to periodically request a list of all nodes to such tools, and then call Node.connect/1 whenever there is a new entry. Those tools and platforms are not required for setting up clusters, but when already in place, they play well with the Erlang runtime by removing the hurdles of cluster membership.

While this mechanism is relatively straightforward to set up, there are existing packages in the community, such as peerage[16] and libcluster,[17] that provide integration with external services as well as their own discovery alternatives via multicast. If you'd rather roll your own, we recommend exploring the source code of those tools for guidance.

---

16. https://github.com/mrluc/peerage
17. https://github.com/bitwalker/libcluster

The solutions described in this and the last section are orthogonal. For instance, you may use Kubernetes, an alternative deployment system, without EPMD by relying on the fixed port technique outlined in the previous section.

Wrapping Up

In this chapter, we addressed deployment, the first step toward moving our development application into production. It was a long process with several steps.

First, we looked at an overly simplified approach to deployment with nothing but a few Mix tasks. We pushed that solution further to include a build server, and worked in some configuration. Then, we added run_erl to direct standard out to a file with rotating logs. Finally, we looked at heart, which provides heartbeat support. We soon learned that Mix couldn't take us as far as we wanted to go.

Next, we formalized the production deployment process a bit. We introduced the concept of a release, a set of artifacts that run on a production server. We implemented a Distillery deployment and used it to build a release, and then discussed how that improved structure allows a simplified layering of typical deployment scripts you'll find in this Elixir ecosystem. We then discussed the different strategies for configuration, and why major Elixir frameworks such as Ecto and Phoenix use init callbacks in the most recent versions.

Finally, we reviewed distributed Erlang, this time from an operations perspective. We introduced key security guidelines and the options for running with and without EPMD, the Erlang port mapper.

In the next chapter, we're going to stay on the production side, and shift to application performance. You're almost done. Turn the page!

Metrics and Performance Expectations

We're coming to the end of the road in our adoption journey, but there's still some work to do. After you have decided how to deploy your application, it's time to shift your focus to keeping things running quickly and uniformly. That task will take you into gathering metrics for performance analysis. Before we dive into tools, let's talk a bit about why we need to do so.

Maybe you chose Elixir precisely because you were facing performance issues or battling scalability challenges. There are many reasons those things are important.

First, consider the impact of uniformly strong performance on your customers. If you are building a web application, performance directly impacts the user experience and that relates to revenue.

Large players such as Google and Amazon report that latencies as low as 100ms are enough to impact the user engagement. A/B tests and studies organized by multiple companies show that load times have a direct impact on conversion rates. On the other hand, we know that the time spent on the server is only part of the journey in delivering web content to your users. We should also expect that Elixir developers building embedded systems have a whole different set of performance expectations.

Second, your development productivity also contributes directly to your bottom line. The performance of your system also has a direct impact on the developer experience. The fact that Elixir can compile your code in parallel and Hex can download packages concurrently improves each programmer's experience immensely. Imagine for a second how your productivity would be affected if the Elixir compiler and your test suite was two or four times slower than it is today. *Feedback cycles matter.*

In this chapter, we're going to examine how to assess your application's performance. To do so, you need tools that help you collect and visualize the right low-level details so you can piece together what's happening. That task has three parts: code instrumentation, data collection, and data visualization. Many commercial solutions roll up the collection and visualization system into a package called a *metrics system*.

When the Elixir community was young, those metrics systems were hard to find, but as we grew, we accumulated more options for instrumenting and monitoring. For example, Bleacher Report uses exometer[1] to collect the data and uses stats to push the data to DataDog.[2] The Football Addicts engineers prefer Telegraf and InfluxDB.[3] Still others use Prometheus and Grafana[4] or a SaaS solution, such as AppSignal,[5] PryIn,[6] WombatOAM,[7] or Scout.[8]

The truth is that there are many different tools, each with their own strengths and weaknesses. You could write a book on any one of these solutions so we can't cover them all but we can focus on code instrumentation. We will tell you how to provide the metrics that your system can use. Along the way, we'll discuss the different kinds of metrics you can get out of your production system and the various APIs you can use to gather that data.

That process is in some ways passive, providing insight when things go wrong. That's often not enough. We will also take you through proactive stress testing so you can see how your application performs under load so you can find potential bottlenecks before your customers do.

To eliminate those potential bottlenecks, you'll need specific data on functions, both counts and times. Together we'll examine a test case, using profilers to identify a problem. That's a full agenda so let's get started.

Instrumenting Your System

Many different applications can show you what's going on provided you feed it the right data. Although we can't recommend which tool you should use, we can try to give you an overview of the data you can gather. In short, instead

---

1. https://github.com/Feuerlabs/exometer
2. https://www.datadoghq.com/blog/statsd/
3. http://tech.footballaddicts.com/blog/gathering-metrics-in-elixir-applications
4. https://aldusleaf.org/monitoring-elixir-apps-in-2016-prometheus-and-grafana/
5. https://appsignal.com/elixir
6. https://pryin.io
7. https://www.erlang-solutions.com/products/wombatoam.html
8. https://scoutapp.com/elixir

of discovering *how to view* the different performance views of your system, we'd like to focus on *what to measure*. We'll show you what useful data you can coax out of the VM and how to use it to inform your decisions. Let's get started.

Using Observer as a Guide

Because Elixir chose early on to build onto the Erlang ecosystem you can take advantage of many tools. One of those is Observer, a tool for understanding how your application is using resources like processes and memory. While you won't use Observer to gather metrics in production, it's a great tool to explore what the VM offers you. If the information is available to Observer, it is available to you.

In this section, we will create a new Phoenix application and we'll use it through the rest of the chapter. We will start by observing this application and translating ideas we find into code.

We chose a Phoenix application because it comes with enough code for us to jump straight into measuring. In any case, the lessons here apply to any Elixir application.

If you are not yet familiar with Phoenix, see their website to get started.[9] Once you have the Phoenix installer available on your machine, create a new application like this:

```
$ mix phx.new demo
```

You'll then need to follow the instructions printed out to get your app up and running with iex -S mix. When the iex prompt becomes available, type :observer.start(). That command will start Observer in all of its glory as shown in the figure on page 174.

When Observer opens, you'll see several tabs. The system tab is open by default. For the two panels on your left, most of the information comes from a function called :erlang.system_info/1.[10] They're fairly static, and just a small subset of all the information system_info/1 returns.

Measuring Memory Usage

The first pane on the right shows memory usage. That's definitely the kind of information you want to push to your metrics system. You can retrieve all

---

9.   http://www.phoenixframework.org/
10.   http://erlang.org/doc/man/erlang.html#system_info-1

of this information programmatically by calling :erlang.memory/0.[11] Try it in your terminal, like this:

```
iex> :erlang.memory()
[
  total: 17479216,
  processes: 4837512,
  processes_used: 4831320,
  system: 12641704,
  atom: 264529,
  atom_used: 248278,
  binary: 64888,
  code: 5903532,
  ets: 350960
]
```

Total is the total amount of memory dynamically allocated, not including the VM itself or the system libraries the VM has started. It is the sum of the memory currently allocated by processes and the system. The process key shows the amount of memory allocated for processes and process used shows how much of that memory is in use.

The system memory is broken into the memory allocated for atoms, the binaries that are not in the process heap, the code loaded by the VM, and finally the memory allocated for ets tables.

---

11. http://erlang.org/doc/man/erlang.html#memory-0

You can use this information to identify resource leakage. For example, if the amount of atoms keep growing, your application may be leaking atoms. The code key is the same. If your application somehow dynamically defines modules, you want to make sure to purge them from the system, otherwise the amount of memory used by code will keep growing and growing. Having this information in your dashboards can help you identify leaks before they bring the system down.

Some of those resources have hard limits. For example, the last pane on the right shows Statistics about the system. Part of those statistics is exactly how many processes exist and what is the maximum number of processes allowed. If you reach that limit, the VM will simply refuse to start processes. In a web application, it means you are unable to accept more requests. Therefore, you want to make sure to measure the number of processes and ensure that they are safely below the maximum number of processes, say 80% of your process capacity.

Tracking Process, Port, and Atom Limits

We can compute the ratio of existing processes by the maximum amount of allowed processes like this:

```
iex> 100 * :erlang.system_info(:process_count) /
iex>         :erlang.system_info(:process_limit)
0.0167
```

If your servers are reaching the stipulated threshold and the machine still has plenty of resources available, you can increase this limit at boot time by passing --erl flags. For example, to set the limit north of one million processes:

```
$ iex --erl "+P 1000000"
Erlang/OTP 19 [erts-8.0] [source] [64-bit] [smp:4:4] [ds:4:4:10]
            [async-threads:10] [hipe] [kernel-poll:false]

Interactive Elixir (1.5.0) - press Ctrl+C to exit (type h() ENTER for help)
iex(1)> :erlang.system_info(:process_limit)
1048576
```

You can also use :port_count and :port_limit to track the number of ports your system is using. This metric is especially useful if you are integrating with external code using ports, as outlined in *Strategy 2: Communicating via I/O with Ports*, on page 130.

Erlang/OTP 20 also introduced the ability to compute usage rates for atoms:

```
iex> 100 * :erlang.system_info(:atom_count) / :erlang.system_info(:atom_limit)
0.0167
```

Most applications should expect their atom usage to be constant after their application has warmed up in production. Pairing the ratio above with memory usage can help you quickly discover if your application is leaking atoms.

Getting the Run Queue Length

Another important statistic to track is the *run queue*. When your VM boots, it starts a scheduler per core, and each core has a queue of actions the scheduler should perform. That's the run queue. An overloaded system will show a steadily increasing number of actions in your run queue.

To understand the impact of the Run Queue, let's revisit a discussion that happened on the Elixir Forum.[12] In that thread, Myron Marston reported that some calls to a GenServer were exceeding the default limit of 5 seconds and timing out. Throughout the week, they tried to find the source of the slow down but they were getting stumped. After gathering more information, they noticed that the GenServer message queue was not getting backed up and that each GenServer callback executed quickly. The numbers didn't add up. If the GenServer was never busy and the callbacks were fast, why were the calls still timing out?

José Valim jumped into the discussion and suggested Myron and team to look at the run queue metric. If the system is overloaded, it may take a while until each process gets a chance to run. So even if the GenServer is not busy and can answer fairly fast, by the time the GenServer executes, the timeout value of 5 seconds may have already passed! After measuring the run queue, they concluded the system was indeed overloaded. They could fix it by either getting more powerful machines (scaling vertically) or by adding more nodes (scaling horizontally).

You can retrieve the Run Queue by calling :erlang.statistics/1.[13] Use :erlang.statistics (:total_run_queue_lengths) to get the total run queue length. Avoid using :erlang.statistics(:run_queue) as it is atomic and therefore can be quite expensive.

If you are expecting to push the VM to the limit, it is worth carefully reading the docs for the statistics function to learn more about all of the available metrics.

At this point you may be wondering what is an appropriate value for run queue. That's a very hard question to answer since it depends on your machine, your application, and the kind of loads you expect. However, graphing the run queue

---

12. https://elixirforum.com/t/troubleshooting-a-slow-genserver/3939
13. http://erlang.org/doc/man/erlang.html#statistics-1

can still be very useful when diagnosing problems. For example, if you have an increase in error rates or requests are taking too long, if you've also noticed a simultaneous surge in the run queue, you will have more insight into what may be happening.

Tracking Process Health

Another area worth exploring is the Processes tab. The following figure shows it in action:

Pid	Name or Initial Func	Reds	Memory	MsgQ	Current Function
<0.321.0>	observer_trace_wx:init/1	251704	68048	0	wx_object:loop/6
<0.315.0>	observer_pro_wx:init/1	129387	16912	0	wx_object:loop/6
<0.320.0>	observer_tv_wx:init/1	122044	24736	0	wx_object:loop/6
<0.319.0>	observer_port_wx:init/1	110766	7056	0	wx_object:loop/6
<0.4.0>	erl_prim_loader	92854	426472	0	erl_prim_loader:loop/3
<0.308.0>	observer_sys_wx:init/1	15228	147424	0	wx_object:loop/6
<0.305.0>	wxe_server:init/1	9177	56600	0	gen_server:loop/6
<0.307.0>	erlang:apply/2	8494	6896	0	timer:sleep/1
<0.279.0>	Elixir.DBConnection.Connection:ini...	5655	21840	0	gen_server:loop/6
<0.280.0>	Elixir.DBConnection.Connection:ini...	5655	21840	0	gen_server:loop/6
<0.281.0>	Elixir.DBConnection.Connection:ini...	5655	21840	0	gen_server:loop/6
<0.282.0>	Elixir.DBConnection.Connection:ini...	5655	21840	0	gen_server:loop/6
<0.283.0>	Elixir.DBConnection.Connection:ini...	5655	21840	0	gen_server:loop/6
<0.284.0>	Elixir.DBConnection.Connection:ini...	5655	21840	0	gen_server:loop/6
<0.286.0>	Elixir.DBConnection.Connection:ini...	5655	21840	0	gen_server:loop/6
<0.287.0>	Elixir.DBConnection.Connection:ini...	5643	21840	0	gen_server:loop/6
<0.278.0>	Elixir.DBConnection.Connection:ini...	5622	21840	0	gen_server:loop/6

By default Observer lists all processes in your system, showing their memory usage, message queue length, and the amount of reductions (instructions) they have executed. High values in any area may indicate a bottleneck or memory leak.

You can find all processes in the system by running Process.list/0, or fetch all locally registered processes with Process.registered/0, which returns a list of process IDs. You can use these PIDs to get additional information with Process.info/1. For example, you can get the top five processes by memory usage like this:

```
iex> Process.list |> Enum.sort_by(&Process.info(&1, :memory)) |> Enum.take(-5)
[#PID<0.48.0>, #PID<0.81.0>, #PID<0.36.0>, #PID<0.4.0>, #PID<0.31.0>]
```

In practice, it is unlikely that you will instrument all of the processes in your system. Instead, you want to choose processes that are more likely to be a central part of the system. Those often come up when stress testing the system.

Observer has many other tabs and we won't explore them all. The lesson here, though, applies regardless of the tab: for any information you see in Observer, you can likely find an API to push it to your metrics system as well.

Instrumenting Ecto

The metrics in the virtual machine are important building blocks, but they do not always tell what you need to know about the rest of your application. Moving up one level, let's learn how to get data from the database layer. While you might find it comforting that the metrics system will tell you when your database queries are waiting for more than a second in the connection pool queue, it is better to know this will happen before you ever put your system into production. Ecto[14] is the best place to start. To get detailed metrics, hook into the Ecto logging API. Let's see how that works using our sample application.

First, we'll generate some blog code to test. Use Phoenix generators to build a context that interacts with Postgres via Ecto, like this:

```
$ mix phx.gen.html Blog Post posts title
```

Make sure to follow the instructions shown at the end of the command, then open up config/config.exs and change your repository configuration to the following:

```
config :demo, Demo.Repo,
  loggers: [Ecto.LogEntry, Demo.EctoInspector]
```

This code tells Ecto to include Demo.EctoInspector in its list of loggers. Don't remove the original Ecto.LogEntry if you want to write messages to the console.

Next, define Demo.EctoInspector in your application. Ecto will call Demo.EctoInspector.log/1 passing an Ecto.LogEntry struct. The function must return the given struct. Our implementation will simply call IO.inspect/1 with the struct to see which fields are available to us. Then, we'll just return it without modification. Create a lib/demo/ecto_inspector.ex file and key this in:

```
defmodule Demo.EctoInspector do
  def log(log) do
    IO.inspect(log)
    log
  end
end
```

---

14. https://github.com/elixir-ecto/ecto

We're ready to see some data. Start the server with mix phx.server and access "posts" to fetch all posts. Internally your application will call Demo.Repo.all(Post), which will cause the following to be printed to your terminal:

```
%Ecto.LogEntry{
  ansi_color: nil,
  connection_pid: nil,
  decode_time: 32319,
  params: [],
  query: "SELECT p0.\"id\", p0.\"title\", p0.\"inserted_at\", ...",
  query_time: 3691285,
  queue_time: 64728,
  result: {:ok, %Postgrex.Result{...}},
  source: "posts"
}
```

The struct includes the query, the result, and a couple other fields, including the following measurements:

:query_time

> The amount of time the query took to execute. This time is reported by the database itself. If those times are too high, you need to change your query, add an index, or optimize your database.

:queue_time

> The amount of time spent retrieving the database connection from the pool. If those times are high, it means a capacity problem. Either your load is too great, or your pool is too small.

:decode_time

> This measurement shows how much time was spent converting your results into Elixir data structures. The database drivers, such as Postgrex and Mariaex, are quite optimized when it comes to decoding. Custom decoding functions may be a problem, though, such as those defined in custom Ecto.Types.

The measurements just shown are in native units. They are reported in the maximum resolution supported by the OS. To convert it to a known measure, use System.convert_time_unit/3, like this:

```
iex> System.convert_time_unit 64728, :native, :microseconds
64
```

Those are the measurements you will want to push to whatever metrics system you've decided to use. Third-party performance tools will likely extract all of this information for you. In case they do not, you can tweak Demo.EctoInspector to publish the data to your data gathering services.

That's the gist of the information Ecto makes accessible to developers. Notice that you may also bring in what you learned in the previous section. For example, you should consider monitoring the underlying Demo.Repo.Pool process, keeping count of its memory usage, the amount of reductions, and message queue length. That will tell you more about the resources Elixir is consuming to manage your database.

Now that we are extracting useful information from Ecto, it's time to keep moving up the application stack. Let's see what Phoenix has to offer.

Instrumenting Phoenix

The heart of a Phoenix application is the endpoint module. It is the entry point for web requests and it encapsulates the supervision tree of our web application. In our app, it is called DemoWeb.Endpoint. This module also contains a function named instrument/3, which we can use to instrument any event inside our web stack:

```
require DemoWeb.Endpoint
DemoWeb.Endpoint.instrument(:long_operation_in_controller,
                           %{metadata: "foobar"}, fn ->
  # code to be instrumented
end)
```

Phoenix itself instruments a handful of events, listed here:

- phoenix_controller_call measures how long the controller takes to process your request.

- phoenix_controller_render measures the time the controller takes to render your view.

- phoenix_channel_join records each time a user joins a channel.

- phoenix_channel_receive records each message received by a client on a channel.

To consume those events published by your own application or by Phoenix, you'll probably want to instrument them through a specific Elixir module. This module should export functions with the same name as the events themselves. Phoenix will call each function twice per event, once when the event starts, and again when it finishes.

For example, to instrument the phoenix_controller_call event, we would define a module with two functions:

```elixir
defmodule DemoWeb.PhoenixInspector do
  def phoenix_controller_call(:start, compile_metadata, runtime_metadata) do
    IO.inspect {:start, compile_metadata, runtime_metadata}
    :ok
  end

  def phoenix_controller_call(:stop, time_in_native_unit, _result_of_start) do
    IO.inspect {:stop, time_in_native_unit}
  end
end
```

Note the result of the :start callback is given to the :stop callback with the time elapsed between events in native units. Just as you did with the Ecto events, convert them to known units using System.convert_time_unit/3.

Create the module above in lib/demo_web/phoenix_inspector.ex. Then, tell Phoenix to use it in config/config.exs:

```elixir
config :demo, DemoWeb.Endpoint,
  instrumenters: [DemoWeb.PhoenixInspector]
```

Start the server once again and you should see our instrumenter kicking in and printing the controller information:

```elixir
{:start,
 %{
   application: :demo,
   file: "demo/lib/demo_web/controllers/page_controller.ex",
   function: "call/2",
   line: 2,
   module: DemoWeb.PageController
 },
 %{
   conn: %Plug.Conn{...},
   log_level: :debug
 }
}
{:stop, 335169}
```

You can see the start event includes compile time information such as the application name, source file, function name, and so on. The stop event includes the time the action effectively took.

Phoenix instrumenters provide a mechanism to instrument and hook into existing events, allowing you to push this data to anywhere you would like, including external systems. Similar to Ecto, if you are picking up an existing tool, it is most likely those hooks are already in place.

At ElixirConf EU 2017, Chris McCord announced metrics and monitoring would be the next focus of the Phoenix team. This means the process of getting information out of Ecto and Phoenix will likely become much more streamlined. Still, understanding the measurements and their impact on the system is essential, so what you have learned here will still serve you well, even if the plumbing in the future is not quite the same.

Even though we have focused on Ecto and Phoenix, the process for other libraries will be quite similar. If they provide their own metrics and instrumentation hooks, then you should look into integrating with them and pushing the data to your own systems. If they do not, then your best bet is to measure important function calls and track any important process that may be part of the third-party library. If you are not sure which processes are part of those libraries, you can use Observer to explore the different supervision trees in your system.

Now that we have hooked up our metrics, it is time to assess if our system will behave how we expect it to.

Performance Assessment Workflow

Good performance analysis is about taking mountains of facts and focusing on the most important grains of truth. In the previous sections we established what to measure so you'll know how your system behaves through different traffic patterns. There's plenty of data to gather, should you be so inclined. In fact, there would be too much information to decipher if you decided to measure everything we've outlined. Remember, the name of the game is focus. It's time to find out which processes to target for more detailed instrumentation.

Regardless of whether you are optimizing a web server, an embedded system or the tools used by your team, the journey is quite similar. Before you begin, load test a feature and compare that to your performance requirements. If it is behaving as desired, you can gladly move forward. If it is not, you will want to profile the system and identify the hotspots. Then, you can use benchmarks to compare different solutions and remove the bottleneck.

That's the flow we will explore here, using the Phoenix application we created in the previous section as a starting point. Before we move on to load testing with specific tools, consider the following suggestions.

First, *never measure only averages.* Besides the average, you also want to measure at least one of the 90th, 95th, and 99th percentiles. When talking about web applications, most page loads experience 99% latencies[15] so it is essential to include those percentiles in your measurements.

Second, *quantify your gains.* Since determining how fast a system or a feature should be is sometimes hard, you should try to convert that time into monetary gains, even if it is back-of-the-napkin calculus. If you can reduce the page load by 1 second, many companies report gains from 2% to 10% in conversion rates, and you can do assumptions based on existing case studies. Similarly, if you are in a team of five engineers with a slow test suite that you run on average 20 times per day and you believe you can cut the test time from 20 seconds to 10 seconds, that will save your team 8 hours every month altogether. If the speedup takes a day, you will recoup that back by the end of the month and your team will feel more confident.

Finally, *avoid performance regressions.* Every time you find a hotspot, you should consider feeding this information back to your metrics system. If a process is a bottleneck, track its message queue length. If a function turns out to be computationally expensive, instrument it. You should also consider setting up performance tests that you run in your CI server. That will give you confidence the server performance won't regress as you add new features.

Now that you have some basic guidelines to work from, it's time to collect some real data through load testing.

Load Testing

Load testing is the process of determining the system behavior under load. Ideally, you want to run load tests against an environment that closely matches your production environment. You might use a staging environment or a production build from your continuous integration pipeline.

For simplicity, we will run tests against a production version of our Phoenix application running on our development machine. This scenario is not ideal since the load tester itself will compete with the Phoenix app for machine resources but it is good enough to get started and build an expectation of the system behavior. At the end of this section we will cover other tools that will provide better end-to-end testing.

---

15. http://latencytipoftheday.blogspot.com/2014/06/latencytipoftheday-most-page-loads.html

Load Testing with wrk

The tool we will use is wrk,[16] an HTTP benchmarking and load testing tool. You can find it in most package managers. To get started, let's start our Phoenix application in production mode:

```
$ MIX_ENV=prod mix ecto.setup
$ PORT=4040 MIX_ENV=prod mix phx.server
```

The environment variable signals Phoenix to start in production mode. Now let's put wrk to work:

```
$ wrk -t5 -c10 -d30s --latency http://127.0.0.1:4040/posts
Running 30s test @ http://127.0.0.1:4040/posts
  5 threads and 10 connections
  Thread Stats   Avg      Stdev     Max   +/- Stdev
    Latency     2.65ms    1.11ms  30.03ms   80.87%
    Req/Sec    768.82     58.71     0.89k    71.20%
  Latency Distribution
     50%    2.46ms
     75%    3.08ms
     90%    3.81ms
     99%    6.46ms
  114871 requests in 30.03s, 158.65MB read
Requests/sec:   3824.80
Transfer/sec:      5.28MB
```

This example uses five threads to run requests over ten connections against our application for 30 seconds. We can see the application averages to 3824req/s with a latency of 2.46ms on average and of 6.46ms on the 99th percentile. Fair enough.

Now, let's increase the concurrency factor to 100:

```
$ wrk -t5 -c100 -d30s --latency http://127.0.0.1:4040/posts
Running 30s test @ http://127.0.0.1:4040/posts
  5 threads and 100 connections
  Thread Stats   Avg      Stdev     Max   +/- Stdev
    Latency    28.70ms   10.15ms 152.78ms   90.48%
    Req/Sec    710.45    157.64     0.95k    71.47%
  Latency Distribution
     50%   25.68ms
     75%   30.66ms
     90%   38.21ms
     99%   72.88ms
  106215 requests in 30.05s, 146.69MB read
Requests/sec:   3534.14
Transfer/sec:      4.88MB
```

---

16. https://github.com/wg/wrk

Our server now has more work to do. The throughput reduces, the latency increases, but the 99th percentile is not even an order of magnitude away from the average. That's why we say the Erlang VM provides predictable latency. The VM preempts slow processes to allow all processes to still move forward, even when the system is under load. Although the throughput and latency here are reasonable, you may want to consider some changes to achieve better performance:

• Set the logger level to :warn in your config/prod.exs. If you have a metrics system in place, as outlined in the previous section, there is no reason to log the same expensive information to disk on every request.

• Increase the number of keepalive requests. Load testing tools work by opening connections to the server and issuing many requests repeatedly over the same connection. Cowboy, by default, allows at most 100 requests on the same connection before requiring the client to start a new one. This is a completely reasonable behavior for most browsers and most clients, but it may show up in benchmarks. You can increase this limit by setting protocol_options: [max_keepalive: 5_000_000] under the :http options in the lib/demo_web/endpoint.ex file.

• You should also consider changing your database pool size in config/prod.secret.exs. Keep in mind a larger pool does not imply better performance. Both the database and Ecto perform a lot of caching per connection and increasing the pool means those caches are used less frequently while also putting more load on the database. Phoenix's :pool_size of 15 is a reasonable default but you may want to raise it if you see increased queue times in your Ecto metrics.

Let's do the first two changes and see how our server behaves. Restart the server and re-run the first command:

```
$ wrk -t5 -c10 -d30s --latency http://127.0.0.1:4040/posts
Running 30s test @ http://127.0.0.1:4040/posts
  5 threads and 10 connections
  Thread Stats   Avg      Stdev     Max   +/- Stdev
    Latency     1.84ms    1.58ms  59.31ms   98.14%
    Req/Sec     1.13k    101.69    1.28k    85.73%
  Latency Distribution
     50%    1.70ms
     75%    2.04ms
     90%    2.42ms
     99%    4.15ms
  168932 requests in 30.02s, 233.28MB read
Requests/sec:   5627.71
Transfer/sec:      7.77MB
```

We saw an increase of almost 50% for two lines of code. We'll take it. Saša Jurić, author of *Elixir in Action [Jur15]*, has written an excellent article on Phoenix latency[17] that can complement what we discussed in this section.

Wrk is also scriptable using LuaJIT.[18] This technique is useful for testing endpoints that require more complex setup such as an authenticated session. However, if you want to test complex user interactions or other protocols such as WebSockets, you need to bring in the big guns.

Scripting Load Tests with Tsung

Tsung is a load testing tool written in Erlang. It comes with:

- A dashboard to see an overview of your tests
- The ability to coordinate multiple clients over multiple machines, and
- An XML configuration system to control complex user interactions.

Tsung is the tool used by the Phoenix team to load test its channels implementation over WebSockets. In a particular benchmark, the Phoenix team used Tsung to coordinate forty-five machines to push two million connections to a single Phoenix server.[19]

If you are looking for more streamlined solutions that do not require you to set up and coordinate all machines, you should take a look at Blazemeter,[20] which is built on top of JMeter[21] and provides a complete set of features. There are many other options available, such as loader.io[22] and flood.io.[23]

Assuming load testing is in place and you find a particular feature or endpoint that is not behaving as expected, you will need to go deeper. That's when profiling can be handy.

Profiling

Profiling is a performance tuning technique that measures primarily the frequency and duration of function calls. Erlang/OTP ships with three profilers. cprof counts the number of invocations, eprof measures execution time, and fprof measures both frequency and time. Each has its own advantages and disadvantages. cprof runs quite fast and has a minimal impact on execution times,

---

17. http://theerlangelist.com/article/phoenix_latency
18. https://github.com/wg/wrk/tree/master/scripts
19. http://phoenixframework.org/blog/the-road-to-2-million-websocket-connections
20. https://www.blazemeter.com/
21. http://jmeter.apache.org/
22. https://loader.io/
23. https://flood.io/

but doesn't tell you as much as full execution times. On the other hand, fprof provides much more data, but expect it to impact your execution time.

Elixir provides integration with cprof, eprof, and fprof via the Mix tool. In this section, we'll provide a quick example of using cprof and fprof.

Imagine that your load tests found one fairly slow route. After looking at the data, the slowdown was in the index action of the PostController. We need to figure out exactly what is happening.

In our Phoenix application, create a file named post_index.exs in a new perf directory. We want to write a piece of code that will execute the action we want to profile. We'll rely on the same functions we use to test our controllers to do so, like this:

```elixir
defmodule PostIndex do
  use Phoenix.ConnTest
  @endpoint DemoWeb.Endpoint

  import DemoWeb.Router.Helpers
  import ExUnit.Assertions

  def run do
    conn = build_conn()
    conn = get conn, post_path(conn, :index)
    assert html_response(conn, 200)
  end
end
```

Now let's run the profiler with cprof. We will run it in production, to make sure our measurements won't be affected by any development configuration, such as logging:

```
$ PORT=4040 MIX_ENV=prod mix \
    profile.cprof -r perf/post_index.exs -e "PostIndex.run"
Warmup...

                                              CNT
Total                                         1327
Enum                                           140
  Enum."-reduce/3-lists^foldl/2-0-"/3           92
  Enum.reduce/3                                 27
  Enum.map_reduce/3                              5
  ...
Plug.Conn
  Plug.Conn.valid_header_key?/1                 59
  Plug.Conn.put_private/3                       11
```

We invoked the count profiler in production, using the -r flag to determine which profilers to load into memory and the -e flag to run it. Notice the results of cprof are quite limited and potentially misleading. For example, in the preceding snippet we can see Plug.Conn.valid_header_key?/1 is called 59 times. At first, that seems like a large value. After all, the sum of request and response headers in most HTTP requests should be far less than 59 entries. However, once you check the definition of that function, you will see its high count is due to its recursive implementation that traverses each byte in the response header.

Furthermore, a high count for one function does not imply it is the bottleneck. At best, think of cprof as a tool that gives you a rough sketch of the modules and functions invoked during the request, without much insight.

To fill in details for your rough sketch, you'll need something more detailed. Where cprof is a count profiler, fprof is a more detailed function profiler. Simply replace cprof with fprof and run the command again, like this:

```
$ PORT=4040 MIX_ENV=prod mix \
    profile.fprof -r perf/post_index.exs -e "PostIndex.run"
Warmup...
```

	CNT	ACC (ms)	OWN (ms)
Total	1542	10.843	8.966
:fprof.apply_start_stop/4	0	10.843	0.019
anonymous fn/0 in :elixir_compiler_1.__FILE__/1	1	10.817	0.005
PostIndex.run/0	1	10.812	0.017
Phoenix.ConnTest.dispatch/5	1	9.671	0.013
Phoenix.ConnTest.dispatch_endpoint/5	1	9.634	0.010
DemoWeb.Endpoint.call/2	1	9.132	0.013
DemoWeb.Endpoint."call (overridable 2)"/2	1	9.056	0.002
DemoWeb.Endpoint.plug_builder_call/2	1	9.054	0.026
DemoWeb.Router.call/2	1	8.589	0.013
Phoenix.Router.__call__/1	1	8.508	0.008
DemoWeb.PostController.call/2	1	7.876	0.009

This run tells a different story. It shows call frequency and execution times for both a function with its children (ACC) and the function itself (OWN). The first entry in the profiler results is a call to the profiler itself, which then executes the -e command we specified. The third entry is finally our own PostIndex.run/0. The profiling data is usually quite long so you should scan from top to bottom looking for unexpectedly high ACC or OWN entries. Keep in mind the first entries in the profiling results will always have the highest ACC, since they capture all of their own times plus the children below.

The mix profile.fprof task also provides other options, such as --sort, --callers, and --details to give you deeper insights into the profiled code. Run mix help profile.fprof to learn more.

After you've profiled your code, you'll find out what's broken. You'll want to try out some potential solutions. Don't guess. Make sure you measure improvements against potential solutions and the original code. That's the topic of the next section.

Benchmarking

Use benchmarking tools to compare different implementations to the same problem. Proper benchmarking requires care: we need to guarantee a measurement won't affect subsequent ones. For example, each measurement should run on a new process to make sure data generated in the first measurement won't affect the second one by triggering the garbage collector. We also need to make sure we warm up the code before each measurement, to make sure the VM won't kick in dynamic code loading for some cases but not others. The details are tricky so most folks use a benchmarking tool instead of rolling their own solutions.

Imagine that your application needs to find the longest word from a file. Each word is on a separate line. Initially everything works fine, but due to business demands, the file you have to process steadily grows until your measurements notice the difference.

Profiling trimmed the scope of the problem down to the following code snippet:

```
path_to_file_in_disk
|> File.read!
|> String.split("\n")
|> Enum.max_by(&String.length/1)
```

You read the whole file from disk, split the file by newlines, and then compute the largest one. Each function call in there is a candidate for improvement. You start by looking at the File module to look for alternatives and you quickly find File.stream!. The ability to stream the file line by line should save you memory since you'll load a small fraction of the file instead of the whole file, but will these memory improvements make it any faster? Let's use the benchee tool[24] to answer this question.

First add it to the deps section of your mix.exs:

```
{:benchee, ">= 0.0.0", only: :dev}
```

This tool is a development-only dependency because benchmarks usually run at the low level where the differences between development and production should not impact us much. If you really want to benchmark broader slices of the Phoenix stack, you may want to revisit that restriction, but our function is isolated.

---

24. https://github.com/PragTob/benchee

The next step is to find the data we will use for our benchmarks. Since the issue starts to show up with large files, let's make sure we have a big enough corpus. This repository[25] is a good start. Download the words.txt file and save it to disk. Now we are ready to write our benchmark.

Create a file at perf/file_bench.exs with the following contents:

```
defmodule FileBench do
  @fixture "path/to/words.txt"

  def run do
    Benchee.run(%{
      "with read" => &with_read/0,
      "with stream" => &with_stream/0,
    }, time: 10)
  end

  def with_read do
    @fixture
    |> File.read!
    |> String.split("\n")
    |> Enum.max_by(&String.length/1)
  end

  def with_stream do
    @fixture
    |> File.stream!
    |> Enum.max_by(&String.length/1)
    |> String.trim()
  end
end
```

The file has three functions. run executes the entire benchmark, comparing the with read results with the with stream results. The other two functions provide the implementations we're benchmarking.

We're ready to run it:

```
$ mix run -r perf/file_bench.exs -e "FileBench.run"
Number of Available Cores: 4
Available memory: 17.179869184 GB
Elixir 1.5.0
Erlang 19.0
Benchmark suite executing with the following configuration:
warmup: 2.00 s
time: 10.00 s
parallel: 1
inputs: none specified
Estimated total run time: 24.00 s
```

---

25. https://github.com/dwyl/english-words

```
Benchmarking with read...
Benchmarking with stream...

Name                    ips      average  deviation       median
with stream             1.00      1.00 s    ±5.27%        0.98 s
with read               0.45      2.23 s    ±0.88%        2.23 s

Comparison:
with stream             1.00
with read               0.45 - 2.23x slower
```

Jackpot! The stream implementation is more than twice as fast. We can now plug the stream implementation into our codebase. Benchee can also run benchmarks against multiple inputs and render the results in different formats. Read the excellent documentation to find what features are available.

You've now seen how to collect statistics, profile to isolate a problem, and benchmark different solutions to choose the right one. We've accomplished a good deal in this chapter, so it's time to recap.

Wrapping Up

Elixir provides a wide range of tools to help you instrument your application to measure performance in production. The first section showed how to monitor and fine-tune Observer to ensure everything runs well in production. The Erlang Observer tool uses the same low-level APIs to collect data that you can use to instrument your own solutions. You learned how to use those APIs to measure memory usage, resources by process, and other details such as run queue length.

The next topic was profiling. You can use three important tools to count function call frequencies or call time (or both), and each has inherent trade-offs. Profiling can give you a good idea of where a performance problem might be, down to the offending function.

Finally, we ran a benchmark to fix a problem. Our code benchmarked a potential solution against the offending code to verify that the cure was in fact better than the disease.

Since you now know how to monitor an application that's running well, it's time to shift gears. In the next chapter, you'll learn ways to be aware of application errors and what we can do about it. There's one more chapter to go, so let's dig in!

## CHAPTER 10

Making Your App Production Ready

Over the course of this book, we've covered the broadly diverse landscape of adoption. Much of our discussion has focused on preventing our application from breaking in the first place. When your application *does* fail, and it will, you'll need the right kind of data to diagnose the problem. Just as a good user interface designer anticipates the needs of a user, you the developer must anticipate your future needs when it's time to provide support.

In this chapter, you will learn how to listen for failures and the tools available to debug your system when things go wrong. We'll primarily worry about logging. We'll find ways to keep your logs efficient and easy to read.

When we've considered those sources of information, we'll look at some Erlang libraries built for diagnostics. We'll shift for a short time to debuggers. Finally, we'll end on a discussion of CrashDump, another Erlang tool that can help you analyze the data that Erlang exports each time a VM crashes. This is the last step in your journey and an essential one, so let's get started!

Logs and Errors

The first defense against bugs is application-specific information, and the best way to acquire that is via old-fashioned logging. Elixir comes with the creatively named built-in Logger for logging *messages*. The word "messages" matters, because Logger was designed with a focus on text-based reports and not structured data.

Logger contains four severity levels. From least to most severe, they are :debug, :info, :warn, and :error. When you configure Logger for the :info level, it will log :info and everything more severe, including :warn and :error messages. A developer can log any message at any time through the Logger API, like this:

```
require Logger
Logger.debug "hello"
```

Logger also handles errors for all processes that terminate abruptly in the system. To see an example, try this in iex:

```
iex> Task.start_link fn -> raise "oops" end
...

23:27:12.221 [error] Task #PID<0.83.0> started from #PID<0.81.0> terminating
** (RuntimeError) oops
    (elixir) lib/task/supervised.ex:85: Task.Supervised.do_apply/2
    (stdlib) proc_lib.erl:247: :proc_lib.init_p_do_apply/3
Function: #Function<20.52032458/0 in :erl_eval.expr/5>
    Args: []
```

Logger writes the previous error report to the terminal. You can use the Logger API in your own application. As any other tool, developers can misuse it. Many applications such as Phoenix and Ecto tend to log events with measurements but these kinds of messages are *for development use* precisely because the data is unstructured messages.

Using extensive logging to the default standard output on production is an expensive operation in a concurrent system since the standard output is a *single entity that forces serial access*! As such, it may become a bottleneck under high load.

Limiting Logger for Production Mode

Luckily, in Chapter 9, *Metrics and Performance Expectations*, on page 171, you saw how to get structured metrics out of your system, including data coming from third-party libraries such as Ecto and Phoenix. In production, you don't need to rely on Logger for :debug and :info messages. Those messages are quite frequent and not nearly structured enough for useful metrics systems. The only remaining messages are warnings, which most likely do not require immediate intervention, and errors, which most likely require a developer to look at. Furthermore, restricting logger to warnings and errors makes it unlikely we will write to standard output frequently enough for it to become a bottleneck. In the unlikely scenario that happens, logger has built-in mechanisms to drop messages and ensure the system won't collapse.

Let's take a closer look at common needs when using logger, such as cheap logging, custom formatters, and custom backends.

Cheap Logging

If you still haven't set up monitoring or if the application is too small to warrant one, logging :info messages in production will likely be fine. If you do have a metrics system properly set up, the first best-practice in Logger is to bump the log level to :warn in your production environment:

```
config :logger, :level, :warn
```

Be careful, though. Simply setting the logger level to :warn doesn't completely alleviate the performance cost of :debug and :info messages. It's best to make the messages we are not interested in consuming as cheap as possible. In Logger, you can do so in two ways.

The first option is to set :compile_time_purge_level to :warn or :error. This option removes all Logger calls below your configured severity *at compilation time*. For a production environment with :warn severity, an application invoking Logger.debug("hello") would see no performance hit whatsoever. The log message effectively becomes a no-op!

The downside of the compile time purging is that you are unable to access purged messages without recompiling the source code. For example, imagine that you are introspecting a live system and you would like to temporarily turn on :info messages. If you purged them, they simply won't be available.

The second approach to cheap logging is wrapping each log message in an anonymous function. For example, in Plug,[1] instead of logging like this:

```
stop = System.monotonic_time()
diff = System.convert_time_unit(stop - start, :native, :micro_seconds)

Logger.info [connection_type(conn), ?\s, Integer.to_string(conn.status),
           " in ", formatted_diff(diff)]
```

it wraps the whole computation in an anonymous function, like this:

```
Logger.info fn ->
  stop = System.monotonic_time()
  diff = System.convert_time_unit(stop - start, :native, :micro_seconds)

  [connection_type(conn), ?\s, Integer.to_string(conn.status),
   " in ", formatted_diff(diff)]
end
```

In the first approach, if the Logger level is :warn, the whole message will be computed, including the time measurements, only to be discarded. The second approach wraps everything in an anonymous function which will only be executed if we are interested in the message in the first place.

---

1. https://github.com/elixir-plug/plug

With anonymous functions, the cost of each missed log message is kept to a minimum, without any compile restrictions. Therefore, you should wrap all debug or info Logger calls in your application in anonymous functions.

Custom Formatters

So far, you've learned how to configure our logger level to :warn and guarantee the :debug and :info messages are as cheap as possible. Logger is ready to support your custom needs. Well, almost. The external system expects all log messages to be in a specific format, one that might not match your application. Luckily, Logger supports custom formatters. To see one in action, let's create a new Elixir application:

```
$ mix new formatter
```

Start a new IEx session with iex -S mix and log a message, like this:

```
iex> require Logger
iex> Logger.error "hello"

15:37:39.791 [error] hello
:ok
```

Next, we want to log messages as JSON and include as much metadata as possible. To do so, we will need to write our own formatter. We need to bring some dependencies into the project so open up mix.exs and add Poison[2] as a dependency, like so:

```
{:poison, ">= 0.0.0"}
```

We'll define our formatter in the Formatter module defined in lib/formatter.ex. Our function will receive the log level, the log message, the current timestamp, and metadata as a keyword list. The formatter should convert it to JSON, like this:

```
defmodule Formatter do
  def json_formatter(level, message, time, metadata) do
    [encode_to_json(level, message, time, Map.new(metadata)), ?\n]
  end

  defp encode_to_json(level, message, _time, metadata) do
    Poison.encode! %{
      level: level,
      message: message,
      metadata: metadata
    }
  end
end
```

---

2. https://github.com/devinus/poison

Next, configure the :console backend in config/config.exs to use the new formatter. Let's also make sure to include some metadata, like this:

```
config :logger, :console,
  format: {Formatter, :json_formatter},
  metadata: [:application, :file, :line, :module]
```

Run a quick command to try out our slick new formatter:

```
$ mix run -e "require Logger; Logger.error ~s[hello]"
{"metadata":{"module":null,"line":1,"file":"nofile"},
 "message":"hello",
 "level":"error"}
```

It works! Careful, though. Our formatter has a dangerous limitation. It may poorly format some messages, or worse, crash the system:

```
$ mix run -e "require Logger; Logger.error ~c[hello]"
{"metadata":{"module":null,"line":1,"file":"nofile"},
 "message":[104,101,108,108,111],
 "level":"error"}
```

In this example, we passed the logger a char list. The logger formatted that list as JSON but the message field showed up as a list of integers instead of a string. We'll need to fix that.

There's another problem too. Let's make Logger crash. Ask it to log more metadata, including a :pid, like this:

```
config :logger, :console,
  format: {Formatter, :json_formatter},
  metadata: [:application, :file, :line, :module, :pid]
```

Now let's try again:

```
$ mix run -e "require Logger; Logger.error ~c[hello]"
```

Our logger crashed, so nothing was logged! That's why it is extremely important to never crash the logger nor the logger formatter because should that happen, you'll get nothing to help you debug the problem.

Let's fix those limitations:

```
defmodule Formatter do
  def json_formatter(level, message, time, metadata) do
    message = IO.chardata_to_string(message)
    [encode_to_json(level, message, time, Map.new(metadata)), ?\n]
  end
```

```elixir
  defp encode_to_json(level, message, _time, metadata) do
    Poison.encode! %{
      level: level,
      message: message,
      metadata: metadata
    }
  rescue
    _ ->
      Poison.encode! %{
        level: level,
        message: "error while formatting #{inspect message} with
          #{inspect metadata}",
        metadata: %{}
      }
  end
end
```

Give it another try:

```
$ mix run -e "require Logger; Logger.error ~c[hello]"
{"metadata":{},
 "message":"error while formatting \"hello\" with
   %{file: \"nofile\", line: 1, module: nil, pid: #PID<0.70.0>}",
 "level":"error"}
```

This time we at least got a message, making it clear we could not format the metadata. At this point, there is not much we can do. Either we choose not to log the PID, or we explicitly handle data we can't format, such as PIDs, in our formatter. For now, remove the :pid entry from the :logger configuration in config/config.exs and try it once more:

```
$ mix run -e "require Logger; Logger.error ~c[hello]"
{"metadata":{"module":null,"line":1,"file":"nofile"},
 "message":"hello", "level":"error"}
```

We are back to properly formatted data. We customize logged console data but that requires care in handling the different kinds of inputs, especially making sure our formatter never crashes.

Error Notification with Custom Backends

While customizing the logger formatter is handy, it is not enough to cover all logging use cases. Sometimes, you need to write your own implementation. For this reason, Logger supports custom backends, letting you push log messages anywhere you want.

If your metrics are in place, the logging system will focus on warnings and errors. This means the most common use case for logger backends is to push data to exception and error tracking systems. Luckily, the Elixir community provides integration with different services, such as Rollbar[3] via rollbax,[4] Sentry[5] via sentry-elixir,[6] and Honeybadger[7] via honeybadger-elixir.[8]

If you are interested in writing your own backends, you should consult the Elixir documentation[9] and look at any of the previously listed examples, or `Logger.Backend.Console` that ships as part of Elixir itself.

Tracking errors is essential in any production system, so developers have an understanding of what is going wrong and when. Combined with logging, if you have the foresight to capture information in advance, logging can be an excellent source of information, but sometimes, completely unplanned bad things happen. That's the topic of the next section.

SASL Reports

SASLs, or System Architecture Support Libraries, ship as part of Erlang/OTP, providing detailed progress and crash reports. They extend Erlang and Elixir loggers to provide detailed reports from supervisors. We can enable it either with a command-line flag or a configuration option.

You can start Elixir or IEx with SASL enabled by passing the --logger-sasl-reports true flag. Create a new application to try it out:

```
$ mix new sasl_sample
```

Start it in an IEx session with the SASL reports flag enabled, like this:

```
$ iex --logger-sasl-reports true -S mix
00:10:51.385 [info]  Child Logger.ErrorHandler of
                     Supervisor Logger.Supervisor started
Pid: #PID<0.79.0>
Start Call: Logger.Watcher.start_link({:error_logger, ...})
Restart: :permanent
Shutdown: 5000
Type: :worker

00:10:51.392 [info]  Application logger started at :nonode@nohost
```

You'll immediately notice our system is logging more frequently. You can see every started application and which supervisor starts which child. Those

---

3. https://rollbar.com/
4. https://github.com/elixir-addicts/rollbax
5. https://sentry.io/
6. https://github.com/getsentry/sentry-elixir
7. https://www.honeybadger.io/
8. https://github.com/honeybadger-io/honeybadger-elixir
9. hexdocs.pm/logger

messages, called progress reports, are particularly useful when you're debugging startup issues or when you can't figure out why some application is not running in development or test.

We also get crash reports every time a supervisor notices a terminated child. Type this example in the same iex session:

```
iex> {:ok, sup} = Task.Supervisor.start_link()
{:ok, #PID<0.83.0>}
iex> Task.Supervisor.start_child(sup, fn -> raise "oops" end)
{:ok, #PID<0.88.0>}

00:23:19.798 [error] Task #PID<0.88.0> started
                     from #PID<0.81.0> terminating
...

00:23:19.799 [error] Process #PID<0.88.0> terminating
...

00:23:19.799 [error] Child Task.Supervised of
                     Supervisor #PID<0.83.0> terminated
...
```

In the preceding example, you should see three reports:

- The first report says the task we started (#PID<0.88.0>) terminated with reason "oops."

- The second contains low-level information about the terminated process.

- The supervisor (#PID<0.83.0>) emits the third report with supervision metadata.

Take a detailed look at those reports and notice the wealth of information available to us. If you would rather have SASL started whenever your application boots, either add it to your mix.exs file under the :extra_applications list or list it as a deployment dependency in tools such as Distillery. Whenever you do so, you need to explicitly configure Logger to handle the SASL reports for you. If you don't configure Logger, Erlang's :error_logger will be the one reporting and it will do so using Erlang terms. You can configure Logger in your config files as follows:

```
config :logger, handle_sasl_reports: true
```

It is also important to guarantee the :sasl application is started *before* the :logger application. Otherwise you will get duplicate reports. Your mix.exs should look like this:

```
extra_applications: [:sasl, :logger]
```

Now, you've seen the logging tools at your disposal for Elixir and OTP. Those *passive* tools can record information you determine in advance. You also have *active* tools to call on, ones that will allow you to step through execution. Let's not stop there, though. We will focus on the tools that will help you debug *live* systems.

Tracing

When it comes to debugging, Elixir developers have two main options: use the debugger GUI[10] that ships with Erlang or the new IEx.break![11] Elixir tools. Debuggers let you stop the execution of one or more processes and inspect their environment, but debugging is clearly not a good match for a production system. If you interrupt an important process in your application while debugging, you could start to accumulate requests, leading to timeouts or even restarts. In the end, *your* email inbox may begin to rapidly fill.

Because the risks of interacting with live systems and security concerns are acute, many companies simply do not give developers access to production nodes except under special circumstances. Even if you work at one of those companies, these next few useful lessons can help you debug systems in staging environments or under load tests.

To debug such systems, we need tools that are light-weight and have little to no effect in the system operations. And as one would expect from a technology that has been battle-tested for decades, the Erlang VM has some good options available. One of those options is :erlang.trace/3.[12] Tracing allows you to ask the VM to send a message to a chosen process whenever some event happens. Let's take an example. We'll use the API to trace all of the messages to a process:

```
iex> {:ok, agent} = Agent.start_link(fn -> %{} end)
{:ok, #PID<0.83.0>}
iex> :erlang.trace(agent, true, [:receive])
1
iex> Agent.get(agent, & &1)
%{}
iex> flush()
{:trace, #PID<0.83.0>, :receive,
 {:"$gen_call", {#PID<0.81.0>, #Reference<0.0.2.98>},
  {:get, #Function<6.52032458/1 in :erl_eval.expr/5>}}}
```

---

10. http://www1.erlang.org/doc/apps/debugger/debugger_chapter.html
11. https://hexdocs.pm/iex/IEx.html#break!/4
12. http://erlang.org/doc/man/erlang.html#trace-3

We started an agent, asked the VM to track all messages received by that agent, and then invoked Agent.get/2. Since Agent.get/2 sends a message to the agent to retrieve its state, the tracing system sent the IEx process a message. We then call flush() to immediately deliver it. This example is just a small subset of what's available. In fact, this much power needs structure so you won't usually invoke those functions directly.

Instead, you'll use modules and libraries with more accessible APIs. One such tool is the marvelously inappropriately named :dbg module[13] that ships with Erlang/OTP as part of the :runtime_tools application. Let's give it a try. Notice you will need to start a new IEx session since the VM supports only one tracing process at a time:

```
iex(1)> {:ok, agent} = Agent.start_link fn -> %{} end
{:ok, #PID<0.83.0>}
iex(2)> :dbg.c Agent, :get, [agent, & &1]
(<0.87.0>) <0.83.0> ! {'$gen_call',{<0.87.0>,#Ref<0.0.3.98>},
                              {get,#Fun<erl_eval.6.52032458>}}
                    (Timestamp: {1501, 610975, 867375})
(<0.87.0>) out {gen,do_call,4} (Timestamp: {1501,610975,867384})
(<0.87.0>) << {#Ref<0.0.3.98>,#{}} (Timestamp: {1501,610975,867404})
(<0.87.0>) in {gen,do_call,4} (Timestamp: {1501,610975,867412})
%{}
```

With :dbg, instead of manually setting up the traces, we asked it to invoke the :get function in the Agent module with the given arguments. Then :dbg logged all events directly to the terminal, including:

- The message sent to the agent

- The fact that the process was scheduled *out* because it is now waiting for a message

- The reply the process received from the agent

- The process was scheduled back *in* because it has receive a message

When you're working to understand message queue flows between processes, :dbg.c is an excellent tool.

Sometimes, such brief flows are not enough. It is also possible to set long-running traces, such as tracing when certain modules or functions are called by any process in the system. The first step is to get a tracer and then explicitly set the events we want to track:

---

13. http://erlang.org/doc/man/dbg.html

```
iex> :dbg.tracer
{:ok, #PID<0.83.0>}
iex> :dbg.p :all, [:call]
{:ok, [{:matched, :nonode@nohost, 46}]}
iex> :dbg.tp URI, []
{:ok, [{:matched, :nonode@nohost, 22}]}
iex> URI.decode_query "foo=bar"
(<0.81.0>) call 'Elixir.URI':'__info__'(macros)
(<0.81.0>) call 'Elixir.URI':decode_query(<<"foo=bar">>)
```

This time, we called :dbg.p and asked it to trace all processes for the :call event. Whenever you set up a call event, you also need to set a trace pattern. Our trace pattern will print whenever the URI module is called, regardless of the function or the arity.

You have to be careful when passing the :all option to any function in :dbg. Don't believe us? Try this out:

```
iex> :dbg.p :all, :all
```

You are now tracing all events in the system on all processes, *even the trace itself.* Since the tracing of events itself generates more events, you just started an infinite loop.

There are a couple things you can do to make sure this does not happen in live systems. The first rule of the all flag in trace club: *do not pass the :all flag.*

The other one is to set up custom tracers. You can configure these tracers to print tracing messages in Elixir terms, which has the benefit of printing structs and other data structures as they were meant to be. Let's give it a try:

```
iex> fun = fn _, 100 -> :dbg.stop_clear()
iex>           msg, n -> IO.inspect(msg) && n + 1 end
iex> :dbg.tracer(:process, {fun, 0})
iex> :dbg.p :all, :all
{:trace_ts, #PID<0.84.0>, :send,
 {:dbg, {:ok, [{:matched, :nonode@nohost, 51}]}}, #PID<0.81.0>,
 {1501, 612544, 238908}}
```

This time, even though we did make the mistake of tracing all events on all processes, we configured our tracer function to stop :dbg after 100 events. That means you won't get fired for melting your server.

In practice, if you are tracing production systems, we recommend you define a MyApp.DBG module in your application. It should have the tracer function above as well as any convenience functions you and your team will discover to be necessary in future sessions, like this:

```elixir
defmodule MyApp.DBG do
  @moduledoc """
  Conveniences and safety around Erlang's :dbg.
  """

  @doc """
  Sets up a new tracer.
  """
  def tracer(limit \\ 100) do
    fun = fn
      _, ^limit ->
        :dbg.stop_clear()
      msg, n ->
        IO.inspect(msg)
        n + 1
    end
    :dbg.tracer(:process, {fun, 0})
  end
end
```

Now, whenever you need, you can import the MyApp.DBG module into your IEx session for careful tracing. For instance, you could trace the last 100 messages received by a named process like this:

```elixir
iex> import MyApp.DBG
iex> tracer()
iex> :dbg.p MyApp.Process, [:receive]
```

And you're off to the races. You can now be using the console tracing systems at a moment's notice.

Due to the complexity and risks behind the tracing API, many developers will tell you that tracing is an acquired taste. This shared sentiment led to the creation of alternative tracing libraries such as recon[14] and tracer.[15] If you find :dbg too complex or error-prone for tracing, you should be able to find a library that suits your tastes.

One other alternative is the :sys module[16] that ships as part of Erlang/OTP. :sys allows you to trace the default Elixir behavior, such as GenServer and Supervisor, and collect statistics. The Elixir docs on the GenServer module[17] provide a good starting point for those interested in learning more.

Now that you've seen both logging and tracing, we're almost done. Before we close out this chapter, let's see a few more tools at your disposal.

---

14. http://ferd.github.io/recon/
15. https://github.com/gabiz/tracer
16. http://erlang.org/doc/man/sys.html
17. https://hexdocs.pm/elixir/GenServer.html#module-debugging-with-the-sys-module

Using Other Advanced Tools

We have learned how trace can be used to debug live systems with minimum impact. There are many other libraries in Erlang/OTP and in the community you can use to understand production systems. We'll look at three Erlang tools: the :runtime_tools library, the :crash_dump viewer, and the :recon project.

Debugging with Runtime Tools

You've already seen one of the :runtime_tools. The :dbg module enables tracing. We only scratched the surface. The useful library also includes more advanced functionality such as:

- An Observer backend for remote debugging. If you want to remotely analyze a production node using the Observer tool, the node must have runtime_tools running. For the details of remote observing, see this article by Plataformatec.[18]

- Integration with OS-level tracers, such as Linux Trace Toolkit,[19] DTRACE,[20] and SystemTap.[21]

- Microstate accounting,[22] a tool that measures how much time the runtime spends in several low-level tasks in a short time interval.

As your adopters get more advanced, :runtime_tools is an important application for learning about your production systems.

Exploring Crash Dumps

Whenever a production system terminates abruptly, the Erlang VM will write a crash report to disk. It is a quite detailed file with a lot of useful information. In truth, for a typical dump, you'll likely get more information than you can handle. Let's generate one:

```
$ elixir -e 'System.halt("oops")'
Crash dump is being written to: erl_crash.dump...done
oops
```

The crash dump for a system that is simply running Elixir is roughly 540KB. You can imagine that one for an actual running system with users is going to take several megabytes and no developer would be able to study it by hand.

---

18. http://blog.plataformatec.com.br/2016/05/tracing-and-observing-your-remote-node/
19. http://erlang.org/doc/apps/runtime_tools/LTTng.html
20. http://erlang.org/doc/apps/runtime_tools/DTRACE.html
21. http://erlang.org/doc/apps/runtime_tools/SYSTEMTAP.html
22. http://erlang.org/doc/man/msacc.html

Fortunately Erlang ships with a crash dump viewer as part of the :observer application. Let's view one from iex:

```
:crashdump_viewer.start
```

Now select the crash dump we just generated and open it. You will see a screen like this one:

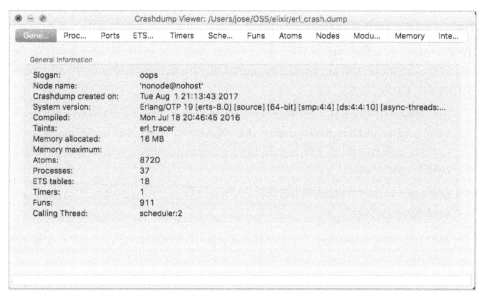

In the crash dump, you'll find information about running processes, ports, ETS tables, atoms, modules, memory usage, and more. You can tell exactly how the crash happened. If a system terminates for an unknown reason, the crash dump alongside the log and SASL reports we enabled earlier in this chapter should provide enough data to isolate the issue to a specific part of your application.

Other Tools

While we have covered the tools that are part of Elixir and OTP, we can find many other tools and alternatives in the community:

- wObserver[23] observes production nodes through a web interface.
- visualixir[24] is a development-time process message visualizer.
- erlyberly[25] is a GUI for tracing during development.

---

23. https://github.com/shinyscorpion/wObserver
24. https://github.com/koudelka/visualixir
25. https://github.com/andytill/erlyberly

The author of the recon tracing library, Fred Hebert, wrote a great book called *Erlang in Anger*[26] covering advanced topics for running Erlang and Elixir systems in production. If you are interested in digging deeper into the VM and into other diagnostic options, we can't recommend this book enough.

Wrapping Up

This area, called DevOps, could be a book of its own. It's easy to skip these important lessons as you adopt Elixir, but a little time spent with these tools can save you considerable effort as your system starts to grow. Erlang has a wonderful reliability and scalability history, owed in part to strong investments in DevOps.

In this chapter, we took the next step in your journey toward preparing your system for production. Our logging discussions showed you how to make the best out of the Elixir Logger, limiting logging to warnings and errors. We took a step-by-step tour through log customization, including custom formatters and back ends.

Then, we moved into tracing tools that can give you a good overview of what's happening in your production system when things go wrong. You learned to use the break! debugger and SASL reports. You saw how tracers such as dbg are great fits when debugging concurrent systems with message queues.

Finally, we concluded the chapter by taking a look at three advanced tools to use when logging and tracing are not enough. Crash dumps with Observer give you a graphical view of a crash dump, runtime_tools provides good tools for runtime debugging and analysis, and the recon library offers a series of tools to simplify and analyze the many sources of production data.

With this wrap up, we're through with this topic and this book. We hope you've enjoyed learning about the language, community, and ecosystem as much as we've enjoyed sharing it with you. You probably have an increased appreciation for those who've put in the thankless hours into building tools, writing prose, and blazing new ground with exciting applications. If so, consider giving back to the community that is supporting all of us, whether it's a simple Stack Overflow post or a grand open source project of your own based on Elixir.

May your adoption story be as rewarding as ours was. Happy coding!

---

26. https://www.erlang-in-anger.com/

Bibliography

[Jur15]   Saša Jurić. *Elixir in Action*. Manning Publications Co., Greenwich, CT, 2015.

[Tat10]   Bruce A. Tate. *Seven Languages in Seven Weeks*. The Pragmatic Bookshelf, Raleigh, NC, 2010.

[TV16]   Chris McCord, Bruce Tate, and José Valim. *Programming Phoenix*. The Pragmatic Bookshelf, Raleigh, NC, 2016.

[Val13]   José Valim. *Crafting Rails 4 Applications*. The Pragmatic Bookshelf, Raleigh, NC, 2013.

Index

Thank you!

How did you enjoy this book? Please let us know. Take a moment and email us at support@pragprog.com with your feedback. Tell us your story and you could win free ebooks. Please use the subject line "Book Feedback."

Ready for your next great Pragmatic Bookshelf book? Come on over to https://pragprog.com and use the coupon code BUYANOTHER2018 to save 30% on your next ebook.

Void where prohibited, restricted, or otherwise unwelcome. Do not use ebooks near water. If rash persists, see a doctor. Doesn't apply to *The Pragmatic Programmer* ebook because it's older than the Pragmatic Bookshelf itself. Side effects may include increased knowledge and skill, increased marketability, and deep satisfaction. Increase dosage regularly.

And thank you for your continued support,

Andy Hunt, Publisher

A Better Web with Phoenix and Elm

Elixir and Phoenix on the server side with Elm on the front end gets you the best of both worlds in both worlds!

Functional Web Development with Elixir, OTP, and Phoenix

Elixir and Phoenix are generating tremendous excitement as an unbeatable platform for building modern web applications. For decades OTP has helped developers create incredibly robust, scalable applications with unparalleled uptime. Make the most of them as you build a stateful web app with Elixir, OTP, and Phoenix. Model domain entities without an ORM or a database. Manage server state and keep your code clean with OTP Behaviours. Layer on a Phoenix web interface without coupling it to the business logic. Open doors to powerful new techniques that will get you thinking about web development in fundamentally new ways.

Lance Halvorsen
(218 pages) ISBN: 9781680502435. $45.95
https://pragprog.com/book/lhelph

Programming Elm

Elm brings the safety and stability of functional programing to front-end development, making it one of the most popular new languages. Elm's functional nature and static typing means that run-time errors are nearly impossible, and it compiles to JavaScript for easy web deployment. This book helps you take advantage of this new language in your web site development. Learn how the Elm Architecture will help you create fast applications. Discover how to integrate Elm with JavaScript so you can update legacy applications. See how Elm tooling makes deployment quicker and easier.

Jeremy Fairbank
(250 pages) ISBN: 9781680502855. $40.95
https://pragprog.com/book/jfelm

From Beginner to Expert

Need to introduce functional programming concepts to the team? Or leapfrog the competition with GraphQL? We've got you covered.

Learn Functional Programming with Elixir

Elixir's straightforward syntax and this guided tour give you a clean, simple path to learn modern functional programming techniques. No previous functional programming experience required! This book walks you through the right concepts at the right pace, as you explore immutable values and explicit data transformation, functions, modules, recursive functions, pattern matching, high-order functions, polymorphism, and failure handling, all while avoiding side effects. Don't board the Elixir train with an imperative mindset! To get the most out of functional languages, you need to think functionally. This book will get you there.

Ulisses Almeida
(198 pages) ISBN: 9781680502459. $42.95
https://pragprog.com/book/cdc-elixir

Craft GraphQL APIs in Elixir with Absinthe

Your domain is rich and interconnected, and your API should be too. Upgrade your web API to GraphQL, leveraging its flexible queries to empower your users, and its declarative structure to simplify your code. Absinthe is the GraphQL toolkit for Elixir, a functional programming language designed to enable massive concurrency atop robust application architectures. Written by the creators of Absinthe, this book will help you take full advantage of these two groundbreaking technologies. Build your own flexible, high-performance APIs using step-by-step guidance and expert advice you won't find anywhere else.

Bruce Williams and Ben Wilson
(250 pages) ISBN: 9781680502558. $47.95
https://pragprog.com/book/wwgraphql

Better by Design

From architecture and design to deployment in the harsh realities of the real world, make your software better by design.

Design It!

Don't engineer by coincidence—design it like you mean it! Grounded by fundamentals and filled with practical design methods, this is the perfect introduction to software architecture for programmers who are ready to grow their design skills. Ask the right stakeholders the right questions, explore design options, share your design decisions, and facilitate collaborative workshops that are fast, effective, and fun. Become a better programmer, leader, and designer. Use your new skills to lead your team in implementing software with the right capabilities—and develop awesome software!

Michael Keeling
(358 pages) ISBN: 9781680502091. $41.95
https://pragprog.com/book/mkdsa

Release It! Second Edition

A single dramatic software failure can cost a company millions of dollars—but can be avoided with simple changes to design and architecture. This new edition of the best-selling industry standard shows you how to create systems that run longer, with fewer failures, and recover better when bad things happen. New coverage includes DevOps, microservices, and cloud-native architecture. Stability antipatterns have grown to include systemic problems in large-scale systems. This is a must-have pragmatic guide to engineering for production systems.

Michael Nygard
(376 pages) ISBN: 9781680502398. $47.95
https://pragprog.com/book/mnee2

Long Live the Command Line!

Use tmux and Vim for incredible mouse-free productivity.

tmux 2

Your mouse is slowing you down. The time you spend context switching between your editor and your consoles eats away at your productivity. Take control of your environment with tmux, a terminal multiplexer that you can tailor to your workflow. With this updated second edition for tmux 2.3, you'll customize, script, and leverage tmux's unique abilities to craft a productive terminal environment that lets you keep your fingers on your keyboard's home row.

Brian P. Hogan
(102 pages) ISBN: 9781680502213. $21.95
https://pragprog.com/book/bhtmux2

Modern Vim

Turn Vim into a full-blown development environment using Vim 8's new features and this sequel to the beloved bestseller *Practical Vim*. Integrate your editor with tools for building, testing, linting, indexing, and searching your codebase. Discover the future of Vim with Neovim: a fork of Vim that includes a built-in terminal emulator that will transform your workflow. Whether you choose to switch to Neovim or stick with Vim 8, you'll be a better developer.

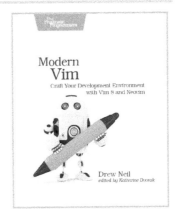

Drew Neil
(190 pages) ISBN: 9781680502626. $39.95
https://pragprog.com/book/modvim

Exercises and Teams

From exercises to make you a better programmer to techniques for creating better teams, we've got what you need.

Exercises for Programmers

When you write software, you need to be at the top of your game. Great programmers practice to keep their skills sharp. Get sharp and stay sharp with more than fifty practice exercises rooted in real-world scenarios. If you're a new programmer, these challenges will help you learn what you need to break into the field, and if you're a seasoned pro, you can use these exercises to learn that hot new language for your next gig.

Brian P. Hogan
(118 pages) ISBN: 9781680501223. $24
https://pragprog.com/book/bhwb

Creating Great Teams

People are happiest and most productive if they can choose what they work on and who they work with. Self-selecting teams give people that choice. Build well-designed and efficient teams to get the most out of your organization, with step-by-step instructions on how to set up teams quickly and efficiently. You'll create a process that works for you, whether you need to form teams from scratch, improve the design of existing teams, or are on the verge of a big team re-shuffle.

Sandy Mamoli and David Mole
(102 pages) ISBN: 9781680501285. $17
https://pragprog.com/book/mmteams

The Joy of Math and Healthy Programming

Rediscover the joy and fascinating weirdness of pure mathematics, and learn how to take a healthier approach to programming.

Good Math

Mathematics is beautiful—and it can be fun and exciting as well as practical. *Good Math* is your guide to some of the most intriguing topics from two thousand years of mathematics: from Egyptian fractions to Turing machines; from the real meaning of numbers to proof trees, group symmetry, and mechanical computation. If you've ever wondered what lay beyond the proofs you struggled to complete in high school geometry, or what limits the capabilities of the computer on your desk, this is the book for you.

Mark C. Chu-Carroll
(282 pages) ISBN: 9781937785338. $34
https://pragprog.com/book/mcmath

The Healthy Programmer

To keep doing what you love, you need to maintain your own systems, not just the ones you write code for. Regular exercise and proper nutrition help you learn, remember, concentrate, and be creative—skills critical to doing your job well. Learn how to change your work habits, master exercises that make working at a computer more comfortable, and develop a plan to keep fit, healthy, and sharp for years to come.

This book is intended only as an informative guide for those wishing to know more about health issues. In no way is this book intended to replace, countermand, or conflict with the advice given to you by your own healthcare provider including Physician, Nurse Practitioner, Physician Assistant, Registered Dietician, and other licensed professionals.

Joe Kutner
(254 pages) ISBN: 9781937785314. $36
https://pragprog.com/book/jkthp

The Pragmatic Bookshelf

The Pragmatic Bookshelf features books written by developers for developers. The titles continue the well-known Pragmatic Programmer style and continue to garner awards and rave reviews. As development gets more and more difficult, the Pragmatic Programmers will be there with more titles and products to help you stay on top of your game.

Visit Us Online

This Book's Home Page
https://pragprog.com/book/tvmelixir
Source code from this book, errata, and other resources. Come give us feedback, too!

Register for Updates
https://pragprog.com/updates
Be notified when updates and new books become available.

Join the Community
https://pragprog.com/community
Read our weblogs, join our online discussions, participate in our mailing list, interact with our wiki, and benefit from the experience of other Pragmatic Programmers.

New and Noteworthy
https://pragprog.com/news
Check out the latest pragmatic developments, new titles and other offerings.

Save on the eBook

Save on the eBook versions of this title. Owning the paper version of this book entitles you to purchase the electronic versions at a terrific discount.

PDFs are great for carrying around on your laptop—they are hyperlinked, have color, and are fully searchable. Most titles are also available for the iPhone and iPod touch, Amazon Kindle, and other popular e-book readers.

Buy now at *https://pragprog.com/coupon*

Contact Us

Online Orders:	*https://pragprog.com/catalog*
Customer Service:	*support@pragprog.com*
International Rights:	*translations@pragprog.com*
Academic Use:	*academic@pragprog.com*
Write for Us:	*http://write-for-us.pragprog.com*
Or Call:	+1 800-699-7764

Milton Keynes UK
Ingram Content Group UK Ltd.
UKHW031808010224
437116UK00008B/437